Skin Colored Pointes

ALSO BY NYAMA MCCARTHY-BROWN
AND FROM MCFARLAND

*Dance Pedagogy for a Diverse World:
Culturally Relevant Teaching in Theory, Research
and Practice* (2017)

Skin Colored Pointes
Interviews with Women of Color in Ballet

NYAMA McCARTHY-BROWN

Foreword by Zita Allen;
Afterword by Melanye White Dixon

McFarland & Company, Inc., Publishers
Jefferson, North Carolina

This book has undergone peer review.

Land and Labor Acknowledgment: This book was written on the ancestral lands of the Kaskaskia, Miami, and Wyandotte Nations. The people of these nations are past, present, and future caretakers of this land. I stand in gratitude to these nations and honor them. This book was written in the United States on lands stolen from Native Americans and built by the unpaid labor of African Americans. I acknowledge the labor of my ancestors who worked this land against their will for generations. I hold the understanding that the economic vitality of the United States was and is predicated on the enslavement of human beings. Those socially constructed arrangements of centuries past, impacting the social arrangements of today, left a need for this book to be written. I sit in gratitude to the Native American caretakers of the land, the labor of enslaved people, and undocumented people as well as the unpaid labor of caretakers.

ISBN (print) 978-1-4766-8705-6
ISBN (ebook) 978-1-4766-5181-1

LIBRARY OF CONGRESS AND BRITISH LIBRARY
CATALOGUING DATA ARE AVAILABLE

Library of Congress Control Number 2023058854

© 2024 Nyama McCarthy-Brown. All rights reserved

No part of this book may be reproduced or transmitted in any form or by any means, electronic or mechanical, including photocopying or recording, or by any information storage and retrieval system, without permission in writing from the publisher.

Front cover image of Claudia Monja (photograph by MA2LA)

Printed in the United States of America

McFarland & Company, Inc., Publishers
Box 611, Jefferson, North Carolina 28640
www.mcfarlandpub.com

To all the Black, Brown, Yellow, and Red
young ones who are called to dance;
the teachers who will train them up;
the directors who will put them in the light;
and the audiences who will receive them
with open eyes, hearts, and appreciation

Acknowledgments

First and foremost, I want to thank the dancers who shared their stories with me. They are the primary inspiration of this book, and when I wanted to stop the work on this project and move to something else, they are the people who motivated me to complete this work. This book took over seven years to complete. Many of the dancers have totally different lives now than when I interviewed them, and I want to extend my appreciation for staying with me on this lengthy journey. I also want to thank the thousands of ballerinas of Color whose stories are not shared here. May this book give you comfort that you are not alone but are one among many mighty and inspiring women, and may you continue to share your story in all the ways possible: through your body, words, writings, and beyond.

I want to thank my colleagues and fellow Temple University alumni Melanye White Dixon and Joselli Deans, whose dissertation research projects were the impetus of my interest in this topic. Thanks go to the inspiring scholars in my life who nudged me along: Takiyah Nur Amin, Thomas DeFrantz, Nadine George-Graves, Brenda Dixon Gottschild, and Kariamu Welsh as well as Nina Gilreath, Waverly Lucas, and the Ballethnic family who included me while I was living in Atlanta, Georgia. Some of my unforgettable ballet teachers who gave me insights that supported me on this journey are Natalia Njissang of San Francisco, Augusta Moore of San Francisco, Carol Szkutek of Atlanta Ballet, and Reginald Ray Savage of Savage Jazz. I extend immense gratitude to my amazing editor, Sherrie Barr. Through the process of writing and revising this book, she taught me the power and gift of a soft-handed guide and how to deliver succinct formative feedback that advances the work. For the many dance educators and dancers who expressed interest in my work and encouraged me to keep going, thank you. I would also like to thank my mother, Eileen McCarthy, and my son, Kasim McCarthy-Brown, as well as my family, friends, and dear colleagues and students who are constant inspirations for this research.

Table of Contents

Acknowledgments	vi
Foreword by Zita Allen	1
Preface	5
Introduction	9
Background of Ballet in the United States	27
Herstories: The Interviews	41
Set I—Retired Dancers	42

    Lauren Anderson 42; *Lourdes Lopez* 53; *Caridad Martinez* 77; *Crystal Michelle Perkins* 93; *Stephanie Marie Powell* 110; *Endalyn Taylor* 128

Set II—Dancers Who Are Still Performing or Recently Retired	141

    Shelby Colona 141; *Monike Cristina* 153; *Yinet Fernandez* 160; *Kristie Latham* 170; *Claudia Monja* 186; *Margaret Severin-Hansen* 192; *Melissa Verdecia* 203

Reflections	221
Themes and Variations: In the Experiences of the Women Interviewed	222
A Liberatory Approach to Teaching Ballet	240
Afterword by Melanye White Dixon	248
References	251
Index	255

Foreword

by Zita Allen

In a candid assessment of the challenges facing Women of Color who venture into the heretofore Eurocentric world of ballet, riddled as it is with racialized traps that can challenge the Black dancing body and soul, dance scholar Brenda Dixon Gottschild has declared that very process to be like staging a civil rights protest. Like Rosa Parks, the African Americans, Cuban, Asian, and Brazilian ballerinas whom scholar Nyama McCarthy-Brown has interviewed here have occupied forbidden spaces and now share their stories as both evidence and examples for others who follow in their footsteps. Before I describe the strategic significance of this monograph's structure and content, I'll explain why I think these reflections on lived experience are such a valuable resource.

I first experienced the racial barriers in the Eurocentric world of ballet as an adolescent in the South when members of my Jack 'n' Jill group were so in awe of the ballerina's ethereal grace, astonishing acrobatics, and flights of fancy that we didn't mind adding ballet classes to our weekly regimen of piano, tap, and swimming lessons. But the only ballet instructor our parents could find in our little Texas town was a white woman who agreed to teach "12 little Black girls. No more and no less." She insisted that we arrive at her studio after the white students and their parents had gone. Nevertheless, for a brief while, dancing in my black leotards, pink tights, and pink ballet slippers, I was in heaven. The ballet studio was the one place where my Black dancing body, skinny as a rail and all arms and legs, seemed perfect. But it wasn't long before one girl got sick and the ballet teacher told our parents "I said 12, no more, no less" and dropped our classes entirely. I was devastated, my love of ballet unfulfilled until a few years later when my dad accepted a teaching job at a college in New York and our family became another statistic in the 20th-century African American Great Migration saga. My love of ballet was rekindled, and I began to study at the Joffrey School, the New Dance Group, and the Clark Center and with ballet and modern teachers such as Vera Nemchinov, Meredith Baylis, Thelma Hill, Joyce Trisler, and Maggie Black. Supportive African American teachers and dancers answered my questions and shared their stories of racism, rejection, determination, and resilience. Their lived experience put mine in perspective. It also sparked a desire to share their stories with others, for like the ones included in McCarthy-Brown's collection, these stories and oral histories of lived experiences illuminate personalities, document history, and provide aspiring dancers with role models and road maps and provide dance scholars and researchers with documentation and insights. These stories are powerful tools.

McCarthy-Brown's collection reflects an awareness of the power of our stories, especially when not filtered through the lens of another's interpretation but instead told in our own words. It is evident in both the structure and content of her interviews with a representative group of ballerinas of Color from around the globe. The question-and-answer format centers their meaning-making anecdotes, their words, silences, and gestures, while highlighting their agency as they tell how they've transcended the structural racism and more embedded in the Eurocentric art form of ballet even as they offer directions to those who would follow in their footsteps. Interviews are not interrogations; when done well, they are conversations. Here, they begin strategically with an open-ended question that sets the stage for interviewees to share what they deem to be the salient facts of their lived experience and seem to follow their lead rather than forcing them down a meticulously and rigidly predetermined path that leaves no room for them to linger or veer off course. In this environment, asking Houston Ballet's Lauren Anderson simply "Why do you dance?" leaves room for the charismatic and gregarious ballerina to share a revealing anecdote about the first major part artistic director Ben Stevenson cast her in and the great awakening it inspired. The interview with Caridad Martinez, former soloist with the National Ballet of Cuba and teacher extraordinaire, is similarly revealing as she recalls her audition for Cuba's Escuela Nacional de Arte in front of *prima ballerina assoluta* Alicia Alonso and a subsequent encounter with what Martinez calls the "problem with race," candidly sharing her thoughts about the insidious nature of structural racism and colorism as the persistent vestiges of Euro-American colonialism.

Like other scholars who have also effectively utilized a format that leaves considerable space for the voices of their interviewees, as the eminent Brenda Dixon Gottschild does in *Joan Myers Brown & the Audacious Hope of the Black Ballerina* and *The Black Dancing Body: A Geography from Coon to Cool,* McCarthy-Brown's format suggests a theoretical position that answers postcolonial scholar Gayatri Spivak's question "Can the subalterns speak?" An interview is a storyteller's invaluable tool. It constitutes a delicately mediated dance that incorporates an interviewee's experience filtered through the multifaceted lens of memory, nostalgia, and ego and the interviewer's ability to inspire trust and establish a rapport. Judging from the interviews included in this volume as well as the interviewees' sometimes disarmingly frank and always informative responses, McCarthy-Brown's strategically structured and illuminating conversations have tackled that difficult task. While signaling that there is still more to be done, with this collection of interviews by essentially stepping aside and letting the subjects largely tell their story in their own words, McCarthy-Brown adds another important dimension to dance scholarship's complex mission of documenting a rich legacy and providing a valuable resource.

Zita Allen is a dance writer and critic.

Preface

In writing this book, I went back and forth with what language to use to describe the population I was getting ready to write about—Women of Color, Women of the Global Majority,* non-White—or write out the three specific racial groups I am using: African American, Asian American, and Latina. I landed on "Women of Color" for the following reasons. First, "Women of the Global Majority," an offshoot of People of the Global Majority, is a widely inclusive term. However, as this book features 13 women from three racial groups, this felt too small a group to make a claim for global majority. While it is true that all of the women featured in this text are non-White, this term describes a group through exclusion, pointing to the racial group one does not belong to, and centers whiteness. African American, Asian American and Latina are accurate; however, due to frequent use of this identifying phrase, I felt a shorter term would be better. As a result, I use the term "Women of Color" throughout this book when referring to African American, Asian American, and Latina women.

Another note about my editorial choices throughout this book. In following the accepted rule adopted in 2020 by the Associated Press, the *New York Times* (Coleman 2020), and other reputable publishers, I capitalize "Black" in reference to Black people and do not capitalize "white." I also capitalize the "C" in "people of Color." I do this to point to the specific cultural experiences of these groups that are significantly different from the variety of colors in a box of crayons (Coleman 2020).

Power, Positionality, and Resilience

Women of Color (WOC) have a precarious existence in ballet. In some instances, they are featured for their strength and exotic difference; in many instances they are excluded, and in other instances they are blended into a corps of

---

*I use the term "Women of the Global Majority" as a qualifier pulled from the term "People of the Global Majority." This term grew out of the discomfort of some Black, Latinx, Asian, and Indigenous folx being called "minorities." The term seeks to empower and affirm the standing of these people, who together comprise a majority of the global population.

white women, only to be asked not to stand out too much. It is an unfair balancing act that WOC negotiate daily throughout the world in countless sectors of society, and it indeed includes the profession of ballet.

Brittney Cooper, Black feminist scholar, writes on the inner workings of race relations in the United States:

> Before we fully learn to love ourselves, all people of color in the United States learn that we are supporting characters and spectators in the collective story of white people's lives. The problem is that only the experiences of white people are treated as universal. Meanwhile, Black movies, shows, and books are typically seen as limited and particular [Cooper 2018, 52–53].

This deep understanding of where we stand, one's positionality, is viscerally understood. It is why, as noted in Beverly Daniel Tatum's book *Why Are All the Black Kids Sitting Together in the Cafeteria?* (1997), no one actually has to tell the Black kids to sit together in the cafeteria. Also examined in Isabel Wilkerson's *Caste: The Origins of Our Discontents* (2020), the social codes that gather and group us, while they are often invisible to the eye and unspoken, are clearly understood. So, what does this mean for WOC seeking careers in a predominantly white profession and art form?

Below are the words of young WOC early in their careers seeking opportunities in ballet. As you read their words, consider who holds power in auditioning (for training/school and employment) and casting settings. What is the positionality of young WOC working to achieve excellence in the art form they love? They possess an unchosen place in history, positioned to break barriers in ballet others could not (or do not have to) or to quit. Each woman's ability to achieve also depends on her ability to access a spirit of resilience to overcome embedded and institutionalized racism. As Caridad Martinez shared during her interview, "The receptionist at the National Ballet School of Cuba, a Black woman, said to my mother at my audition for the school, 'They don't have black dancers. So, you know, I don't think she's going to be able to make it'" (Martinez interview).

Ruth Page berated Endalyn Taylor: "You don't look like snow, you look like slush" (Taylor interview).

Aesha Ash, in a group of corps dancers preparing to dance *Swan Lake*, was told by the ballet mistress "I don't want to see one tan body on the stage" (Craig 2018).

Misty Copeland shared this story about a part she was cast in early in her career:

> In a Paul Taylor ballet, called *Company B*, there's a role for an "ethnic girl" in the piece called "Rum and Coca-Cola." I know the ability of a lot of the dancers in the company and I know in terms of rhythm and coordination they probably would not have been able to do the part, but I do feel like because of the color of my skin, I definitely "fit the part" [Copeland interview 2009].

Skin Colored Pointes shares primary source interviews detailing the experiences of a select group of WOC working in ballet. Through oral history interviews, women who self-identify as African American, Latina, and Asian as well as two dancers from Latin America dancing in South Africa share their stories—their "pointes" of view. *Skin Colored Pointes* is the only book that shares excerpts of oral history interviews with numerous women from different parts of the world who held ballet careers during different time periods. Some of these women share their stories of confronting racism, while others minimize racism as a barrier, refusing to give power to the system. Many of the dancers provide encouragement as well as explicit advice to the younger dancers of the world. The experiences shared in this text defy stereotypes, inspire humanity, and insist on a revised history that includes their stories.

The book begins with an introduction and a theoretical framework exploring the tensions experienced by women from culturally diverse backgrounds, committed to a profession anchored in a Eurocentric art form that historically privileges white dancing bodies. The heart of the book contains interviews of 13 women exploring various themes, including but not limited to casting, training, employment, company life, moments of triumph, and the breaking of barriers. I fully acknowledge that the interviews were edited for clarity and to center the focus on race. In addition, the accounts shared in this book are only one perspective of moments in time, others may have different accounts of the events described by interviewees. Following the interviews, there is a theoretical essay discussing the themes identified in the lived experiences of the 13 women interviewed. The book closes with a chapter on progressive and antiracist teaching practices for the ballet class that offers a new paradigm through which to see this art form in the 21st century with the American dancing body and all of its cultural identity markers.

Introduction

All cultures, peoples, and dances possess stories. Featured in this book are the stories of selected women in ballet. The women interviewed share firsthand accounts of their lives in ballet, recounting how their training and careers were informed by their racial identity. Each woman's story stands on its own. Yet, at times I compare and contrast the experiences of these different women. In addition, I offer critical analysis of some of the experiences featured herein of Women of Color (WOC) navigating a Eurocentric art form, with most residing in locales entrenched in social structures of racism (the United States, South Africa, and Cuba). My analysis is grounded in whiteness studies and critical race theory. *Skin Colored Pointes* engages the intersectionalities of humanity, race, gender, class, nationality, and artistry interwoven within and throughout the stories of these women.

The experiences shared by the interviewees do not fit into stereotypical ideas of a minority group in an elite dance form. Instead, the individual experiences documented point to the variety of ways the human spirit manages to address and adapt to a set of circumstances (WOC seeking professional employment and advancement in a white-centered profession) in numerous ways. The narratives herein work against essentialism and avoid "lumping" the experiences of WOC into any one category. As you will read, each dancer found balance in this world and on her own terms.

While achievements of the women featured herein ground this book, their stories are inextricable from the structural social constructs around race that impeded, alienated, and often isolated these great women during their careers. As each of them demonstrates, racism impacts different people differently for a multitude of reasons. Social factors of race were a catalyst for personal drive for some and an unbearable obstacle for others. These women navigated a predominantly white art form with their Black or Brown dancing bodies; their stories demonstrate both the diversity of experiences and interpretations of racism. For some, racism was an ever-present entity that they considered in career planning and daily life. For others it was a nonissue, not acknowledged or consciously given much weight in determining life plans. To be sure, location, skin color, nationality, and class were all factors for the 13 women interviewed. *Skin Colored Pointes* seeks to frame the racial obstacles as opportunities to widen space for WOC. These women are heroic and achieved a livelihood in spite of the social ills of their time.

Background of the Project

My initial research began in 2008 as a graduate student studying African American women in ballet. As I started to examine the obstacles for African American ballerinas, I began thinking of Latina, Native American, and Asian ballerinas. Once interviewing Karen Brown, who began her career with Dance Theatre of Harlem (DTH) in the 1980s and was the first African American woman appointed as artistic director of a mainstream company (Oakland Ballet in 2000), and Caridad Martinez, working her way up from being a member of the corps to principal dancer in the National Ballet of Cuba who was previously the director of education at Ballet Hispánico and is currently on faculty teaching ballet at the Ailey School, I soon found myself in the midst of a research project greater than initially envisioned. One particular feature of this book is that it includes dancers from the 1970s as well as the 2020s, providing readers with an expansive picture of racial identity in relation to ballet over time and through multiple perspectives.

I began this study with a core set of open-ended interview questions and then shaped them around each interviewee. To identify some general themes while also potentially establishing connections amid their experiences, I employed a basic interview script that was customized slightly for each encounter. In instances where a dancer's history was well documented, I added questions to dig into particular moments in the interviewee's life. For example, ballerina Lauren Anderson has been interviewed numerous times, and there were certain experiences I was hoping she would share and elaborate on, such as being present when Misty Copeland performed the principal role of Odette in *Swan Lake* for the first time in 2015.

Core questions are as follows:

1. How did you come to ballet?
2. Can you describe the environment of your training/company employment?
3. Did you have a teacher or advocate in your life who helped you get where you are today?
4. Do you think you have ever been color-casted?
5. What prompted your retirement?

Or,

What are you looking forward to next in your ballet career?

I withheld questions about race until the end to learn if this topic would emerge as a component of their experiences if I did not ask about it. I also wanted to provide a space for dancers to talk about their experience the way they wanted to, on their terms; if they did not choose to center race, that option was available to them. Toward the end of each interview if the topic had not organically come up, I did pose a question about their experience in ballet as a woman of Color or asked for their thoughts on the racial landscape of the field of dance. Responses to my questions varied widely.

As previously mentioned, my interest in the stories of African American ballerinas bloomed in my first year of a doctoral program at Temple University in Philadelphia, Pennsylvania. I dove into the dissertation research of two previous Temple University graduates, Melanye White Dixon, who brought forth foundational research about Marion Cuyjet, and Joselli Deans, who built on Dixon's work to bring forth the oral histories of Cuyjet's student, Delores Browne. I quickly learned that Philadelphia is historic ground for Black ballerinas. Philadelphia was the locale of Marion Cuyjet's ballet school Judimar School of Dance, opened in 1948 (Dixon 1987) and one of the first Black-owned businesses in downtown Philadelphia (Deans 2001).

Cuyjet was an African American ballet pioneer. She set out to train one of the first African American ballerinas (*I'll Make Me a World* 1999), which was no small feat in the 1940s. To be sure, Delores Browne and Judith Jamison were students of Cuyjet's through the 1940s and 1950s. In a documentary about the time, Jamison recalled that Cuyjet was a firm teacher with high expectation (MOBBallet 1948). She explained that the location of the Judimar School of Dance moved on several occasions because when Cuyjet would lease a space and people in the area learned that the school served Black people, she would either lose the lease or be forced to move (Dixon 1987).

Cuyjet built a legacy of Blacks in ballet during that time, specializing in "Brown skinned girls" (*Classic Black Panel* 1996). This is of particular note in the context for an art form that historically favors white people and those who can approximate whiteness (Gottschild 2003). Cuyjet, a light-skinned woman who could pass for white, deliberately decided to focus on dancers who had the most limited access at the time, "brown-skinned girls." With an acute understanding of colorism in the African American community,* Cuyjet worked to give darker-skinned Black students more support; she intuited from the social structure of the time that they would be met by more obstacles (*Classic Black Panel* 1996). The more I learned about this pioneer, the more I was drawn into the rich histories of many WOC in ballet.

Most interestingly, Cuyjet was not the only ballet pioneer in Black Philadelphia. Gottschild describes a "black dancing-school movement in Philadelphia" led by four light-skinned women, Edith Holland, Jenny Squirrel, Willa Walker Bryant Jones, and Essie Marie Dorsey (Gottschild 2012, 6). Dorsey was Cuyjet's teacher and also taught another aspiring Black balletomane, Sydney King. King and Cuyjet followed in their teacher's footsteps to establish Black schools of dance in Philadelphia in the 1940s. Joan Myers Brown, one of King's students, went on to teach and

---

*Colorism is a system of favoritism whereby those who can most closely approximate whiteness are privileged (Gottschild 2003, 190). This type of discrimination can be seen in institutions throughout the United States ranging from lighter-skinned Black people having lesser sentences than darker-skinned people for the same offenses (Burch 2015) to casting discrimination based on skin color.

choreograph for Cuyjet's school and recitals, respectively, and eventually founded Philadanco (Gottschild 2012, 75).

There is great significance to the Black dance schools offering ballet in the first half of the 20th century, as Gottschild states in her book *Joan Myers Brown and the Audacious Hope of the Black Ballerina: A Biohistory of American Performance* (2012). Gottschild points to the interest in "upwardly mobile aspiration" during these years (xxviii). She frames the struggle of African Americans seeking a place of acceptance and dignity within our culture and society as a part of the integration process: the need to be included and not relegated to the margins. To be sure, the arts symbolize civility to many. However, people's basic needs must be met before they can satisfy their humanistic urges for creative expression. Thus, such aspirations often indicate a certain amount of attained economic stability.

Most of the women featured in this text and many women throughout the world are introduced to ballet by their mother or another parental figure. For young girls, the study of ballet is widely understood as a dignified socializing agent, a signifier of status and class. Historically, breaking the racial barriers embodied and exemplified in ballet was a mark of achievement within working-class communities and communities of Color throughout mainstream society. Described by Gottschild as serving the same purpose in Black and white America, "it was a symbol of privilege signaling a level of acculturation inaccessible to the masses" (2012, 5). The experiences of the women featured in this book would further indicate that this symbol of privilege also existed in the lives of the Latinx community.

At the onset, my research was focused on colorism in ballet. It is a theme I still relate to, examining how the variance of skin color within the African American racial group impacted the opportunities that many women in ballet received or were denied. However, as I quickly learned, the stories of Black ballerinas went far beyond skin color. As a result, my focus shifted and widened as well. I became more interested in gathering the oral histories of these women and wanted to disseminate their lived experiences.

In addition to being a dance scholar, I am also an educator and had something of an ulterior motive. I wanted to share these stories to inspire my students, who often struggle to find Black and Brown bodies in this art form. My desire to relate to students required me to expand my focus to the multitude of WOC in ballet, extending to Latina, Asian, and Native American dancers, although the latter two were challenging for me to find for reasons I will later discuss. To be sure, one of the most important learning experiences for our young white ballet students is to understand that the art form does not belong to any one group, race, nationality, or culture. Black dancing bodies, Native American dancing bodies, Latinx dancing bodies, and Asian dancing bodies can all perform ballet on an absolute scale. Additionally and of greater significance, the absence of more dancing bodies of Color is not an accident, nor will the diversification of the form be accidental. We are in the midst of a painstakingly slow process of equity, inclusion, and transformation.

Author's Positionality

Before I continue, I feel compelled to share that I am not a ballet dancer, nor have I ever been. There were moments along this research journey when I thought to myself "why am *I* doing this? There are other scholars who lived this life of a ballerina." The names of Theresa Ruth Howard, Endalyn Taylor, Kimberleigh Jordan, and Joselli Deans come to mind. But somehow, with the encouragement of "my village" and the knowledge that we do not have nearly enough researchers documenting, collecting, and sharing the stories of our Brown and Black women in ballet, I gathered and wove together the tapestry of stories told by courageous women of perseverance and creative artistry who are presented in this text.

While I never performed ballet in the professional sense, I am an African American female dance professional (scholar-educator-performer) who began dancing in the United States at the age of six. For me this means that I, along with many WOC raised in the world of dance, spent much of my developmental years wearing form-fitting clothing in predominantly white dance studio spaces with mirrors everywhere. I, like many WOC (and women in general, for that matter) have a complicated relationship with ballet. I started taking ballet as a child as a hobby, a recreational "something to do" with no knowledge of how it would or could direct the trajectory of my life. As I got older, I became more serious about dance. A myriad of experiences, such as auditioning for the local arts high school and interacting with other young dancers and teachers, led me to understand that ballet was often used as a leveling tool, a gatekeeping post for those who wanted to advance in concert dance as an art form or career in the United States. I was implicitly taught to believe that my dancing would be more acceptable and legitimate if I studied more ballet. I am not talking about being a ballet dancer; that was never on the table in my wildest dreams or the wildest dreams of anyone who saw me dance. I am talking about the need to be competent in ballet in order to pursue modern, contemporary, or even jazz in some places. After over a decade of off-and-on study of ballet (requirements in graduate school at the time) with varying levels of commitment (in addition to my studying contemporary dance), I earned a master's degree of fine arts in dance but only through a process of taking courses in ballet each semester, reinforcing the idea that my dancing needed to be legitimized through this form.

After graduate school I moved to Atlanta, Georgia, and found myself teaching ballet at the Ballethnic Academy of Dance. Ballethnic is an amazing dance school and company founded by former DTH dancers Nena Gilreath and Waverly Lucas. I also sought out a wonderful Saturday morning open adult ballet class offered through the Atlanta Ballet Center of Dance Education taught by Carol Szkutek, the best ballet classes of my life. I loved those classes dearly; they felt like therapy to my soul. Several years after my move to Atlanta, I was hired to direct a dance program for a new small performing arts high school in Atlanta with a conservatory focus. The school had to be established fast, over a summer, and although we held auditions, most of the students who auditioned were accepted so we could open the school. I immediately moved into the mode of training I had been taught—"ballet is the foundation"—and sought to instill Western dance values into my new students. Ultimately, my approach did not work. Many students in that community, who came to the school for the love of their own culturally informed dance forms, were turned off by this traditional Western-focused training approach and left the program.

In 2021, I was selected as San Francisco Ballet's "Scholar of the Year" and given the platform to widely share my research on WOC in ballet. This was a great honor and experience for me. But it is not lost on me that the beautiful building on Franklin Street in downtown San Francisco is one I seldom went into as a child. I attended *Nutcracker, Romeo and Juliet,* and other ballet productions here and there, often when complimentary tickets were distributed to my school. But I did not have a real opportunity to be connected to San Francisco Ballet (SFB) as a child or to see dancers who looked like me on the stage. My reflection fuels my research and enables me to appreciate the work that (SFB) a and many comparable ballet institutions are doing today to be more accessible to the local community.

I share these stories to provide an understanding of how I come to this work. I love ballet, and I hold nothing but respect and admiration for the women whose stories are presented herein. Yet, I am aware of the ways in which ballet has been utilized as a gatekeeper; regretfully, I too have utilized it in this way. However, through a process of critical reflection, I understand that ballet is not racist, yet it has at times been employed by racists to uphold whiteness.* It is this gatekeeping process, utilized to maintain white space, that has served to disenfranchise many young dancers who would have otherwise enjoyed learning and dancing ballet. This book seeks to work against those gatekeepers, to demonstrate and document the greatness in ballet of many WOC.

Theoretical Framework

Many ballet dancers speak of the indirect comments and whispers in the dressing room, suggesting that they might be more suited to jazz or another genre; among this group are Virginia Johnson, Delores Browne, Raven Wilkinson (*I'll Make Me a World* 1999), and Misty Copeland (Copeland 2010). For all the WOC who have heard that narrative—received those implicit messages of disaffection—this is the counternarrative. You belong, you are beautiful, and you can dance ballet as well as anyone else.

This book is framed by critical race theory, through the lens of counternarrative, and was conceived to shine a light on Black and Brown dancers of yesterday and

---

*Whiteness is structural arrangements that oppress those who are not white while maintaining a veneer of neutrality (Castogna 2014).

today and light the path for all dancers of the future. As Solórzano and Yosso state, "critical race methodology provides a tool to 'counter' deficit storytelling" (2002, 23). Specifically, such theory anchors the presentation of research grounded in the experiences and knowledge of people of Color narratives, storytelling, and oral histories that are modes of communication and historicizing the human experience. Moreover, counternarrative is a tenet of critical race theory. This text is a counternarrative, a documentation of ballet in full color, an inclusive story that seeks to widen the space for all peoples in this majestic form. It is fitting that these counternarratives are shared through oral history interviews. In the words of scholars Izabela Dahl and Melin Thor,

> In oral history, the purpose is often to "give voice" to marginalized or forgotten individuals or groups, to listen to their stories and give them the possibility to speak from their perspectives. We agree with these emancipatory aims of oral history [2009, 1].

As we learn more about the history of dancers within this genre that has often been aligned with a white supremacy culture, we can work to deconstruct and reconstruct how it is viewed and to value the art form.

Intersectionality is evident in the identity markers of WOC, but it goes beyond race and gender. Some of the interviewees' stories shared here also bring forth issues of language, nationality, and class. Similarly, there are other theoretical frames in which these dancers can be understood: Black feminist thought and Latinx critical race theory. Theories are engaged herein to understand experiences further, to consider the complexity of humanity situated in the midst of social constructs, nation-states, and institutions of organized high art, including ballet. The tacit boundaries, borders, and checkpoints in ballet are continuously negotiated. From the stories of the dancers, it is apparent that identity markers were more of an issue for some dancers than others; some dancers were in more supportive environments to grow, while others grew in spite of spaces that were abusive verbally or psychologically. To be sure, each dancer had support, either someone cheering them on from inside the studio or family and friends at home. There were two consistent anchors in all of the stories: the human spirit is resilient with the ability to adapt and prevail in the midst of significant adversity, and dancers needed someone who saw possibility and success in them.

An additional theory that emerged during this process was the identification of in-group messaging. Education scholar Mary Earick (2009) describes a social mechanism, in-group messaging, that provides further insight into how some of these implicit messages work. "In-group" refers to a group of individuals who share the same identity markers for race, gender, or both. In-group messages are communications that regularly indicate where one should go (or not go) as directed by the behavior of other members from the affiliated in-group.* Misty Copeland shared

---

*In-grouping categories can extend to other identity markers like sexual orientation, religion, etc.

that on a number of occasions she overheard her dance mates talk about how she stood out too much and did not fit in (Wilson 2015). This example demonstrates the in-group messages and ideology that Copeland's dance company colleagues shared. The impact of in-group messaging works to not only inhibit the behavior of ones outside the in-group (in this case Copeland) but also bolster the confidence and extend the reach of gatekeepers who belong to said in-group. Within the realm of dance, even audience members are impacted by these messages; an audience member was noted as being distracted by a dancer's Black skin color onstage (Craig 2020).

This theory surrounding in-group messaging argues that people identify with others who possess the same salient identity markers, such as race and gender (Leary 2012; Earick 2009). Once making the connection of the self to a group, such as an individual to the Latinx community, socially constructed ideas of limitations and opportunities as well as behavioral norms—expressions of leadership and superiority or subordination and inferiority—are communicated through membership to the group. In-group messages are a mechanism to send like group members messages about where one might seek employment or where members of a particular group might not belong. Much of in-group messaging is subconscious and implicit, although it can be explicit as well. Throughout this research process I identified moments when dancers received in-group messages of limitations as well as those of opportunity and resilience. I encourage you to take note of these moments as you read the lived experiences of the dancers.

Pervasive Stereotypes

Our society, a group of people linked together by a social contract, expresses its understanding of humanity and society on the performance stage. It is not surprising, then, to witness stereotypes reinforcing the discrimination, marginalization, and subjugation of Black and Brown bodies onstage. I argue that this is one reason why many members of Color are excluded from ballet. The controlling images about who gets to perform ballet often do not include people of Color. These ideas of who gets to dance are most salient in the United States, although the reach of white supremacy is vast and does extend beyond U.S. borders.

What are the controlling images of the ballerina? This excerpt, taken from a chapter written by Ann Daly, explores gender dynamics and roles in ballet:

> In ballet, the female form has long been inscribed as a representation of difference: as a spectacle, she is the bearer and object of male desire. The male on stage—the primary term against which the ballerina can only be compared—is not inscribed as a form, but rather as an active principle [1997, 111].

Ballerinas are often described as elegant, delicate, innocent, and pure. These are not words typically used in any of the prejudicial stereotypes that permeate our society describing WOC.

It is of great significance to understand that a typical practice in the ballet industry is dancers signing contracts to maintain a particular appearance. The job of ballet dancers includes their image, their look, which is used and presented for public consumption. Dancers commit to explicit requirements pertaining to hair, often including facial and body, as well as hair color and hair length, weight, tattoos, piercings, and other considerations that would change one's appearance. The image of a dancer is part of the job. Thus, when only one racial image is selected for certain roles, implicit messaging rings through with great clarity.

Consider Patricia Hill Collins's theory of historical controlling images of the Black female. These controlling images are powerful and limit what one can perceive of as possible for Black women (Collins 2000). Controlling images for Black women are in conflict with those of American ballerinas (Deans 2001, 82–85). Consider the racial climate of the United States and add an African American identity marker to the female ballerina; one can see how positioning her as the object of male desire challenges mainstream stereotypes. American philosopher Cornel West identifies these stereotypes as "Jezebel (the seductive temptress), Sapphire (the evil, manipulative bitch), and Aunt Jemima (the sexless, long-suffering nurturer)" (West 2001, 119). West's Sapphire is often called the "angry black woman," while the Aunt Jemima stereotype is most widely referred to as "mammy."* None of these three primary stereotypes for Black women—the Mammy, the Jezebel, or the Sapphire—fits into the feminine identity of classical ballet (Deans 2001, 82; McCarthy-Brown 2011, 8). This socially constructed paradigm of controlling images relegates Black women to roles of anger, servitude, or exoticism and may provide insights as to why many Black women are not cast in classical ballet roles that often feature the female lead as young, delicate, and innocent. Similar socially constructed challenges are an issue for Latina and Asian women in ballet.

Let us examine how our Latina and Asian sisters fare under the white gaze.† The Jezebel stereotype is comparable to the "Vamp" or "Hot Latina" stereotype (Merskin 2011) pervasive in mainstream American culture. "Orientalism" is a term coined by Edward Said (1978) in establishing the "Other," but the term also opened the space to exoticism and a fetishizing of the Other. This controlling Asian image relates to the dragon lady or the geisha girl. The model minority, good in math or a nerd and the aggressive/rude Asian, are also Asian stereotypes (Merskin 2011).

Taken together, there is a range of stereotypes across these various ethnicities. However, none of these dominant mainstream stereotypes blend well with the idea

---

*Within my experience in the Black community, the Jezebel is usually a light-skinned woman, and the Sapphire and Mammy are darker-skinned. However, these terms in general are dated. Often used today across the skin color spectrum is the term "strong Black woman." This term is particularly harmful, as it ascribes a superpower to Black women that denies their humanity and positions them to be given less financial, physical, and emotional support than their white counterparts.

†"The white gaze traps black people in white imaginations" (Grant 2015). In this book, I apply the impact of the white gaze to all those outside the dominant culture who are positioned as subjects of the white gaze.

of the American ballerina. This paradigm also supports the understanding that ballerinas outside the United States experience issues around race differently. It is well documented that performance spaces in Western culture have a history of "exoticizing or fetishizing the Other, trivializing the Other, or ... not engaging the Other at all" (Johnson 2003, 243). These alienating stereotypes paired with stereotypes about white women as the archetype for ladylike femininity have had a large impact on the positionality of women and who gets ushered into which spaces and opportunities.

It is significant to note that historically, it was Russians, not Americans, who offered the first opportunities for WOC in American ballet. Ballet Russes, developed by Russian Sergei Diaghilev, was the forerunner in hiring WOC, including ballerinas such as Raven Wilkinson, Sono Osato, Maria Tallchief, Marjorie Tallchief, Yvonne Chateau, Moscelyne Larkin, and Rosella Hightower. George Balanchine, who opened the door to Arthur Mitchell, the first African American to dance with New York City Ballet, desired to work with a racially integrated ballet company (Banes 1994), and it is certain that his support of Mitchell ensured generations of African American women achieving in ballet.

The arts and, more specifically ballet, have been slow to undo the insidious racism that lives within all parts of our U.S. society. To contextualize this statement, I challenge you to go to the websites of three widely known and reputable mainstream ballet companies and look at the images put forth to represent the companies. Is whiteness affirmed? In what ways are people of Color included? What culture and cultural backgrounds are being celebrated? To this end, consider whose bodies are marked as "universal." Look at the leadership of the company. Are board members and the artistic directors white? If we are serious about equality and equity in all sectors of society, we cannot turn away from these truths.

Rationale and Methodology

The goal of this book is to focus light on 13 WOC and to share their experiences in ballet. My overarching research question involved how WOC have prevailed and transcended the racial boundaries embedded in the Western-framed artistic genre of ballet. This research is part of a crucial effort to preserve the knowledge of these women for dance history. It is an investigation of lived experience in the arts.

Through oral history interviews, I documented a wide range of experiences from WOC from different parts of the Americas while also differing in global descent. Oral histories are used as a qualitative research method to honor the lived experience of the dancers and the oral history traditions prevalent in cultures of the Latin American and African diasporas. Thirteen WOC share their stories of training, growing, and aging in the dance form of ballet. In addition to exploring the intersectionality of each dancer, this book is also in dialogue with the fields of sociology, Africana studies, Latin diasporic studies, dance studies, and performance studies, examining the experiences of performers of Latin, Asian, and African descent and constructing meaning through sociological inference and applied theories relating to racial constructs.

My methodology was informed by preliminary research conducted for my article "Dancing in the Margins: Experiences of African American Ballet Dancers" (McCarthy-Brown 2011), published in the *Journal of African American Studies*. During that process, I interviewed Misty Copeland. She stated her goal of being a principal dancer in a top-tier company. This made a lot of connections for me, drawing me into looking at top-tier ballet companies differently from other companies. I began to pay more attention to the difference between top-tier companies and companies outside that status. Not surprisingly, resources are at the heart of that difference, resources that enable top-tier companies to bring in the best choreographers, directors, and dancers; resources for public relations and advertising; resources to support dancers' body wellness; and resources for larger-scale productions, including live music, musical compositions, lights, sets, costumes, etc. This examination of companies fueled questions around the visual images and representation of dance companies, particularly on the World Wide Web. With a focus on companies in the United States, I started with American Ballet Theatre, San Francisco Ballet, and New York City Ballet. Within my website searches, I found few images reflecting the diversity of the United States, and I began to squint and question whether any of the photos included people of Color.

When beginning to look outside the United States, Joburg Ballet in South Africa leapt off the screen. Although I was uncertain as to its "status" in terms of "tiers," it was the most racially diverse company I found in terms of images. I was intrigued to research the company further. I approached Meryl Lauer, an assistant professor of dance at the Johns Hopkins Peabody Institute, who is working on an ethnography of South African ballet. She explained that most of the ballet dancers of Color in South Africa were not native to the country. This led me to a whole new set of questions. It also led me to consider how the United States found representation for Latinx and Asian dancers. This discovery extended my research focus from the United States to other countries, a notion that makes sense as I consider today's global nature of the arts and society. Thus, although my research is grounded in the United States, I include the stories of women from other countries for contrast and context of this global form.

I employed oral history guidelines and interview techniques as outlined by Valerie Yow in her book *Recording Oral History: A Guide for the Humanities and Social Sciences* (2005) to prepare for and conduct all interviews. As an oral historian, Yow writes, "Oral history testimony is the kind of information that makes other public documents understandable" (Yow 2005, 11). I made a number of visits to the New York Public Library to read background on the various dancers and companies and to view photographs and newspaper clippings. These research trips guided the development of my interview scripts and gave me a sense of how my interviews might provide additional context to the ballet history that is widely available. To that end, this book seeks to make dance history more understandable to those who have always wondered where all the dancers of Color are.

Interviews were conducted between 2016 and 2022. Research funding support was secured from Indiana University's College of Arts and Humanities Institute and from Ohio State University Global Arts and Humanities Discovery Themes. Nine out of thirteen interviews for this book were conducted in person. One interview was conducted by phone with a dancer I had previously interviewed in person; three were conducted via Zoom. Half of the interviews were conducted in conference rooms of the dance companies (Ballet Hispánico, DTH, and the Joburg Ballet); one took place at a public library in Queens, New York; and one was conducted at an interviewee's home in California. Interviews ranged in length from 45 minutes to two hours, with each interview focused specifically on the training and performance career of the subject.

I considered dynamics of position and power during the interview process. To this end, my identity as a woman of Color was importantly aligned with the identity of those interviewed. Where language, nationality, or both differed, so did the relationship between the narrator and myself. Similarly, I experienced a shift in power dynamics in relation to the age of interviewees, with younger interviewees seeming more timid and unsure of themselves and deferring to me for directions, while interviewees who were senior to me took a more assertive role throughout our time together. I got the sense that the dancers who had long since left company life had time and distance to process experiences more deeply. This is in line with findings from other researchers, for "with the passage of time people tend to be more candid" (Yow 2005, 19). This was especially the case with those still in the midst of their dancing careers and directly connected to a company. For these dancers, I got the sense that they were also in the midst of negotiating their story and public relations for their company. Moreover, the dancers still under contract with a company seemed to be more guarded and careful with their responses than the retired dancers I interviewed.

Oral history as a methodology was essential to this project in revealing the stories behind the absences and low representation of WOC in ballet. The words of the women featured here take you beyond the curtains, sharing details of how some were able to get through the well-protected gates of institutional racism and achieve careers in a dance form that requires at a minimum the utmost commitment and discipline if not blood, sweat, and tears. Of significance here is the invaluable power of personal voice. Yow, building on the research of linguist Deborah Tannen, writes,

> [W]hen the narrator makes a point by sharing a personal intimate memory—rather than offering some general statement—he indicates a high level of emotional involvement in the interview and trust in the person spoken to.... Events in which there are high levels of mental activity and emotional involvement will be remembered [2005, 51].

As *Skin Colored Pointes* seeks to understand and illuminate the experiences of WOC in ballet, oral history as a methodology is the anchor of this research. Numerous scholars acknowledge the relevance of oral history when bringing forward underrepresented populations. Researching on oral history in action, Kathryn Haynes wrote,

> It is particularly appropriate for exploring the experience of those who have been marginalized, silenced or ignored ... because an oral history methodology has the potential to uncover some rich, powerful data, which allows the participants to stress in their narratives not so much events themselves but their meaning to the individuals concerned [2010, 229].

Throughout this text, I sought to reveal meaning and tell the stories of the women featured by maintaining their voice and keeping their stories intact. Building on the scholarship of Catherine Riessman, Yow writes that narratives are "essential meaning-making structures ... researchers must not break them up but respect respondents' ways of constructing meaning and analyze how it was accomplished" (2005, 17). In this spirit, I do not parse the words of interviewees for analysis but instead seek to reveal the meanings the interviewees have constructed from their stories. Any additional framing done through a theoretical lens is presented apart from the interviews and positioned at an intentional distance.

Further, it is widely accepted that people from cultural backgrounds outside the dominant culture have a more salient sense of identity than those of the mainstream culture (Tonkin 1992). Thus, this text seeks to make meaning of how some experienced the world of ballet within life experiences not typically centered in traditional dance history texts and with the understanding that identity is shaped and manifested through narrative storytelling processes (Tomé 2011).

Who Was Selected and How?

The experiences of the women I interviewed were wide-ranging. The WOC do not have monolithic experiences. There is no "Black experience" or "Latina experience" in ballet; each woman has her own story. I interviewed women from different eras of dancing and with various distances from their performing career. Five women were previously employed by professional ballet companies and now are in different chapters of their lives. These retired dancers were Caridad Martinez, former principal dancer with the National Ballet de Cuba and former director of education at Ballet Hispánico, on faculty at the Ailey School; Stephanie Marie Powell, former dancer with the Oakland Ballet, DTH, *The Lion King* on Broadway, the Alvin Ailey American Dance Theater, and professor of dance at Long Beach Community College; Endalyn Taylor, Dean of Dance at North Carolina School of the Arts and former DTH principal dancer; Lourdes Lopez, trained at the School of American Ballet (SBA), former performer in the corps and as a soloist with New York City Ballet and now artistic director of the Miami City Ballet; and Lauren Anderson, the first African American principal dancer in the Houston Ballet, a mainstream dance company.

I interviewed six dancers who are currently still performing or recently retired from dancing: Shelby Colona, an Asian dancer recently retired from Ballet Hispánico; Melissa Verdecia, a Latina dancer recently retired from Ballet Hispánico; Monike Cristina, born and trained in Brazil and now a senior soloist with the Joburg Ballet in Johannesburg, South Africa; Claudia Monja, born and trained in Cuba, whom I interviewed in Johannesburg while she was performing with the Joburg Ballet and has since joined the Nashville Ballet in Tennessee; Yinet Fernandez, also born and trained in Cuba, formerly a dancer for the National Ballet de Cuba and currently dancing with DTH; and Margaret Severin-Hansen, an Asian principal dancer with the Carolina Ballet in Raleigh, North Carolina. I also interviewed Kristie Latham, an Asian soloist with BalletMet who retired in the summer of 2022.

As previously mentioned, I began my foundational research in 2008 while I was a doctoral student. Misty Copeland was quite popular at the time, and my adviser, Dr. Kariamu Welsh, said to me, "Just ask her for an interview. You know, Nya, these people are not rock stars; dancers are not famous like you think. They are famous to you because you are in dance, but they really are accessible." Her advice opened doors for me as a neophyte scholar as only another woman of Color in the academy can. She gave me permission to move out into what appeared to be exclusive space and see opportunity. With her advice I was off, and indeed Misty Copeland did give me an interview. Then, I set out for the Dance Division of the New York Public Library to examine DTH programs. Programs in hand, I then googled and called person after person until I came to Duncan Cooper, former principal dancer with the SFB and DTH, who answered the phone. Cooper was generous, agreed to an interview, and provided the contact information for Stephanie Marie Powell, whose interview is featured in this book. I connected with Cooper early in the project before I made the decision to limit my focus to women (McCarthy-Brown 2011).

As I continued to look for interviewees, I was reminded time and time again that the dance world is small. When doing research at the New York Public Library, I learned about Karen Brown's work with the DTH. I realized I had been in class with her from time to time while studying dance in Oakland, California, with Reginald Savage. At that time, Karen Brown was artistic director of the Oakland Ballet. When I figured this out, we were both in Philadelphia. I was working on my doctorate, and she was teaching at the University of the Arts. She agreed to interview with me. In examining early DTH programs, I saw Lydia Abarca-Mitchell's name a lot. I realized that I knew her, having rehearsed under her direction a number of times. She was the rehearsal director for the Ballethnic Dance Company in Atlanta, Georgia, where I taught ballet for several years in the early to mid–2000s and performed with the company in its annual productions. Joselli Deans was an alum of Temple University's Graduate Dance Program; I leaned on her dissertation a lot during my tenure at Temple and still return to her work as a resource. She too agreed to be interviewed. In those moments, I decided that my research would take a path encountering many voices that are marginalized and folks we do not see and hear from as much. Each person I interviewed connected me to more people to interview, the snowball effect. The web of dancers I talked to was wide, and all were quite generous, each one connecting me to another.* These interviews led to my 2011 publication "Dancing in the Margins," mentioned earlier.

That initial article was specifically focused on issues of colorism. I felt uncomfortable during those interviews because I got the sense that there was so much more to the women I was interviewing beyond this issue of colorism. I felt that the article did not shed light on the aspects of their career most important to them: their achievements. I decided to start this book with a new set of interviews and hold space for the stories that they desired to tell. That said, I did still want to bring light to experiences they had that were particular to WOC in ballet.

To start this book project I went back to a previous interviewee, Stephanie Marie Powell.† Previously interviewed in 2009, she had spoken to me in a phone interview, but as my research focus evolved into an oral history collection process, I wanted to conduct in-person interviews. A friend, Corrine Nagata, introduced me via email to her colleague from DTH, Endalyn Taylor. I wanted to interview world-renowned ballerina Lauren Anderson, now in an educational role at the Houston Ballet, and so I emailed her; she responded and agreed. When I started to put feelers out about expanding my research to include women of the Latin diaspora, a colleague, Elizabeth Schwall, suggested I interview Caridad Martinez. Martinez suggested I interview Lourdes Lopez. Many of my contacts, including Lopez, suggested I interview Virginia Johnson, now the artistic director of DTH. I wanted to. I met her at a couple of events, and we talked about the possibility, but due to scheduling and crossing emails, it never worked out. However, I was happy to focus on dancers who are not as widely known, as interviews of Johnson are plentiful and relatively easy to access.

I wanted to include women currently performing in ballet, so I looked on Ballet Hispánico's website to learn about Melissa Verdecia and Shelby Colona; I soon connected with them. I was attending a dinner in honor of DTH in Columbus, Ohio, and met Yinet Fernandez; I asked her to interview with me, and she agreed. In an online search I noticed that the Joburg Ballet had one of the most diverse-looking rosters. I returned to the thought of investigating issues of diversity and inclusion in South African ballet companies because I found issues of ballerinas immigrating to find employment quite interesting. I reached out to the Joburg Ballet, which kindly arranged for me to interview two of its dancers, Monike Cristina and Claudia

---

*That initial research resulted in my first publication on the topic, "Dancing in the Margins: Experiences of African American Ballerinas" (2011) in the *Journal of African American Studies*. The initial interviews that were the impetus of this book but were not used in this text (with the exception of Stephanie Powell) were Misty Copeland, Karen Brown, Lydia Abarca-Mitchell, Joselli Deans, Duncan Cooper, and Waverly Lucas. After these interviews I decided to limit my focus to women and was unable to get back to these interviewees for various reasons.

†My first interview with Stephanie Powell was by phone in 2009. I interviewed her for a second time in person in 2014, with funding from Bowdoin College.

Monja. In addition, the Joburg Ballet's executive director, Esther Nasser, interviewed with me as well. She provided me with an understanding of the company's vision to diversify to include Black South Africans.

I had a hard time finding Asian dancers willing to interview with me. For several years during this research process, I only had one interview completed. Yet, over time and during the course of this project, I developed more relationships with more dance organizations and dance professionals. In 2021 Edwaard Liang, artistic director of BalletMet, led me to two Asian dancers to interview, Kristie Latham and Margaret Severin-Hansen. Both were still dancing at the time of their interviews and affiliated with their company/employer.

After 12 interviews were completed and I was in the final stages of this book, I made the decision to add one more interview. I interviewed my friend and colleague at Ohio State University, Crystal Michelle Perkins. Her interview was different for many reasons. First, she is most often thought of as a contemporary dancer even though she started out and planned to have a career as a ballet dancer. Yet, as she reveals in her interview, other opportunities opened up on her path. Second, I worked for four years as a colleague of Perkins and had close proximity to her. This relationship also offered me insights into knowing what questions to ask to bring forth detailed accounts of some of the cross-cultural challenges that dancers outside the mainstream can at times experience. She also provided insights into what teachers and allies can do to support dancers outside the mainstream. Thus, Perkins's interview was conducted with a slightly different approach than the others.

Implications of Company Affiliations

Arranging interviews with the support of the company (i.e., the dancer's employer) came with challenges. When I conducted interviews with dancers still performing and in particular when taking place in the interviewee's place of employment, there seemed to be an impact on the dancer's comfort to share freely. I got the sense that public relations for the company was at play during these interviews, that dancers might have been given direction on how to represent the company. I questioned if dancers could openly share that they were experiencing racism or color-casting when they were dependent on that employer for their livelihood. As you read the interviews you may notice that some interviewees seem more guarded or open than others. This was the case with the interviews with Monike Cristina and Claudia Monja. It is important to note that these women were in South Africa, likely on work visas and more vulnerable than dancers interviewed in their home country and in their primary language (Portuguese for Cristina and Spanish for Monja).

In general, I found that all my interviewees did not want to say the wrong thing. This was a particular issue when they were talking about their companies, affiliations, teachers, mentors, and so forth. Again, this was amplified if the dancer was still performing and working for a company. I noticed this tension at play with Kristie Latham, who mentioned concerns about not wanting to cast a negative light on her company. Fernandez, Monja, and Cristina spoke to me about their work with their current company, in English, outside their primary language, which could have been the cause for concern.

Throughout the research process I continuously received suggestions from friends and colleagues on more dancers to interview, and there are many more I would have loved to interview, but that will be for another book.

Regrets

When I decided to extend my interest in African American ballerinas to WOC in ballet, I did not consider a number of challenges. I sought to create a book that told the stories of those heard from least and marginalized the most. For me that meant extending space to all WOC in ballet (or as many as I could find). I began looking within my own country, the United States of America. Almost instantly I realized that Latina and Asian women dancing in the commercially successful mainstream dance companies were more often than not born outside of the United States. In this book, I share a smaller number of interviews from Asian ballet dancers; this is a direct correlation to the disproportionately low number of Asian ballet dancers in the United States. That is not to say that Asians are less connected to ballet; in fact, there are rich legacies of ballet in Asian countries such as China and South Korea. But this does speak to a perceived stigma present in the United States that suggests that the arts are not a viable option for people of Color. Moreover, historically the United States has not trained ballet dancers of Color at the same rates as their white counterparts; of the WOC in ballet trained in the United States, African Americans make up the largest group. The presence and legacy of DTH, being the largest training institute for African American women and employing the largest number of African American women in ballet to date, has also impacted the notable presence of Black women in ballet.

Although you will find a limited number of Latina and Asian women born in the United States represented in this text, the small number of Asian women interviewed was a limitation of the research. In this way, the text is a representation of ballet in the United States. There are a limited number of professional U.S.-born Latina and Asian ballet dancers. Similarly and despite the rich history of the Oklahoma Five Moons—Maria Tallchief, Marjorie Tallchief, Rosella Hightower, Moscelyne Larkin, and Yvonne Choteau—I was unable to find Native American representation for this book. I hope the absence was simply my shortcoming as a researcher and that Native American ballet dancers were just unreachable for me. If that is the case, I hope that those more knowledgeable will bring forth these needed biographical stories. The lack of Native American representation is a great misfortune of this research and an opportunity for a future endeavor.*

Skin Colored Pointes focuses on the experiences of WOC in ballet. To be sure, men of Color also have important stories of breaking barriers in the art form. I limited my focus to women not because men of Color were not discriminated against but instead because instances of entry and acceptance seem to be more plentiful for men of Color, likely because of the demand for male dancers in Western societies (far exceeding the demand for female ballet dancers). Ballet training institutions and companies tend to have a disproportionately lower ratio of men to women, making men more of a commodity.

Decisions around delimiting the research subject prevented me from exploring Black women in British ballet; this is also an area that deserves attention. However, contributions in this area have been made. For example, Adesola Akinleye's anthology, *Narratives of Black British Dance,* including a variety of perspectives on the topic. Dawn Lille Horwitz has also written in this area. In the chapter "The New York Negro Ballet in Great Britain" in *Dancing Many Drums: Excavations in African American Dance,* edited by Thomas DeFrantz (Horwitz 2002), Horwitz provides a detailed account of the company's British tour in 1957 and its historic presence. Additionally, there was a wave of Latin American dancers that transformed the look of ballet in the United States around the turn of the millennium: Paloma Herrera, Xiomara Reyes, Erica Cornejo, Lorena and Lorna Feijóo, and a number of other dancers who became leading figures in the Boston Ballet, the Houston Ballet, the San Francisco Ballet, the Miami City Ballet, the American Ballet Theatre, and other companies not explored in this book. To be sure, when you look for WOC in ballet, you will find that they are not only present but have been for quite some time.

---

*Russ Tallchief has shared publicly that he is working on a book about Maria and Marjorie Tallchief that will share stories of their lives in ballet.

Background of Ballet in the United States

It is well documented and understood that ballet in the United States privileges the white dancing body, a mode of artistry that harkens back to Europe and embraces Eurocentric aesthetics. In 1840, a "ballet craze" was documented when Australian ballerina Fanny Elssler toured the United States (Klapper 2020, 3), and another craze occurred in the 1920s as a resurgence of ballet started to sprout. Its popularity grew with the active touring schedule of the Ballets Russes in the 1930s. The presence of ballet in the United States expanded further with the establishment of the New York City Ballet (NYCB) in 1948 (Homans 2010). Yet, when ballet was emerging as an art form, obstacles around segregation and socioeconomic status prevailed that could explain this racialized paradigm. Imagine where the nation was in terms of race when ballet was emerging, given that *Brown vs. Board of Education* was tried in 1954 and desegregation was pursued throughout the 1950s and 1960s. When such a racial landscape is considered, it is all the more monumental that WOC were able to make strides in ballet in the 1930s, 1940s, and 1950s.

Unsustained efforts to integrate ballet did occur from time to time. In 1940, Agnes de Mille created a ballet with 16 Black women, *Black Ritual*. The group of dancers were Ballet Theatre's Negro Unit. Shortly after the season, like many dance companies, the unit was disbanded so that Ballet Theatre (the sponsoring larger company) could pull its financial focus toward the main company (Maher 2014). In 1954 the Negro Ballet Company emerged, only to disband several years later due to financial challenges shortly after its first tour to the United Kingdom (Horwitz 2002). As mentioned earlier, Russian-born George Balanchine wanted an integrated ballet school in the 1930s (Gottschild 1996). While he was known to have an interest in African American vernacular dance and culture and jazz, it was not until Arthur Mitchell joined NYCB in 1955 that an African American gained entry to a mainstream ballet company. As the United States became more integrated, many ballet companies since the 1970s have made efforts to employ dancers of Color. Yet, racial obstacles prevailed, and the question remains as to why there are still so few WOC in ballet.

In the United States, a race-based society, most industries of high capital or artistic merit possess some barometer that is employed to maintain whiteness. For dance in the United States, ballet is that barometer employed to reify whiteness. Ballet is a Eurocentric art form. It is important to note that a focus on Europe does not make the form inherently racist. The form was birthed in Europe and is an ethnic dance form with origins in Europe (Kealiinohomoku 1983); the European dance characteristics of upward, heavenly orientation, partner work, and symmetry (Glass 2007) are evident in the technical execution of the dance form. The arguable difference is how the term "Eurocentric" is interpreted. Some definitions refer to a focus on European culture and history. Others note that such a focus is to the detriment of other cultures, equating Eurocentrism to whiteness. In the context of whiteness, ballet is positioned at the top of the dance hierarchy to uphold and maintain a position of superiority over other forms. While ballet is not always used in this manner, it is often used in this manner within the United States.

To be sure, American ballet has been impacted by the Black dancing body and the rich, culturally informed movements and rhythms derived from the African retentions living in African American communities in the United States. Esteemed dance scholar Brenda Dixon Gottschild writes about this at length in her landmark 1996 book *Digging the Africanist Presence in American Performance:*

> [T]he Balanchinian flexed foot, angled arm, retracted hip, or thrust pelvis are essential parts of a larger, polycentric whole, not merely interesting twists on an otherwise Europeanist turn. American culture is both heated and cooled by the Africanist presence, and this particular intertext of borrowings, receivings, and exchanges influences us all.... When we are able to see the African reflection as the image of our culture, then finally we will behold ourselves fully—as Americans—in the mirror. At that point it will be silly to talk about Africanist presences as "the African contribution." That is the outdated language of disenfranchisement, the mindset that implies that the European is something bigger or better into which the African—Other—is subsumed. But there is no Other, *we are it* [Gottschild 2012, 78].

Gottschild highlights the insult of and injury in not seeing the Africanist presence in ballet as it perpetuates the lie of white supremacy. Adding to this insult is that the people who opened the doors for people of Color in ballet in the early 1900s were oftentimes not from the United States (e.g., George Balanchine and Ballet Russe de Monte Carlo directors). Thus, their instincts about race were often in conflict with their lived experiences within a race-based society.

However, what I learned from ballet dancers from other countries, such as South Korea, Cuba, China, and Brazil, is that the racialized issues that many people have with ballet flourish in settings where racism is actively operating, such as the United States. In these places, sports, education, health care, politics, financial institutions, music, theater, and visual arts are all tinged with racism. So, why would ballet be exempt from the racial hierarchy rooted in the soil of the United States? Ballet in the United States is funded by the government and private donations of people who are often gratuitously wealthy, and this wealth and government support are often white-controlled. To be sure, the hand of white supremacy is far-reaching beyond the United States and does indeed extend to all of the previously named countries (South Korea, Cuba, China, and Brazil); however, racism operates differently in each of these countries.

As such, these countries have been able to share the art form of ballet with many of their citizens in a way that does not promote the exclusion of WOC in the ways that have historically been an obstacle in the United States; this will be seen in the stories of the women featured in this book. To be sure, after the Cuban Revolution any art that did not promote the state values of Cuba was not supported (Tomé 2011). As a result, some of the women interviewed do not relate racial issues to ballet. For these women, ballet training and employment was/is funded and supported by the state. In addition, the structures that uphold whiteness globally are complicated; women of darker skin color have been excluded in some spaces and sought after in others in some rather creative ways. This is most vividly seen in the work of South Africa's Joburg Ballet. There, few Black South African dancers were employed in the ballet company; financial barriers and historically limited access to training for Blacks resulted in a smaller pool of trained Black South African dancers. However, the Joburg Ballet is committed to providing diverse representation and imagery. To remedy this, the company brings in dancers from other countries while simultaneously developing training programs in several townships to ensure a presence of Black South African ballet dancers in the future (Nasser interview).

Even with obstacles, WOC did establish a visible presence in ballet in the 20th century. There are three institutions I wish to highlight here, as they have been instrumental in widening spaces for WOC in ballet. First, the Ballets Russes, as you will read herein, was instrumental in hiring WOC to perform with the company from the 1930s through the 1950s. Among those dancers were Alicia Alonso, Yvonne Chateau, Rosella Hightower, Moscelyn Larkin, Sono Osato, Lupe Serrano, Raven Wilkinson, Marjorie Tallchief, and Maria Tallchief. Second, DTH, founded by Arthur Mitchell with Karel Shook in response to the assassination of Dr. Martin Luther King, Jr., was established in 1969 as a beacon of hope and infinite possibility in Harlem, New York. Third, Ballet Hispánico was founded in 1970 by Tina Ramirez to promote Latinx cultures through the teaching and performing of dance. The legacy of these institutions is clear: open the space, and the dancers will come and thrive.

Historical Background of Women of Color in Ballet

To understand the full context of where we are in terms of diversity in ballet, it becomes necessary to look at how far we have come in regard to the presence of WOC in ballet throughout the 20th century. WOC began to be seen in growing numbers during the 1940s and 1950s. The five Native American women from Oklahoma—Maria Tallchief, Marjorie Tallchief, Rosella Hightower, Yvonne Choteau, and Moscelyn Larkin—affectionately known as the "Five Moons," were employed by

Flight of the Spirit, mural by Mike Larsen, 1991 (Oklahoma State Capitol Art Collection; courtesy the Oklahoma Arts Council).

various professional companies such as Ballet Russe de Monte Carlo, NYCB, Paris Opera Ballet, and Chicago Opera Ballet. Maria Tallchief danced with NYCB and performed for the Bolshoi Theatre. The Oklahoma Ballet was founded by Moscelyn Larkin. The Five Moons made monumental contributions to American ballet, commemorated by the Oklahoma Legislature. Lili Cockerille Livingston wrote a biographical book, *American Indian Ballerinas* (1997), that stands as an excellent resource for anyone who wants to learn more about these women.

In 1991, Mike Larsen was commissioned to paint a permanent mural in the rotunda of the Oklahoma State Capitol to celebrate the achievements of the Five Moons. The women, dressed in white, are positioned in front, with the centered ballerina reaching up with the upward-bound embodiment of the genre. Native community members in traditional and regular clothing are behind the dancers, with young and smaller dancers positioned on the side. It is as if they are preparing to move toward the Five Moons, ready to follow in their footsteps. A reddish-orange horizon looms in the background, evoking an Oklahoma prairie feel.

Culture, race, nation, politics, history, and place work together through varying intersections to comprise a nation's identity. Examinations of national identity find that these markers of identity can be expressed through art (De Baca and Best 2015). Alicia Alonso, Cuban prima ballerina and artistic director, crossed color and cultural barriers in the 1940s to achieve international recognition for her prowess in ballet. She also crossed the European border to bring ballet to her nation-state and became the catalyst who initiated the emergence of ballet in Cuba. Through Alonso's curation of a unique ballet aesthetic that expressed the Cuban culture and national identity after the Cuban Revolution in 1959 (Tomé 2017), the National Ballet of Cuba connected to the ethos of the nation, valuing community and countrymen

(*Classically Cuban* 1982). Moreover, through the ballet company's embracing and mastering of a European form, a model of excellence and cosmopolitanism came into play, one that subverted any and all ideologies of Cuba being inferior.

Similarly, in 1962 the South Korean government established the South Korean National Ballet Company. This government-sponsored company was and still is intended to provide the country with a vehicle for South Korean artistic expression. The South Korean National Ballet Company works to exalt a South Korean national identity, operating within a Western dance medium, but the "subjects, themes, and ethos" are South Korean (Kyunghee and Hyunjung 2008, 412). This company stands as another example of a nation appropriating a Eurocentric form to express a non-European cultural identity for the purpose of national cohesion.

This is not to say that the presence of ballet throughout the world has come without critique and challenge. Certainly, questions around Western cultural imperialism have been consistently raised. In 1997, dance anthropologist Jane Desmond found more than the imitation of Western culture when researching aspects of Chinese culture; China created a hybridization and recontextualization of ballet. Using ballet vocabulary blended with Chinese acrobatic traditions and martial movements, the National Ballet of China told Chinese stories and affirmed a national identity with ballets such as *The Red Detachment of Women* during the Cultural Revolution (Desmond 1997). Considering the context in which many come to know ballet outside the United States, one can understand how ballet can be recontextualized to affirm national identity. In contrast, ballet is often positioned to reify whiteness in the United States.

The New York Negro Ballet Company began performing around 1954 with six members and toured in the United Kingdom in 1957 with 21 dancers (Horwitz 2002). Among those included on the company roster were Guy Allison, Delores Browne, Sylvester Campbell, Theodore Duncan, Ward Fleming, Thelma Hill, Michaelyn Jackson, Frances Jimenez, Bernard Johnson, Graham Johnson, Yvonne McDowell, Charles Neal, Edna Phillips, Gene Sagan, Cleo Quitman, and Elizabeth Thompson. One of the contributing choreographers for this company was Louis Johnson, who studied early on in his career at the School of American Ballet and later choreographed dances for Broadway, established ballet companies, and film.

Raven Wilkinson danced for years in Ballet Russe de Monte Carlo during the 1950s. She was initially offered a position in the company that was contingent upon her being able to socially pass for white while traveling with the company across the United States. Years into her time with Ballet Russe there was an incident while traveling through the South when a "colored" woman identified and reported her as a Negro staying with the company at a whites-only hotel. As race relations became more and more tense during her tenure with Ballet Russe, Wilkinson eventually left the company after seven years not because of a lack of talent or skills but due to the racial politics of the time and the dangers of passing.

In the docuseries *I'll Make Me a World* (1999), Arthur Mitchell talks about this beautiful dancer, Raven Wilkinson, and notes that although she was "passing" while traveling with Ballet Russe de Monte Carlo, he could tell she was Black. This is a typical dynamic of passing; people from the in-group, in this case African Americans, generally can tell when one is passing, while the individual passing is vulnerable to being exposed at any given moment. Noted in Deans' dissertation, 2001, Wilkinson agreed not to announce her race as a contingency of her employment by the ballet company. Wilkinson's story is poignant and significant, providing insight into how race operated in the United States at the time. Opportunities for light-skinned Black people were then and continue to be more plentiful for those who can approximate whiteness (Gottschild 2003). In the documentary *Ballet Russe* (2005), Wilkinson talks about a day in rehearsal when the Ku Klux Klan stormed the stage and demanded that the Negro be identified. She spoke of feeling protected and valued when no one from the company outed her, describing the atmosphere in the company as akin to family.

Janet Collins was a prominent figure in American ballet, the first African American prima ballerina of the Metropolitan Opera Ballet in the early 1950s (Dunning 2003). She was also offered an opportunity to perform with Ballet Russe in 1932. Collins declined the offer because it came with a requirement that she "powder up," a process that has been the reality for many dancers of Color, continuing to be noted by dancers today (McCarthy-Brown 2011). And although Collins appeared in many performances with the Metropolitan Opera in New York, when the company went on the road, she would have to stay back because she was Black. Her life story is documented extensively in Yael T. Lewin's biography *Night's Dancer: The Life of Janet Collins* (2011).

As readers will find, there were many WOC in ballet throughout the 20th century. Among these women was Sono Osato, born to a Japanese father and an Irish French Canadian mother in Omaha, Nebraska. One of the few American dancers to witness the "Diaghilev ballet at its peak," she was actually accepted into Ballet Russes in 1934 at age 15 (Osato 1980). Her beautiful life story is told in her own words in her autobiography *Distant Dances* (1980). Another significant ballerina to the history of WOC danced with the American Ballet Theatre (ABT): Lupe Serrano. As her biography states on ABT's website, she was born in Santiago, Chile, and trained in Chile and Mexico City (American Ballet Theatre 2020). Serrano performed with the Mexico City Ballet and Ballet Russes before joining ABT in 1953 as a principal dancer. She retired from performing in 1971. Afterward she taught at Juilliard, the SFB, the Minnesota Dance Theater, the Cleveland Ballet, the Washington Ballet, the Rome Opera Theater, and Ballet Nacional de Mexico (Telgen and Kamp 1996).

There are many other WOC who have devoted themselves to the art of ballet, and while it delights me to recognize these ballerinas and see their names in print, I endeavor to get to the heart of this work: the women interviewed for this book. Yet, I would be remiss if I did not mention one more significant detail. Two dance institutions were instrumental in connecting me to many of the women in this book: DTH and Ballet Hispánico. Both of these institutions were the locale for several interviews for this book. More importantly, they were integral to the training, employment, and inspiration of most women featured herein. It is notable that these institutions continue to hold needed space for WOC in the world of dance. DTH, founded in 1969, and Ballet Hispánico, established in 1970, are invaluable in the resources and contributions they have bestowed on American dance.

Institutional Racism, Whiteness, and Ballet

In 2016 as dance historian Jennifer Fisher, building on the influential scholarship of Gottschild from the 1990s to today, wrote,

> Almost any way you look at it, ballet is a bastion, a very established hierarchical art form that often patrols its borders on the level of looks and body type, above and beyond the many talents it takes to perform well. And it is very white, meaning that pale-skinned people have dominated both onstage and backstage throughout its history as a profession from the seventeenth century to the present. Does this "whiteness" have an element of racial supremacy built in? Perhaps, inevitably, it does, ballet being an art form that has thrived during many eras when racism has been blatant and even institutionalized [Fisher, 2016].

Institutions are organized entities with a focused mission and purpose. To this end, there are many performing arts "institutes" besides ballet. Within all institutions are people who bring with them their cultures, aesthetics, languages, ideologies, prejudices, and social constructs of understanding. Institutions are a reflection of people, most often white and middle-class, and the patriarchal structures that seek to preserve whiteness. As such, it is not surprising to hear a flood of stories about experiences of racism or alienation within these institutions.

That is not to say that all ballet institutions and organizations are racist but instead that like any other institution and organization in our society, if not decidedly antiracist, the racism that permeates our Western society is too strong to keep outside the institution. Thus, if an organization is not working against the status quo, it is working, at times through stances of "neutrality" and "love for all," to maintain the status quo. Historically, institutional racism has held a strong presence in the following systems in the United States: education, health care, criminal justice, media, and employment (Meadows-Fernandez 2018). Historically, when the structure and composition of an institution is examined, it is clear how institutional racism has been embedded in its foundations.

I came to this research seeking to uncover a few of the many WOC who studied and dedicated their lives to this art form, often seen as "white." For most of the women interviewed, the color-casting of the dance form was insignificant when weighed against its personal value and the joy the women experienced through embodying ballet. These dancers talked about the work of creating magic, artistry, and elegance. That is not to say that they were ignorant or dismissive of the racial barriers around the form but simply that racial obstacles were not the focus of most of these women. Yet and still, this book and its discourse on the topic would be irrelevant if race were not included as a factor in the lives of these women. Ballet is an art form that preserves whiteness; white bodies dominate the dances seen on the concert stage, and ballet "remains one of the most organizing principles for defining concert dance history" (Kerr-Berry 142, 2018).

The academic definition of the term "whiteness" was employed to examine the experiences of the interviewees as individuals as well as the collective. Whiteness goes beyond the dominant presence of white bodies in the ballet dance form and extends to the institutional structures in ballet (funding, school admissions, hiring, lighting design, and casting), which ensures that it is maintained as a white space. Whiteness, as defined by Angela Castogna, "refers to structural arrangements ... [that] maintain power and privilege by perpetuating and legitimating the status quo while simultaneously maintaining a veneer of neutrality, equality, and compassion" (2014, 5). While whiteness is most often perpetuated by white people, people of Color at times participate in whiteness and uphold these set structures in order to survive and thrive in their education or profession (Castogna 2014). In addition, by design, whiteness is often invisible (Case 2013). I can think of many times as an educator and academic gatekeeper when I enacted whiteness on others, requiring a conformation to the status quo that would privilege the ethos of the dominant culture. I share this painful truth because without such honest admissions, we will never see the structures of racism we are complicit in and that must be dismantled.

For all of the interviewees, the artistry of ballet was first and foremost. They were willing to answer my questions about race, but I believe that for many of them the topic would not have come up if I had not asked. For some, I do not think it was on their radar; for others, I think in terms of public relations with their employing company they are encouraged to push the positive aspects of the work. Still others, I believe, consciously or subconsciously choose not to focus on what they alone cannot change. When encountering dismissive interest from interviewees concerning racial barriers in dance, I read this as a coping mechanism. Also of note, the dancers born in the United States all experienced racism in their careers and were able to identify and describe specific moments. Racial barriers were most prevalent for the African American ballet dancers interviewed.

As previously stated, it is significant to note that operations of white supremacy work beyond the borders of the United States. However, the WOC interviewed for this book who were raised and trained in ballet outside of the United States had very different ideas about race. Their thoughts correlated to how ballet is accessed and presented in many countries outside the United States. In Cuba, for example, because of the National School of Ballet, Cubanness and ballet have been brought together, which gives Cubans an opportunity to identify with the form not offered to most people of Color based in the United States. This is not to say that WOC did not experience racism in ballet outside of the United States but rather that their experiences were different and arguably not as stringent.

For some who feel the barriers of racial oppression in ballet, the "how" in this social construct is often obscure, particularly for those who see the Unites States as a progressive and diverse nation where one can do or be anything one wants. To be sure, ballet is a genre of artistic movement, and as a movement practice, it is not racist. So, how is it that within one of the most diverse and multicultural nations in the world—the United States—the form is so white? Race is experienced by persons without white privilege,* a set of messages and codes of conduct. Charles Mills (1997) described it as a contract, the "racial contract," similarly described by Isabel Wilkerson (2020) as a caste system. In the 21st century, these messages by and large are implicit, subconsciously understood even by young children.

This is demonstrated in the widely referenced "Black and white doll experiments" whereby young children are asked if they prefer a Black doll or a white doll and which doll is good and which doll is bad. From the 1940s through to experiments in recent years, Black and white children between the ages of five and seven consistently privileged the white doll (Bergner 2009). Such messages indicate where people "belong," as scholar Beverly Daniel Tatum states in *Why Are All the Black Kids Sitting Together in the Cafeteria?* (1997). Many of these implicit messages can be seen through the doors of commercially successful mainstream ballet dance studios and hanging along the halls of such spaces. Few Black and Brown dancers are seen in the studios, few are seen leading class or directing companies, few are seen uplifted and honored in photo imagery along the walls or even on the websites. As you will read, many dancers of Color receive messages about whether they fit in or belong. These messages are powerful and effective.

Ballet dancers of Color have cited more explicit messaging including Raven Wilkinson, who was told to go and do African dancing by her ballet mistress at Ballet Russe de Monte Carlo after six years with the company (*I'll Make Me a World* 1999). The teacher gave no consideration to the physical impossibility of a ballet dancer simply going off to do a virtuosic dance form that, like ballet, takes years of extensive training to master. Former DTH principal dancer and artistic director Virginia Johnson noted the whispers she heard suggesting that she should take up jazz or something other than ballet (*I'll Make Me a World* 1999). Aesha Ash routinely addressed the overall exhaustion of being the only Black dancer in a ballet company, which took its toll on her (Kourlas 2007). Lauren Anderson shared an experience of being ignored by a guest artist choreographer, who eventually sought an academy student dancer to take her company slot to avoid working with a Black dancer. These examples are more than implicit messages; they are macro-aggressive, explicit racist messages, that amount to, at the very least, verbal and psychological abuse, and at the most, racial violence. These behaviors cause injury. Yet, for many, it is just another day at the dance studio.

---

*White privilege is the status to which the structure was created to favor and to position those with white skin with unearned privileges above all others.

One of the challenges is that in many instances, the training spaces for ballet feel white to many people of Color. In contrast, some white people see the same spaces as "universal" or "normal" (Frankenberg 2001). Students of Color (and white students) see little representation of an attainable goal for individuals who are not white. Education research has been conclusive in noting that students are advantaged when they can identify with their teachers and other aspirational figures (Earick 2009). In several of my interviews, you will read about dancers overcoming feelings of alienation or "being the only one" to succeed in ballet when they were connected to dancers who shared the same racial background.

Whiteness is often reified in the racial representation of the teaching faculty and company members (if the training institution has a ballet company in residence). Traditional paradigms of classical ballet casting center around European characters (i.e., *Giselle, Romeo and Juliet, Sleeping Beauty,* and *Swan Lake*), with Eurocentric aesthetics of the physical space compounding the Eurocentric focus of many companies. Whether one sees a ballet school as a Eurocentric or neutral space, in either instance the reality is that the physical space supports the dominant culture. This is to say that ballet spaces are often void of the vibrant colors typically utilized to signify Latinx, African, and Asian diasporic cultures and have bare studios that feature the barres and the piano. While the barres and the piano are functional, without any countering cultural artifacts that affirm a value of other cultures, European ethos and aesthetics are enshrined. These observations provide a context and an explanation as to why some feel that ballet spaces are white spaces.

Whiteness is simply felt. A ballet company asked me to provide some consulting services around the area of diversifying its school. A school representative noted a challenge in previous diversity and scholarship auditions due to the staff in the building not being prepared to welcome in the auditioning students. Some of the staff were uncomfortable with the number of family members accompanying auditioning students. This may be because oftentimes families outside the dominant culture are structured differently. In many communities of Color, extended family is a staple that is valued in a similar fashion to a nuclear family. This type of cultural clash can be the impetus for the ideas of exclusive white space that some people outside the dominant culture associate with ballet. Implicit messages of discomfort and unwelcome are transmitted. When dancers of Color, including their families, sense a lack of value, they choose not to commit themselves to the space, and whiteness is maintained. Below is an excerpt from Yael Lewin's biography on Janet Collins wherein her consciousness of being in a white space sits at the forefront of her performance experience:

> What in the name of God am I doing here! It is opening night at the Metropolitan—the gala performance of Giuseppe Verdi's *Aïda*. It is the first time in the history of the venerable opera house that it has a black artist on its roster. Let me tell you, my friend, I am just as surprised as anyone else. I can only think, "Oh, dear God, what am I doing here" [Lewin 2011, xiii].

Collins's rise in an exclusive art form occurred during a time when, as Lewin points out in *Night's Dancer*, "the black dancing body was welcome to the stage in the form of popular entertainment, often soothing the stereotype of the exotic primitive" (Lewin 2011, xiii). Requirements of hair buns and pink tights contribute to "othering" notions of whiteness often built into ballet spaces. Collins's thoughts of "what am I doing here" align with Charles Mills' framework of the racial contract (1997). He argues that the racial contract establishes white spaces that are deemed proper, with nonwhites deemed alien in those spaces: "white raced space of the polity is in a sense the geographical locus of polity proper" (Mills 1997, 50). One must question and then understand why Collins felt out of place. I assert that the social "racial" contract was successful in communicating to Collins where she belonged and where she did not.

Ballet and the Color of Swans in the 21st Century

For decades, dance critics have commented on the scarcity of Black ballet dancers. Jennifer Dunning wrote about this phenomenon in her *New York Times* articles "A Dancer Who Had a Dream" (1974) and then again in 1997 when writing "An Uphill Path to Swan Lake" (1997). Many have echoed the words "Where Are All of the Black Swans?," which was the title of a *New York Times* article by Gia Kourlas in 2007. Over the years, there has been a galvanizing push to document the history and presence of Blacks in ballet and create institutionalized paths that ensure equitable access for dancers of Color. Various entities and strategic plans emerged in response to these calls.

One example of proactive change toward inclusion is the website MOBBallet, launched in 2015 by Theresa Ruth Howard. MOBBallet works as a curated digital archive, an online museum, and a forum that provides primary sources, a historical gallery, and invaluable sources of inspiration for dancers and nondancers everywhere. MOBBallet addresses the issue of history. Documenting the presence of Blacks in dance provides a more accurate picture of our history, diminishing the opportunity to whitewash history and the genre of ballet at large. Resources provided at the MOBBallet website offer a picture of the ballet dancing body that is multidimensional and comes in many colors.

MOBBallet works as a repository to preserve the history of Blacks in ballet, while "The Equity Project" seeks to provide access, with a particular focus on training and employment for African Americans who wish to pursue ballet as a career. These two entities underscore the fact that there are no similar networks for Asian or Latinx dancers. This is in part because the lineage and legacy of DTH provides a network of advocates for Blacks in ballet not matched by any other ethnic group outside the dominant culture. The work of these entities also brings forth another question: What are institutions doing to diversify the genre of ballet and to be more inclusive? For decades, most commercially successful mainstream ballet companies have offered a varying number of diversity and need-based scholarships to students. These tactics have yielded little institutional change.

It is documented and shared on the International Association of Blacks in Dance website that in 2018, "The Equity Project: Increasing the Presence of Blacks in Ballet" convened for the first time. "In a press release, 'The Equity Project' describes itself as a partnership between DTH, IABD [International Association of Blacks in Dance], Dance/USA, and twenty-one large budget U.S. professional organizations." The list of participating companies includes but is not limited to ABT, Boston Ballet, SFB, Joffrey Ballet, NYCB, Charlotte Ballet, and National Ballet of Canada.

For dancers in the United States, the dominance of white bodies in the space is a structural outcome of whiteness, a structural arrangement imbedded within our society. For people of Color, this premise can often feel as though one is swimming upstream just to be included in what is presented as mainstream life. Implicit, tacit messages weigh on dancers; there are few opportunities, perceived or otherwise, in mainstream ballet companies that are not exclusionary white spaces. However, while conducting research for this book, I encountered two institutional models for institutional change that address some of these barriers.

Where race is an issue, class is often an inseparable factor. Historically, class is also a prohibitive factor for would-be students of the genre. For as long as I can remember, established ballet companies have offered minority or need-based scholarships; yet, they never seem to impact the composition of the school or company due the challenges of recruitment and retention. There are myriad reasons that could explain this paradigm. One issue with traditional diversity initiatives is funding and transportation. Many programs have scholarships that do not guarantee continued funding over the number of years that students must study. However, the Miami City Ballet developed a program to provide an assured commitment to families. Recognizing that many parents are unable to leave work and transport children across town after school, the Miami City Ballet sought to address this issue of inequity from a financial angle. In 2015 the company launched the Miami City Ballet Bus. Students audition at seven years old and, when accepted, are offered a seat on the "bus." That is, the Miami City Ballet School makes a commitment to the child and parents to offer continued ballet classes and transportation from their neighborhoods to the Miami City Ballet School building (Lopez interview). Few programs assure families that they will not be financially strained for the duration of the child's training. Artistic director Lourdes Lopez is passionate about providing opportunities to young dancers who cannot afford the expense of ballet lessons. In addressing the financial aspect of training, otherwise excluded groups are provided access. With this reality in mind, the Miami City Ballet Bus makes a 10-year commitment to families accepted into the program when a child is seven years old. Consequently, this program provides a solution, as on average it takes 10 years to train a dancer.

The Joburg Ballet is also invested in a long-term solution to diversify ballet in South Africa. There are very few classically trained Black ballet dancers to employ in a South African ballet company. At the time of my visit to the country, Kitty Phelta was the only Black South African company member in the Joburg Ballet. Executive director of the company Esther Nasser said that her goal with the company's training program, currently thriving in two South African townships, was to ensure that Phelta would not be the only representation of Black South Africans in ballet for long. Within the social context of a changing nation, the Joburg Ballet sees training future generations of ballet dancers as not only a solution to the diversity challenges in South African ballet but also a trajectory shift for the nation (Esther Nasser, interview with author, Johannesburg, South Africa, 2017).

As a part of this model for institutional change, the Joburg Ballet has two satellite programs in the Soweto and Alexandra townships outside the major city of Johannesburg. Students are given daily classical ballet training in multiple levels in their communities. Although families pay a small fee, no family unable to pay is turned away. There is a pipeline for students to progress to the National School for the Arts and then on to the company's Aspirant Program, operating like an apprenticeship for dancers before being offered a position in the company. To be sure, only a few dancers in any starting ballet class progress straight through their training to the company. Yet and still, this shift for developing talent from township communities marks a significant structural change. Nasser admits that in decades previous and to date, the remedy for a white ballet company was to go to Cuba or Brazil in order to get Black dancers (Nasser interview). As a result, the Joburg Ballet is quite internationally diverse but considers the strategy of hiring dancers from other countries a short-term remedy that does not advance the nation or the company. However, it is a strategy that will be employed until the township training programs have produced enough dancers to meet the demand for more dancers of Color in the company.

In *The Black Dancing Body* (2012), Gottschild points out the Eurocentric sensibilities and physique encompassed in the ballet aesthetic. It is notable that nations that have widely embraced ballet without its Eurocentric cultural entrapments have consciously altered the technique to apply to the body types commonly seen in their regions of the world. This can be seen in the Chinese ballet *The Red Detachment of Women* and the established Cuban Method of training utilized in the Cuban National Ballet School. Nasser, of the Joburg Ballet, shared with great excitement the development of a South African ballet training method. Developed by two expert South African trainers, it combines the Cuban Method, which evolved from the Vaganova Method,* with new training practices developed. The company is very

---

*There are a small number of internationally recognized ballet training methods including but not limited to the Cuban Method, the Cecchetti Method, the Vaganova Method, the Bournonville Method, the Royal Academy of Dance, and the Balanchine Method.

optimistic about this emerging method, as it has already been very effective with Black South African students. The development of a South African training method and the more established Cuban Method acknowledges the need for adjustments that can benefit dancers of Color and different body types in the pursuit of ballet training.

The historical context of WOC in ballet underpins the challenges of representation and equity seen today. Yet, it is wonderful to celebrate the success and the ways in which race has at times been transcended through dancing bodies of Color. Indeed, dancing bodies of Color defy whiteness on aesthetic, performative, and structural levels. The act of these dancing bodies of Color, mastering this virtuosic form, flies in the face of every obstacle positioned to oppress and limit access. It is an act of power, subversion, and triumph.

Herstories:
The Interviews

The 13 oral history interviews are divided into two sections. Interview Set I features dancers who retired from performing 10 or more years ago. Interview Set II contains interviews of dancers who are still performing or retired within the past five years. In addition, within each set, interviews are in alphabetical order. Interview Set I begins with six retired dancers, four African Americans and two Cuban Americans. One of the interviews is with Crystal Michelle Perkins, a ballet-trained African American dancer who performed in a ballet company for one year before her dance journey evolved to join a contemporary Black repertory company. The next seven interviews, interview Set II, are of dancers that were performing in ballet companies at the time the interviews were conducted. Two of these dancers were interviewed in Johannesburg, South Africa; three are Asian American dancers; one is a Cuban American dancer; and one dancer was born and trained in Cuba and is now dancing with Dance Theatre of Harlem (DTH).

As previously noted, the interview script centered on the following core questions: (1) How did you come to ballet? (2) Can you describe the environment of your training/company employment? (3) Did you have a teacher or advocate in your life who helped you get where you are today? (4) Do you think you have ever been color-casted? (5) What prompted your retirement/What are you looking forward to next in your ballet career?

Each interview begins with general background information and a photograph. Because of the diversity of experiences among the dancers interviewed, this format for chapter introductions and photographs is not identical. Some dancers had more accessible photographs than others. To guide the reader, brackets are used to document unspoken gestures and emotions such as laughing, crying, and gesturing. I use parentheses to explain terms or words used by interviewees. Directly following each interview there is a brief glossary of the teachers and significant places mentioned by the dancers.

Set I—Retired Dancers

Lauren Anderson • Lourdes Lopez •
Caridad Martinez • Crystal Michelle Perkins •
Stephanie Powell • Endalyn Taylor

Lauren Anderson

Past affiliation: Houston Ballet (1983–2006)
Current position: Associate Director, Education & Community Engagement, Houston Ballet
Hometown: Houston, Texas
Age at time of interview: 54

I interviewed Lauren Anderson in Dallas, Texas, in 2017 at the annual International Association of Blacks in Dance conference. She brought her commanding energy into the room, comfortable with public relations but also genuine. There is nothing cookie-cutter about Lauren; she gave me the vibe of down-to-earth diva. Records from that interview were destroyed in an unforeseen event. Lauren was gracious enough to redo the interview by phone on July 20, 2019. Excerpts from the 2019 phone interview are shared here.

NM: *Can you tell me how you began dancing?*

LA: Well, when I started, my father was the assistant principal of the High School for the Performing Arts (HSPA) in Houston. He was hiring dance teachers and pianists for HSPA from Houston Ballet, and I guess he mentioned to someone that he had an overactive daughter, and they wondered if ballet might be a good outlet for me. That's kind of how I got started. I don't really think I said "Dad, I want to be a ballerina."

I played the violin. My favorite things to do were play the violin and play outside. So, ballet wasn't even on my radar. I just have two parents that were into the arts.

Houston Ballet former principals Lauren Anderson as Cleopatra and Timothy O'Keefe as Caesar in Ben Stevenson's *Cleopatra*, 2000 (photograph by Geoff Winningham; courtesy Houston Ballet).

NM: And how old were you when you started to take ballet lessons?
   LA: I started ballet in 1972; I was seven years old.

NM: Why did it stick, what was it about dance? Why do you dance?
   LA: Well, I was going to quit when I was nine, 11, and 13.
   When I was nine, the reason I didn't quit is because we went to see Dance Theatre of Harlem. It was funny, because number one, I didn't actually know I was going to see Dance Theatre of Harlem, and number two, I didn't know who they were. And then I saw this African American ballerina run across the stage. And I was like "Oh! [gasping]," and my mom said I sat on the edge of my seat the entire performance. So, that was kind of a turning point. And when I saw them do *Firebird* I said, "I want to be her." That was one time I was going to quit—and didn't.
   And when I was 11, Ben Stevenson came to Houston Ballet (as artistic director of the company), and he taught classes; he taught classes even in the academy (teaching to the students, not just professional company level). And he made ballet fun but challenging. And it was already challenging, but to me it wasn't very fun, so that was another turning point for me.
   And then when I was 13, the thing that kind of glued me in, probably by the time I was 13 it had already chosen me. I loved the competitive side; I realized I had a superpower—that was jumping. I could jump higher than anybody. Pretty fearless with turns. I decided at that point I wanted to be a dancer. And you know, when you're of a certain age, your parents go in and ask the director or the coach or whoever it is, whatever your kid's doing, if your kid's going to be any good at it. And, of course, my parents went in, and Ben Stevenson was very honest. He said, "No, I would not think Lauren would be a good ballet dancer, but she has a good singing voice and a good personality. Musical theater might be her niche, but she should keep taking ballet because it's a good base of all dance, and she'd have an edge if she went into a musical theater audition with ballet knowledge." Well, I was devastated, of course. They continued the conversation, I left the room, my dad came out and said, "You're taking these classes, because I've already paid for them. We'll visit it again at the beginning of next year."
   Meanwhile, the spring show was going, and every kid in the Houston Academy is in the spring show. The spring show that year was *Alice in Wonderland*. I guess it was, like, January. We all ran to the board to see the casting. And next to Alice it had the last name Anderson. I figured there must be some other student coming in with the last name Anderson. That couldn't be me; I couldn't be Alice. And I looked down and there were no more Andersons. So, I went into the office again and was just devastated. Like, "Why am I the only kid not in the show?" [*in an exasperated tone*], and Ben Stevenson said to me, "Darling, you're Alice." And I was like, "Oh, I can't be Alice, Alice is white." And he said to me, "The only color in art is on a canvas. You're a dancer, and dancers dance. You are Alice." I couldn't believe it. That was like the thing that really ... like I didn't have to be the ballerina. In *Alice in Wonderland*, that

(lead dancer) is a Tiger Lily, but the lead person in *Alice in Wonderland* is Alice. So, it just let me know that there is a spot for me somewhere. It doesn't have to be what I thought it had to be, but I could get there, right? I was like "Okay, well, shoot, if I could be 'Alice' in *Alice in Wonderland,* I could be anything."

NM: How did you overcome the other advice you were given about pursuing musical theater?

LA: Well, I just decided that I was going to be a ballet dancer. I decided that. I'm a little hardheaded. I figured I'll take classes here and then go get a job somewhere else, maybe Dance Theatre of Harlem. That's what I was thinking.

NM: So, Dance Theatre of Harlem. Can you describe your first visit to the space, the building, the company?

LA: Yeah [emotional shift in her voice], wow, ... so I never danced with them, by the way. I've only danced with Houston Ballet. But um, well, I mean I've only been *hired* as a company member at Houston Ballet. So it was, gosh, I don't know, half a decade, I don't know probably five or six years ago, and Virginia Johnson, who is the ballerina I looked up to as a young dancer ... called me and asked me to come teach. And I said "sure," and I got there. Just walking in and seeing that giant picture of Mr. Mitchell ... tears came to my eyes. Walking around and seeing that many little Brown ballerinas in one place, I'd never seen it before; I never ever witnessed that before. So, it choked me up, and when I think about it I still get a little choked up.

NM: You mentioned that you had never danced with them, but you had an appreciation for them throughout your career because they inspired you as a child, so what was it like to teach that master class?

LA: Well, I taught for a week in the summer, and it was amazing actually just to be there. I felt at home immediately, and everyone that I ran into on the staff were dancers that I'd read about in *Dance Magazine* when I was dancing. So, it was a serious mutual admiration moment for all of us, for everyone involved. They knew who I was; I knew who they were. They had no idea the impact they had on my life and my career. Yeah, it was a really special moment. And so, I still have a really good connection with them now.

NM: Another dancer who came from a predominantly white company I interviewed talked about her desire to dance with Dance Theatre of Harlem because she found herself onstage with another African American ballerina, and she thought to herself that that had never happened in her life before, that she was able to dance with another Black woman. And you mention these experiences with DTH: walking into the building and also seeing them for the first time. Have you ever been able to dance onstage with other Black women or Women of Color?

LA: Oh, Houston Ballet had nine dancers in the company of Color. Yeah, in 1976 the first African American was hired, male, Adrian Vincent James, and then Sandra Organ the year before I got in, which was '82, and then I got in, in '83.

(Continuing into) the '90s, we had, like, a lot of us. I mean there was a Latin contingent, an Asian contingent, a Black contingent; there were quite a few dancers. So yes, Ayisha McMillan and Katlyn Addison, a dancer that is with Ballet West right now. Yeah, yeah, absolutely.

NM: Can you tell me a little bit about your performance career? I know that you retired in 2006. How was your entry into the company, the highs and lows?

LA: I got into the company in '83 as a corps member. In '87 I became a soloist, and in '90 I became a principal dancer. Gosh, I don't know, I've danced all the major ballerina roles.

NM: Did you get to do Firebird?

LA: The only thing I haven't done is Juliet. I haven't done Juliet, Clara in the *Nutcracker*, or Clara's Mother in the *Nutcracker*. I've been everything else, pretty much. The performance I've done the most, of course, is *Nutcracker*, 'cause that happens *every* year. And since my first year in the company, I was Sugar Plum Fairy. I've done other things too. And then, I was fortunate enough to have a couple of ballets choreographed for me: one, *Don Quixote*, and another one, *Cleopatra*. And the cool thing about *Cleopatra* was, it had never been done before, so I was the very first one to do the full-length *Cleopatra*, which was way cool.

NM: What would you say was your favorite role?

LA: Oh man, people ask me that all the time, and it just depends what mood I'm in, really. My first favorite was Sugar Plum Fairy because ever since I was seven, I've wanted to do her, and then I got to be her. And I've had the longest relationship with her because I've done her from 1983 to 2009 all over the world, so that's—we have a special relationship. Then after that I got to be the Swan—well, I mean I've gotten to do quite a bit, but the Swan Queen, being the black and the white swan, was a big deal. *Don Quixote,* which Ben Stevenson did for me, was then of course my third favorite because I mean, like I said, that ballet was done for me. And I actually did that one a lot all over the world too. It's hard (to narrow it down), and then of course *Cleopatra* was special; that just holds a special place.

NM: You talked a little bit about the diversity at the Houston Ballet, and you've seen tons of ballet companies and their inner workings. What could you tell me about the culture of Houston Ballet that stands out among others and is special to you?

LA: Well, I mean, I can say this just from firsthand experience: Ben Stevenson had no problem sticking me in the middle of the corps *of Swan Lake*. You know, a lot of people have issues with that; people have come into set ballets on Houston Ballet and said, "Well, I can't have her there and I can't have her do this" because of the color of my skin. And he's like "Why not? She's just another dancer." Are you going to tell a white person with a tan that they can't go on (stage) because they have a tan? That doesn't make any sense. So, Houston Ballet has been very open about anyone dancing any role since I can remember. I mean, come on, they had a Black Alice in *Alice in Wonderland* in 1979.

And Li Cunxin, who's a Chinese guy—I don't know if you know the movie *Mao's Last Dancer*. That movie was based out of Houston because Li Cunxin, the dancer, defected from China and came here (to Houston). So, he was Chinese and there was this huge thing about him being Romeo. Ben got so many letters about it: "You cannot have this Chinese guy as Romeo." How crazy is that? Anyways, that didn't stop Cunxin; he did all three nights. So, Houston Ballet's always been very open about the quality of the dance, not the color of the dancer.

NM: Quite a special experience (at Houston Ballet). I remember doing a talk for college students in Pennsylvania, and I had a student in the room who was from Houston, and when I was talking about the scarcity of Black ballerinas she kind of just looked at me sideways the entire time. And at the end she said, "Well, I'm from Houston, and there are Black ballerinas performing every time I go to the ballet, dancing a range of roles." I thought that was amazing, the work that you all have done in Houston, to imprint in someone's ideology as a child, to come up in a place and think anything is possible, the opposite messaging from what you intuited about being Alice.

LA: Yeah, it is good. But it's a little disappointing when you go other places and find out that's not the case, right? I think it's awesome, but it's just a shame that you cannot convince everyone to feel that way. But apparently (African American ballerinas are) just not common, and I didn't really know that until I retired, that it wasn't common (to have plentiful opportunities for African American dancers).

NM: Wow, that's amazing. You've talked a lot about how supportive and instrumental Ben Stevenson has been to you and your development as a ballet dancer. What have you taken from that relationship that you see in the relationships that you now have with young dancers?

LA: Oh, my goodness, that's a great question. Okay, so he decided in 1987 that I should teach a class in the summer school. I said, "You must be crazy. I can't teach a ballet class." And he asked me, "How many classes have you taken?" I thought "Well, I've probably taken millions of classes." And that was the best thing he could have ever done. 'Cause my thing now is teaching. I *love* teaching. He was a great teacher, and he still is and a person who is really good at visualization. If you can get a child to feel it or imagine it or create the feeling in their mind, then you can get them to do anything. He gave me that "anything is possible in the studio" attitude, and I take that with me into every class I teach.

NM: Do you remember being promoted to principal dancer?

LA: Ohhhh, *yes*. So, I'm in this ballet called *Études*, and it's the summer; I think it's May of 1990. And I'm going to the international ballet competition, and we're rehearsing *Études* or whatever we're rehearsing. And he just walks into the room and he says [in her Ben Stevenson accent] "Lauren, by all accounts you're going to be promoted to principal dancer next season" and walks out of the room, and I thought I was going to pass out. It was awesome. That's all it was, that's all it was. And I signed the contract in August.

NM: *That's amazing.*
LA: I know, it's crazy. It was amazing.

NM: *Have you ever had any struggles with your body in terms of injuries or preparing to dance or getting into the image of a ballet dancer or things of that nature?*
LA: *Yes*, when I was a student. You know, body image to the dancer is so warped. And as a youngster, you know, 14, 15, 16, you don't like your body anyway. No matter what it is, you don't like it. And it's doing all kinds of weird things. So, that was about the age I started doing Pilates to change the shape of my legs, to start working differently in ballet, because I decided I wanted to be a ballet dancer, and the body that I had looked like "come Nana" on pointe. And I couldn't be that. So, I decided that I would do whatever it took to change and lengthen, because ballet is an illusion. And I wanted to create the illusion. So, I did that in a very healthy way, actually. I didn't do any crazy diets or anything like that. I did, however, become a pescatarian for, I don't know, 16 years just so that I wouldn't build too much muscle. And I'm muscular already, which is fine. I mean, you have to be muscular; we're athletes. But I wanted to lengthen my body, and it worked; it worked.

NM: *Did you ever feel as though you had to be twice as good as a white dancer? Or was that not an issue because of the nurturing environment you were in?*
LA: Um … when people came from outside of Houston Ballet, yes, I felt like I had to be … better. But Ben was always about "You need to be the best you can possibly be anyway." There is never a day that you let down your guard on getting better. And my parents raised me that way. It was always about hard work, working hard, and pushing through—all that. Luckily, I didn't have any major injuries until after I retired. And that's because in our classes back then, we were taking classes to improve, not just taking classes to warm up for the day. You were taking class to become a better dancer, which I think is very important for a dancer's career. That way you stay in a tip-top shape.

NM: *Is there something different that you see in the way dancers train today?*
LA: Yes. I feel that, in some places, it's about "Let's just get warm for the day and get ourselves together for what we have to do in rehearsal" and not "I need to improve this thing." I can't say that goes on here; I'm not saying that at all. It just seems like (audience) yelps are around the tricks, how high I can get my leg, how much more split, and all that instead of the quality of what they are trying to achieve. I know they notice it and see the quality is better (when they focus on technical development over tricks) because of what they "oooooh" and "ahhhhhhh" at, but um, yeah, I think that's just kids being kids, you know. And with social media it's all about who can do that really quick trick, that one time on social media where you can keep looking at it over and over again. But does that happen in performance?

NM: To your point, and in seeing the way the terrain of dance and ballet has changed over the years, do you think ballet has been impacted by the rise of competition dance?

LA: Yes, of course. I think competition dance, dance shows, all that has helped bring ballet into mainstream America and mainstream everything. Right, and I know those competition dancers take ballet. I mean, absolutely. Competition dance is an interesting animal to me. I'm just going to leave it at that.

NM: You retired in 2006. Do you ever miss your pointe shoes and performing?

LA: Do I miss my pointe shoes? *No.* Do I miss performing? No, because I perform every day. When you teach a class, you're performing. You've got to inspire when you teach. It's about inspiration, inspiring those kids to do whatever it is you need them to do to get whatever your goal is. Performance is happening all the time as a teacher, I feel.

NM: How did you come to the decision to retire?

LA: My body said "Stop," and I couldn't dance at the same level that I danced before if I wasn't taking complete classes and all that. You know, class is the bread and butter; it keeps you going. You can rehearse all you want, but class is technique. Ballet 101 is what keeps you going, and if your body's done, your body's done. My knees were done.

NM: You were called to present Misty Copeland with flowers for her debut as principal dancer in Swan Lake. *Can you talk a little bit about that experience?*

LA: Yes, that was really neat. I sat with Raven Wilkinson, which was *amazing*!

NM: What did you two talk about?

LA: The performance. We talked about the performance and subtleties and things we could tell her (Misty) to make it better. We were coaching her through the whole thing. It was awesome.

I remember when I danced and I saw Debbie Allen and Judith Jamison at one of my performances, or a couple of performances, like opening night, big performances. It was so huge. It meant so much. So, it was really neat to be there for (Misty) for that. I remember how much that meant to me. And Judith Jamison and Debbie Allen were there too. It was great. So, it was really neat, the three of us, or four of us, with Raven. Being there along with so many people. Cecily Tyson and so many amazing people were there to support her for that big event in her career.

NM: Yeah, I was going to ask you a little bit about Debbie Allen. You talked about what it meant for you to have her present to support you when you were dancing, and I was just curious, aside from Misty, if there are other young up-and-coming ballet dancers that you have your eye on today or you are excited to go see.

LA: There's a young lady named Madison Brown I think could be amazing; I would have to work on her pointe work, but that's like a whole other story. I mean, but she's like 13 or 14. I get to go all over the country and teach, so I see a lot of really talented students. Yeah, there are so many beautiful dancers out there, there really are. I just think Alicia Mack-Graff retired way too early for me. But she's in a great place. She's at Juilliard and still dancing a little bit from what I see but retired way too early for me. A lot of dancers that didn't get the opportunities. I would love to see Michaela DePrince get coached by someone who would be willing to take the time to bring her into all her ballerinadom. But there are so many, so many.

NM: You share publicly about your sobriety.
LA: Ten years two Mondays ago.

NM: Congratulations on the 10 years!
LA: Thank you.

NM: That experience has truly added to the ways that you inspire greatness in others. There is a lot of pressure in performing.
LA: Gosh, yes. When you're looking at someone in the public eye, it looks like everything is perfect and they couldn't have any issues or problems, and that's so not the case. I just want people to know, there's other people out there going through whatever you are going through; you are not alone. Help is not far; help is much closer than you think. People have reached out to me (when I went public), and it was awesome, and I try to steer them in the direction so they could get help.

NM: I'm going back to the issue of racism in casting because you mentioned people from the outside gave you a different experience than when you were insolated within the Houston Ballet. Was there ever an instance where you felt that issues of race were factored into your casting?
LA: Oh yeah. I think it was my first year in the company; we were doing *Theme and Variations*. Someone came to set it. There were some company members being used as soloists in another ballet in the next room, so they let corps members slip into their spots, and all the corps members and apprentices were used and I was standing in the back, and the person that came in to set the piece leaned over and said, "Can we get someone from the academy? I can't put her in." Now, I can do the corps de ballet of *Theme and Variations*. As a matter of fact, after they left, the next time we did it, I was the lead every time. So, it wasn't because I couldn't, it's just that they weren't used to seeing Brown people in absolutely classical ballet.

NM: What are some of the struggles that you see your students going through now and the challenges to inspire them through today when you're teaching?
LA: That whole thing of wanting to be fabulous now and not being willing to put in the work, it takes time. Classical anything is slow; you can't get it quickly. You have to practice repetition. Kids now don't want to repeat. They're so used to getting it once on their phone. And going in a search bar, typing something in and finding it, right? They don't want to have to do the work. They would just rather Google "ballet." And it's not going to happen that way. You can't just Google-search ballet and eat it, and then you're doing it. So, that's the challenge that I find.

Houston Ballet former principals Lauren Anderson as Alice and Keith Lelliot as the White Rabbit in Ben Stevenson's *Alice in Wonderland*, 1979 (courtesy Houston Ballet).

Houston Ballet former principals Lauren Anderson as Kitri and Carlos Acosta as Basilio with Artists of Houston Ballet in Ben Stevenson's *Don Quixote*, 1995 (photograph by Geoff Winningham; courtesy Houston Ballet).

NM: What works to address that?

LA: Changing it up a little bit, changing up music, changing up things that they do in it. Saying some things. I have a pink flip-flop that I throw at people to remind them to do stuff. Not that I beat kids, because I don't. But I do want to get their attention. And they think that it's funny, and it cuts the hard candy shell. So, they start to trust me right away. Plus, because I teach master classes, I'm not their teacher all year. I have to get to them right away. I have like an hour and a half maybe to get through to the students. You need to know your audience.

NM: How do you feel about ballet as an art form?

LA: Ballet is beautiful; you get to physically become music. I think that's with dance, period. One thing about ballet is there are so many absolutes. You can't just be willy-nilly about it; there's one technique and that's it. But what's so wonderful is expressing yourself above that technique, telling a story without words. Being aesthetically pleasing at all points. It's just absolutely beautiful and elegant. I have no other real words for it.

Lauren Anderson Glossary

These brief bio-notes of artists and places mentioned in the chapter are not intended to be comprehensive but instead to offer a small amount of information to spark more thorough research if readers are interested.

Addison, Katlyn—Began performance career as a company member with Houston Ballet in 2007. Joined Ballet West in 2011; promoted to principal dancer in 2021.

Allen, Debbie—Internationally recognized director, choreographer, author, dancer, and actor. Founded the Debbie Allen Dance Academy in 2000.

Brown, Madison—Dancer with American Ballet Theatre.

Copeland, Misty—First African American female principal dancer with the American Ballet Theatre in 2015.

Cunxin, Li—Artistic director of Queensland Ballet. Former Houston Ballet dancer.

DePrince, Michaela—Born in Sierra Leone. Joined the Boston Ballet in 2021.

Houston Ballet—Founded in 1969. The company progressed from a ballet school and a foundation that were established through a state charter in 1955.

Jamison, Judith—Dancer for Alvin Ailey American Dance Theater from 1965 to 1980. Returned to the company to serve as artistic director from 1989 to 2011.

Mack-Graf, Alicia—Former member of Alvin Ailey American Dance Theater, Dance Theatre of Harlem, and Complexions Contemporary Ballet. First African American woman appointed director of Juilliard's Dance Division.

McMillan Cravotta, Ayisha—Academy director at the Charlotte Ballet. Former dancer with Houston Ballet.

Mitchell, Arthur—Cofounder of Dance Theatre of Harlem in 1969. First African American to become a principal dancer with New York City Ballet. Mitchell died in 2018.

Organ Solis, Sandra—Houston Ballet's first African American ballerina, dancing there for 15 years (1982–1997). Founded the contemporary ballet ensemble Earthen Vessels with the Sandra Organ Dance Company.

Sugar Plum Fairy—Featured principal female role in the *Nutcracker* ballet.

Tyson, Cecily—Award-winning film, television, and stage actress.

Vincent James, Adrian—Dancer, choreographer, director, and educator. First African American selected by artistic director Ben Stevenson to dance with the Houston Ballet.

Wilkinson, Raven—First African American woman to join an established, mainstream classical ballet company, Ballet Russe de Monte Carlo of New York, in 1955 at age 20. Wilkinson died in 2018.

Lourdes Lopez

Past affiliation: New York City Ballet (1974–1997)
Current position: Artistic director, Miami City Ballet (2012–present)
Country of birth: Cuba
Current residence: Miami, Florida
Age at time of interview: 59

Excerpts from April 18, 2017, interview with Lourdes Lopez, conducted in person in a conference room at Miami City Ballet (MCB) in Miami, Florida. Lourdes came into the interview with direct focused energy. She was very personable and appeared at ease and comfortable in her workspace, with elongated posture that never wavered. Lourdes was thoughtful throughout our time together and was genuinely interested in answering all of my questions. She was generous with her time; in addition to sitting with me for the interview, immediately after she showed me around the company

Lourdes Lopez (photograph by George Kamper; courtesy Miami City Ballet).

building, including the costume shop, the studios, the lounge for dancers, and the administrative offices.

NM: How did you start dancing?

LL: I started dancing when I was about five and a half. I had very weak legs, actually no calf muscles and very thin legs. I had flat feet. I was seeing an orthopedic doctor to correct my feet, and he suggested that I do something extracurricular after school like gymnastics or dancing, more than just the P.E. that the public schools offered, to try to strengthen my legs. And my mom, I think, just went "no gymnastics." She had always loved ballet in Cuba, and so she put me in kind of a beginner's dance class, more like a preballet here in Miami. The school was run by Sylvia M. Goudie. I actually started up [on pointe], believe it or not at six and a half—and it's horrible now that I think about it—but it was just that type of school.

NM: I didn't even know they made pointe shoes that small.

LL: Apparently they did; I have pictures. I also remember buying them at a department store called Richards, here in downtown Miami. There was no real knowledge of training. Kind of a very beginner and basic type of ballet school, but it got me going. I was with them for a couple years … starting at five and a half. When I was eight, the orthopedic or corrective shoes came off, and I remember being in the kitchen with my family....

NM: So, you were on pointe with orthopedic shoes.

LL: Yes, there were corrective shoes I would wear, except when going out. It's kind of really interesting, but I had never really thought of that. But the shoes came off, and I'm still doing these little classes, I want to say maybe four or five times a week, at this little local ballet school. And I remember my dad in the kitchen said to me, "Well, do you want to continue these ballet classes?" We were immigrants and poor. He said, "This is a bit of a strain, financially, to pay for these classes, but if you like to do it, we're happy to make the sacrifice and find a way." And I remember, I didn't miss a beat. I said, "Yes." And I don't even remember what I loved about it; I just didn't want to stop. I can't in my mind go back to what it was, only that I liked it and wanted to continue. A bit like enjoying playing with dolls, I just loved ballet. My mom loved ballet and had a connection to performing artists. Her brother, my uncle, was a singer in Cuba, had his own musical band and had put out records. Also, her uncle, the brother of her mother (my grandmother), was a very famous pianist, Felipe Dulzaides, in Cuba. My mom had a sense that if you're talented, then there's training that needs to happen, and if Lourdes likes this, let's see how we get her the right training. Somehow, she researched this Russian teacher in Miami called Alexander Nigodoff who was from the Bolshoi, kind of like a transplant in Miami, and had a studio in Coral Gables. And she said, "Well, if you want to continue, then we have to get you real training, because this is not just for fun, and you no longer have to do it for your legs." I started with Alexander Nigodoff, and I remember he was the first one who actually taught me that ballet was an art form. He introduced me to *Sleeping Beauty*, and he introduced me to *Swan Lake*, and introduced me to this whole world called ballet that I could be part of. He also was the one that introduced me to the fact that each of these steps had French names. That was something I never knew. When I first went into Mr. Nigodoff's class I didn't know any of the names of the steps in class and could not keep up. I remember he asked me if I was stupid in front of the rest of the class, and I responded "no," but I could see why he would think that; I couldn't understand what he was asking me to do. He was a much better teacher than I had previously. I was at Mr. Nigodoff's until I was 11.

My father worked as an executive accountant for Ecuatoriana Airlines, which was a cargo service at the time. I don't think it's around anymore. They did a lot of flights from Miami into Latin and South America. And we would get free standby tickets all the time. He had to go to New York one summer, and we were like "Can we go?" The whole family joined him on this trip, which was supposed to be for a few days. My mother used the trip as an opportunity for me to take classes in New York. I think we were only going to be there for a week or so. Again, I'm not sure how my mother knew to do this, but I ended up going to the School of American Ballet, just for an audition without even an appointment. At that time the school was on Broadway and 86th.

It was in the middle of their summer course because we had no idea of their summer intensive dates and literally just showed up. At the time it was Madame Gleboff who was mostly directing the school. My mother could not speak nor could she understand English well at all, so it was my sister Teresa who was doing all the translating. Madame Gleboff told my mother that at 10 years old I was too young, and they didn't take summer students till 12 years of age. Madame Gleboff suggested that I go to ABT (American Ballet Theatre) or Joffrey. I took classes at both schools. I remember my mother asking me to choose where I wanted to continue taking classes, ABT or Joffrey. I said Joffrey. I have no idea why except that I do remember the studios, at that time, seemed brighter and newer. Joffrey offered me a scholarship right away for the rest of their summer course. I remember my mom came into the dressing room at Joffrey, and she said to me in Spanish, "You've been offered a scholarship." I didn't know what the word for scholarship was in Spanish. I asked her, "What's *una beca*?" I didn't understand what that word meant. And so, we ended up staying through the summer so that I could finish the summer intensive at Joffrey. We stayed at a hotel called the Dixie Hotel on 42nd Street at 1st and not a great neighborhood, especially at the time. It was Edith d'Addario at Joffrey who then moved us over to the Great Northern Hotel on West 57th, my sister, my mom, and me. Then, completely by luck, I mean, completely like a bizarre coincidence, my older sister was getting married in Los Angeles, and we're supposed to go from New York to Los Angeles for her wedding, which we did. When we get there, again, my mother somehow finds out where to take me to take ballet class. I end up taking class with Irina Kosmovska ... this is all my mom. My mom is somehow finding out and researching where the ballet studios are and asking around.

NM: And there's no internet, and there is a language barrier.

LL: There's no internet. So, how she's doing this, I'm really not quite sure how. And unfortunately, she's passed, so I can't ask her…. But we find this extraordinary teacher, Irina Kosmovska, from the Mariinsky, from St. Petersburg. And little do we know, she is actually one of the teachers at the School of American Ballet during their summer course and knew Balanchine and Madame Danilova and everyone else at SAB. She was one of those Russians who came in and transplanted themselves in Los Angeles, like David Lichine, Massine, and Riabouchinska. There was a group of them.

So, I take class with Kosmovska, and she says, "Have you been to the School of American Ballet?" And we go, "Yes, we have, but they said 'no' because I was too young, so I went to the Joffrey." Well, she writes to the School of American Ballet, and tells them, "You need to see Lourdes." She asked my mother to send photos of me in several ballet positions and all other information that fall to SAB, asking to audition for their next summer course. On Kosmovska's recommendation and I'm assuming the photos, they take me in the following summer and offer me a scholarship. I'm only 11, but this is how I start with them a year earlier than most. After that summer course at 11 they then offer me a year-round scholarship, which meant that they would pay for my classes in Miami, my pointe shoes, and my dance wear, allowing me to continue my dancing in Miami. By this time, I was taking class every day and more on Saturdays; there were pointe shoe costs, there's transportation. It was outside our financial realm of possibility. But with the School of American Ballet giving me a year-round scholarship it was basically paying for all my training. I would go back to New York for the summer for their five-week summer intensive and during the year stay in Miami, study with a local teacher, and go to school.

So, they paid for my classes, and they paid for my pointe shoes, which, as a kid, is not that much, but still, at the time, it was probably $30 a pair. And that scholarship continued, and SAB was able to do this as part of major funding from the Ford Foundation that was given to the School of American Ballet back in the early 1960s, I guess to create a scouting program for talent across the U.S. So, it's kind of interesting that I'm a trustee of the Ford Foundation now; it's like this full circle.

NM: Do they still have scholarships like that, where they would support students at home?

LL: Yes and no, it's different. The Ford Foundation's mission at the time was about cementing the arts in America and giving them foundational support so these artistic institutions could survive and flourish. Two of the beneficiaries of this major support were SAB and NYCB, among a few others.

Anyway, that's how I started dancing. Every summer I would go to New York, starting at 11 until the age of 14; I would go to NY and study at SAB for five weeks. Then, I would come back to Miami and continue my studies here under scholarship. However, that first year SAB asked that I change teachers when I got on full

Lourdes Lopez, age 12, in a school performance for her teacher, Martha Mahr, at Miami Dade Auditorium (courtesy Lourdes Lopez).

scholarship. I had to leave Mr. Nigodoff and started training with Martha Mahr, who was a Miami-based teacher SAB identified in Miami. It was Ms. Mahr who gave me the foundational training and the technique that in many ways would carry me throughout my career. Ms. Mahr was Argentinian and was a soloist with the Ballet Nacional de Cuba.

NM: And after that first summer, did your mother continue to go with you?

LL: Always. Every summer, my mom would come with me, as well as my sister Teri, who continued to do all the translating for my mother. This went on until SAB asked that I move full-time to New York at the age of 13, and my mom said, "No, she's way too young. We have to give her one more year." And she was right to do that. And so, at 14 I moved to New York with my sister Teri. My mom stayed behind because her aunt who was in Miami was dying of breast cancer, and my mom wanted to take care of her. I moved with Teri, who was 19. We both lived together in New York, which was great to have someone from my family. I studied, and she went to school at New York University.

NM: Oh, that worked out nicely.

LL: Yes, it did, actually. She did a year or two here at Miami Dade and then got some financial aid and got a business administration degree at NYU. Then I got into the company as an apprentice at 15 and a half and then at 16 as a full-time member. My sister Teri also worked as an usher at the New York State Theater while going to school, and because of this I was able to see so many Balanchine and Robbins ballets but also New York City Opera.

NM: Can you talk a little bit about your performance career? Maybe some of your favorite roles or times with the company?

LL: My performance career had a lot of ups and downs. I danced with New York City Ballet for 24 years. And I danced, obviously, under Mr. Balanchine, and then when he passed away under Jerome Robbins and Peter Martins, and then, when Jerry said he didn't want to be artistic director, under only Peter. So, I had those three men as artistic directors. And each one of them was very, very different. In my first couple of years I was lost, because I was so young. I was 16 and going from a ballet school into a company; it's like going from elementary school into college. I didn't know how to handle it. I didn't get into trouble or anything like that, but it was just unsettling. It wasn't really until about, I'd say, my fourth year that I had a real sense of … there's a difference between "I'm just working" and "I'm dedicated." And so, I was just working. I was in classes, I was in rehearsals, I was focused, but I wasn't really driven. And so, I said, you know what? I've always been very pragmatic, and I thought to myself, I'm wasting my time here. If I'm not going to get anywhere, I want to maybe do something else. I also thought a lot about regret. If I wasn't going to make it at NYCB, I didn't want to look back and think "If only I had tried harder," nor did I want to blame my lack of success on someone or something else. I wanted to say "I gave it 150% and it just wasn't for me" and be able to walk away. And so, I really started to drive myself and started to understand that there were things I needed to work on and towards. There is no easy shortcut. And then my dancing changed.

I started taking classes with different teachers. I started watching a lot of other dancers onstage. I immersed myself in it in a very different way—and that always shows. I started getting parts with Mr. B. I actually started dancing quite a lot, not only in the corps, but demisolos and then solos and eventually principal parts, and then I became a soloist, and things were great. And then unfortunately he (Balanchine) passed away. For me, I always say he died way too soon for me. And there was a kind of turmoil at City Ballet when Mr. B passed. It wasn't business as usual anymore. There was a definite loss that was felt, and though Peter was wonderful and kept the company going, he was a very different artistic director, a very different type of mentor, a very different type of leader, a very different type of leader than Mr. B was.

So, that took some time to get used to, you know, after 10 years with one, and then overnight, this kind of abrupt change. Even though Mr. B was not well and in the last year of his life he was not around that much, still his passing was a shock. But, I danced a lot under Peter and Jerry, a lot, and became a principal dancer, so it all worked out in the end.

I ended up with a very bad injury right after the American Music Festival, which was Peter's truly first big artistic statement. I finished the spring season, but the injury sidelined me for quite a few months through the summer. And then, when I tried to come back—I'm giving you this story because it changed my life. When I tried to come back, it was not any better. In fact, I was back to square one. So, the orthopedic surgeon finally decided that I needed to have surgery. But the type of surgery they had to perform had never been done on a dancer. The injury was a cyst, or growth that had developed in the heel bone at the base where the achilles attaches to the heel bone. I went to see several doctors in the United States; nobody would touch me. They wouldn't touch pianists; they wouldn't touch dancers. It was the company's orthopedic surgeon, Dr. William Hamilton, who said he would do it. "At that time—I was 30 and there was a real question mark about whether I could come back to dance or not, since at least Dr. Hamilton had never seen this type of injury before, and the surgery was right where the back rim of the pointe shoe hit the heel." As you can imagine, I was a mess. I spent about two weeks at home not wanting to come out. I was devasted and really not able to function and very depressed. I already hadn't danced for over seven months. Then one day I thought, if there's a possibility that I'm not going to come back to dancing, then I'm going to do the two things—I told you I was pragmatic—I'm going to do the two things that I've never been able to do because I've always been dancing. One of them was to have a child; I was married at the time. And the other one was go to school. I'd always been a great student, loved going to school, and loved learning. I graduated from high school, really mostly correspondence, but I hadn't had the opportunity to really pursue any academic interests.

So, I came out of surgery and planned all of it out beforehand with my friend, Marika Molnar, who was then and is still the physical therapist for NYCB. How and when do I plan to get pregnant and have a child given the surgery and knowing that I had to heal the foot and carry the baby. She and I planned it out on a calendar, and all in all, it ended being a two-year hiatus before I was fully back dancing. Right after Adriel was born in November, I tried to come back for the spring season, but it was too soon after the baby and tore my calf, of course! But I did finally make it back and danced for quite a long time. A child, emotionally, just changes you because you realize that there are other things outside of ballet that matter, and yet both still mattered, baby and ballet. You realize that your priorities change every day and can change every day. One day you're worried about your performance, and the other day you're worried that your child has a fever. You realize that you can do both and pretty well. You realize that no matter where you are, ballet or with baby, you need to be present. And you realize that you're capable of a lot more. And then, school completely changed me as well, because I realized that we are all intelligent; what dancers lack at times is an education. There's a big difference between the two. And it also taught me that many of the things I had learned in a ballet classroom—you know, showing up on time matters, focus, dedication, determination, thinking ahead, preparation, constantly learning—it all matters and it all makes a difference. Sticking to it matters. Respect to those around you matters. All these things that make a person successful in the outside world, I had learned in a ballet classroom, in ballet class. There was an interesting moment for me. I was part of an Excel program at Fordham University, and I'm around, basically, 18-year-olds (the other students on the class), and here I am, 30 years old, pregnant and with a cane. I'm in an English Composition 101 class because I don't even know how to write a correct paragraph, much less what a sentence is, so it was one of the first courses I took, and we have homework that first week. I come into the classroom a week later because it was every Monday when we were off from performances, and I hand in my homework. I then realize that more than half the class hadn't finished the assignment, and I was astounded that they hadn't handed in their homework. I had come from a world where if they said class is at 10 a.m. and your rehearsal is at 11:30 a.m., you're just there. No questions asked and no excuses, and you're there before the start of class or rehearsals, not after. You don't even question it, you know? So, that was a real shock.

NM: Because in your training and life up to that point, it was not an option to be unprepared, correct?

LL: Exactly, exactly. That one chooses to be either prepared or not. So, anyway … those were two things that kind of changed my life and why I say that my career kind of went up and down.

NM: Well, it was a down that you weren't dancing.

LL: It was a down because I wasn't dancing, but it was the best thing that happened to me at the time. It really just changed my perspective about my career, about who I am as a female, as a woman, as an artist. It gave me hope for the future and a sort of freedom. I understood that while I loved to dance, I didn't need to be on the stage; there was joy in other things. It was about me being in the art form. It wasn't about me on the stage.

NM: How was it reentering, then, after the injury and the baby?

LL: A great question. I tell so many dancers that are out for a year or end up with a serious injury and out for a long time. The greatest thing about being away from a ballet company is that when you come back, you realize you've changed; it hasn't. The company stays exactly in the same place, meaning your class is at 10 a.m., your rehearsal is at 12:00 p.m., performance is at 8:00 p.m., you have a weekend. It's this machine that just keeps on going even if the dancers are different; it's a machine that keeps on going, whereas you've changed. So, it's the best, really, of both worlds.

NM: I'm curious about what happens when you see dancers working who are not devoted. Like, what do you think of that? Or do you see it, or...?

LL: Immediately. You know, it's very interesting—when you talk to dancers, hopefully they'll say this—I communicate a lot with the dancers because I just feel that if I don't tell them what I'm thinking or feeling and they don't tell me what they're thinking or feeling, there's going to be a miscommunication, right? Also, because I think it's within your power to be able to change something if it's not right. You ultimately, as a dancer, want something. So, meet the artistic director, the teacher, whoever, halfway to get it. It is a two-way street. It's very interesting to be in the front of the room and see it, because you just see everything—I wish I had known this when I was a dancer. You know, it's not that your teachers had eyes in the back of their head, it's that when you're in the front of the room, you can tell right away by how a dancer walks across the studio if they're hurting, if they're upset, if they're happy to be there, if they're not happy to be there, if they're scared to be there. Immediately, you're zeroing in, or at least I am, on both physically how they're feeling, emotionally and sometimes even mentally. I can tell by their barre work who is present or who leaves in the center. I can tell who leaves and comes back. So, they think that I don't see it, and I'm wondering, did my teachers know? I guess they knew when I left. So, I talk to them a lot and I do tell them. I say, look, you know, my office is always open. They're free to come in and talk to me, but not many do. I'll also meet with them whenever I feel it's necessary to meet with them. Meaning, I'll ask to meet when I see that things are going the wrong way. I'll call them in and say, "What's up?" You know, "Talk to me. If you don't want to talk to me, fine, but talk to someone because I'm concerned about what I'm seeing." And sometimes it works, and sometimes it doesn't. But it's how I like to be.

NM: Okay. How does being a dancer compare to your role as artistic director—you talked a little bit about it—but how did it compare, like, in your body and the experience of being an artistic director now? What do you think of those two roles in your life?

LL: They're just ... they're like polar opposites. You know, opposite ends of the spectrum. There's a connection because it's the art form, and there's a connection because they are steps that I grew up doing and ballet and parts in those ballets that I grew up doing, but it's two very different talents, strengths, weaknesses, and challenges. One is you're communicating, as a dancer you're communicating with your body, your talent, your musicality, your technique, and your expression. I think, as a dancer, as an artist, you must be very in *you*; it is about you. The day is about you. It's about how you get to class, how you warm up, how your body feels. Do you know the ballet, can you do the ballet? Are your shoes ready? Are you prepared? It's all about you and what you're going to do that evening, right? And it must be, because your career is so short, and once the curtain goes up, you have to give it all.

The artistic director is about giving it all 24-7. You must be problem-solving for a lot of people, almost every minute. You're rehearsing other people, you're putting programming for other people, you're raising money from people. As an artistic director you're wearing multiple hats: teacher, mentor, friend, counselor, programmer, fundraiser, visionary, the list goes on and on. So, it's a very different … it's about giving, whereas as a dancer, you're taking in during the day to give at night. An artistic director is constantly giving. Also, you know, I worry, because I still—not that I demonstrate fully, but the visuals are important for me. I always grew up with teachers who could visually demonstrate, to some extent, what they were doing, and that's how dancers learn. So, I worry how much longer my own body is going to hold up. Not that I'm doing jumps and turns, but I'm semidemonstrating a movement to indicate. So, that's a concern that I have, because I think it's an important part of teaching.

NM: Can you describe the culture of Miami City Ballet?

LL: The culture of Miami City Ballet is very familial. It's a very happy, warm, and, I think, an accepting place. What I realized when I got here was that there is a very different culture here, and I've spent the last four years trying to figure out what it is, because I think it contributes to what you see on the stage, and I certainly didn't want to change that; I wanted to add to it.

I think there are a few reasons for why MCB is such a happy, warm and friendly company. First, we have great weather, and I'm being serious. Most of the time it is sunny, and after a hard day at the ballet you see sun, sky, water and nature as you make your way home. It makes a difference in your mood and life. Second, our dancers come from all over the world, and they all have such different training, so sameness is not us. Because they all come from such different backgrounds and training, in that difference lies the commonality—there's an identity beyond their diversity. Because of this they're inclusive, and it's that generosity, warmth, and inclusion you see and feel onstage with them.

So, that's one thing. The other thing is that the way our schedule works, everyone has—I know this is going to sound silly, but I really think this contributes—everybody's lunch is 2:30–3:30. It is a communal lunch time for all. It is very much like an academy. Everybody goes down to the second floor, and you see them, you see 51 dancers in this lunchroom that are chatting with each other, and they're coming together around a meal. These dancers do everything together; they invite each other for dinner and holidays. They vacation together. They watch out for each other. They take care of each other, and they support each other. No one is more or less than any other. When someone can't get to the theater, they'll call: "Can you drive me?" So, they carpool. When someone does a part for the first time, they're in the wings cheering and clapping in support of their colleague. It is like this little family in this one warm and sunny place. And that's why when the curtain goes up, people say it feels and looks like a company. We have principal dancers that will step in for an injured corps dancer. I had one this season, a dancer who stepped in for a corps dancer because the corps dancer was out; nobody knew (his part), and he said, "it's my old spot," and he was off that day. And he went, "I'll do it." So, that is very important to keep that feeling of family of camaraderie and not fiddle with that, because that's what makes it kind of unique.

NM: And you mentioned that the company belongs to the community. So, what does that look like? How does that translate?

LL: When you look at Miami, when I look at Miami, I see it as a mosaic now. Every specific part helps to make up the greater whole, better. When I was growing up here, it was very Cuban. It was very Cuban because of the immigration that took place in the early '60s. The city was dominated by Cuban exiles. Now, you have … people from everywhere. Some are from Europe, Latin and South America, the Caribbean, different countries, so there are these pockets, these little communities that make up the larger community. It's the same thing with the dancers, they've come from all over the world and speak different languages and have different training. They look different, but I like that they all look different. I've never liked companies where everybody looks the same, kind of cookie-cutter. I like companies where the curtain goes up and they're different shapes and sizes, but they're all working towards the same goal. And that's, I think, what makes the company so diverse and gives it the quality it has.

NM: And what challenges and achievements stand out for you the most in your time here? What was the biggest challenge you feel and the most prideful accomplishment?

LL: Oh my god, I think everything was a challenge at the beginning. It's such a hard question to answer. You know, I don't … it's hard for me to answer that, because I don't think that way. I think, what do I need to fix so that the dancers are dancing better? So that they're inspired, so that they're challenged? What do I need to put in place so that the school is producing dancers for the company? What do I need to program, what do I need to create so that the audience has a relationship with the company that they want to come back to see? For me, it's just ongoing work, every day. "Work" is maybe the wrong word, but I don't think "accomplishments" either.

NM: I can identify with that as well. I don't really think about the challenge, I think of what I need to do. But I do see the accomplishments, because I'll notice, oh, I did this, and then this happened. So, like the syllabus you brought into the school. You might not have thought of it as a challenge in the first place, but once it happened, you're like…

LL: That's right. The syllabus was a big one, that was based on how do I get everyone on the same page? Everyone was teaching something different, which is fine. It shouldn't all be the same class, but there must be common ground, a commonality, a common aesthetic. It's not about the Balanchine training, it's about the Balanchine aesthetic. You can have a different training, but everybody must be on the same boat and on the same page or else the student doesn't know what to do. And I go back to the School of American Ballet, where we had so many different teachers from different backgrounds, but aesthetically they were all teaching the same thing.

I've always believed that the more you dance, the more different things you dance, the better dancer you will be. It was a very different philosophy when I was growing up at City Ballet, because we had Robbins and Balanchine and that's all we danced. And frankly, I had little interest in dancing Ashton or Tudor, or Tharp you know. We had Balanchine and Robbins alive in the theater. What more could we want? But I was wrong. The American Music Festival changed this thinking for me. All of a sudden, I was dancing Lubovitch and Lynne Taylor-Corbett and Bill Forsythe. And I realized that it changed my dancing. It changed how I did *Agon*; it informed me. I think the dancers are dancing better at Miami City Ballet because of the rep that has been introduced, the new works that have been introduced.

NM: What was your favorite role to perform?

LL: I didn't have a favorite one. I really didn't. I had several that I liked. I loved *Firebird*, I loved *Serenade*, I loved *Violin Concerto*, I loved *Dances at a Gathering*. Loved doing *Fancy Free*. There were very few roles that I can think of that I didn't enjoy. Some I'm less fond of just because they were hard and difficult and I had to find my way to them…. *Symphony in C*, interestingly enough, was one…. I had to find my way to that. It took me a while to find my way into it and to feel comfortable in it … which is odd, because it's the type of dancer that I was. But for some reason … I danced more than I ever thought I would, and I think that's why it was so easy for me to—at a relatively young age and healthy—to just move away from it. Just say, I think I'm done here.

NM: That was my next question. How did that decision come along?

LL: By the time I reached 38, I was fine. I mean, I wasn't hurting or anything. But you know, your body slows down. All of sudden you realize you're not jumping as high or moving as fast, and it happened rehearsing one of my favorite ballets, *Kammermusik No. 2*. The first section is really fast and it's like math in your head; it's in rhythm so you're counting twelves and sixes and it's fast, and I loved doing it. And I was in a room rehearsing by myself, and I realized I couldn't keep up. I realized that for the first time I just couldn't, and it was something that I used to just, you know, just do and not even think. So, I went in and had a conversation with Peter, and I said, "You know, I have to get out of these ballets." He said, "No, of course you can still do them." And I'm like no, I can't. I said, "You know I really can't do them anymore and I'm OK with that. I'm not doing them the way that I want to do them and the way they deserve to be done." And so, I was about 38 years old, and that's when I started thinking it's down the line. Balanchine was long gone, and Jerry was very ill and slowing down. And I realized it just wasn't getting any better or easier for me. And I'd always been able to ask myself, are you in the right place at the right time for *you*? Are you in the right place at the right time for Lourdes? The answer had always been yes. At Fordham, are you in the right place at the right time for where you are in your life? Yes. And so, I asked myself, are you in the right place at the right time? And I thought, I'm not. I'm not anymore. So, what happened during that year is that I started to figure out what I wanted to do, what I could do. I started doing these very, very beginner arts education classes. Really not very comprehensive, I put the whole thing together myself and I would go to the South Bronx every Monday for a couple of hours, and I would teach these children from low-income communities about the arts after school. I'd bring in pointe shoes, I'd play Bach, teach a few positions, teach them to waltz, and just talk to them about art and artists. I did this for about a year. And I got a community award for it. I had to give some remarks at the award presentation, and the general manager from WNBC Channel 4 was there. He came up to me and said, "You know, I'm kind of interested in putting together a kind of arts magazine on television." Saturdays and Sundays, early in the morning 7 to 8 a.m. or something like that. And he said, "Would you be interested in doing some segments?" And I said, "I have no idea how to produce anything." He said, "We'll give you a producer, but I want you to come in." So, I did one that focused on Allegra Kent. Allegra Kent was one of Mr. Balanchine's most beloved ballerinas, and she had just written a book. She's still alive.

NM: She danced with Arthur Mitchell?

LL: She danced with Arthur Mitchell and Edward Villella, and she wrote a book. A very smart woman, wrote her biography, which had just come out. So, I said, "I'll do that," you know, kind of help her sell her book to the general public. They gave me a producer, and I learned how to conduct the interview, how to transcribe it and gather collateral to use, etc. I also learned how to write out the story, where the interview questions should go, where the video should go, what were the salient parts and what to edit out and how to keep it all at a minute and a half! They then put me in the video room with an editor, and they edit the interview film. And so, then he came up to me and he said, "We're thinking of launching this during the summer. Would you be interested in doing eight more segments or six more segments?" But that meant that I would miss going to Saratoga. By now I'm 39, so I spoke to Peter. Peter said, "Absolutely. Take Saratoga off." It was three weeks; he said, "Not a problem." At that time, I knew that I'd done my last *Firebird* and *Violin*; I had prepared myself for this. The last ballet I did was Jerry's *Brandenburg*, a ballet he created on me along with Wendy Whelan, Peter Boal, and Nikolaj Hubbe. And then I just never came back. I did … I called them back and I said, "You know, it's just … I've made that step." And I knew that if I took that opportunity for the television, I knew that I wouldn't come back. I needed that one step and opportunity. And that was it.

NM: That's a nice ease-out.

LL: It's a very nice ease-out. I didn't like television. I lasted there two years. I felt I needed to be in dance, and the television world was very different … television news is just so different than the arts, a very different world.

NM: It's not as small as dance either.

LL: It's not as small as dance, a lot more cutthroat and very fast-moving. It's hard, especially if you're covering the arts. It's murder and mayhem all the time. And it was hard, because I had a job and I had benefits, and I was getting a paycheck, so it wasn't like I was out on the street. And people would say, "How can you possibly leave that?" You know, every time I would go into that television world and I'd push those glass doors to walk into the station, my DNA changed; who Lourdes was changed. And I didn't like that, and so after two years I left.

NM: Can you tell be about this program, the Ballet Bus?

LL: Oh my god, the Ballet Bus is the greatest. One of the things I'm most proud of—because when I walked into MCB the outreach department was nonexistent and we had no community impact. And now, we reach about 10,000 kids a year with our various outreach programs. One day I was talking with our former school administrator about how difficult it was to get to the ballet school here on Miami Beach from the mainland.

I said, "We're on the beach and so far from the mainland and with traffic, it is difficult to get here if you live someplace else; our students are attending their academic school on the mainland. How do we bring them here?" And more specifically, how do we bring children from our low-income communities? Those children who don't have the finances to be able to study ballet or come to the ballet performances and therefore have not seen it? We're missing a huge population and an important one. This is an expensive art form and not available to all. There are numerous barriers here, geographic, financial, time.

We started thinking and talking about a program where we send school buses to Title I district schools; students get on and we transport them to the ballet. We would offer tuition-free classes, dance wear, and all they need to take class and dance. And then the parents pick them up here at MCBS (Miami City Ballet School). Instead of only offering a one-year commitment to the child and parents, we make it a 10-year commitment. "Make a commitment to the parents, saying, if your child wants to dance, and they can't come to us, we will go pick them up. And this is not a six-week program it's a 10-year program." So, that's what Ballet Bus is. We go to the Title I district schools in Miami Dade and offer scholarships to those young students that want to learn to dance and show talent.

First, we hold annual auditions for the ones that are interested, and we look at the little bodies ages seven to 10. Do they have rhythm? Do they know left from right? Can they skip? You know, a regular audition for children their age. And then we choose. They start at seven. There's a limit in terms of class size: 30. The first year we didn't have that many. Now parents are really interested. We give them their tights, their ballet slippers, their leotards, their bags. Anything that they need to be able to participate. We pick them up, we bring them here, we give them a lunch, a little snack. We have a counselor on the bus with them that helps them with their homework. They take their class. They're part of our *Nutcracker* and *Midsummer* productions. Then their parents pick them up here. And then the next year, they go into the next level, and into the next level. They are annually evaluated like any child. There's a goal that is created for these children of moving up to the next level and an understanding of delayed gratification. You don't get what you want right away; sometimes you need to wait and continue to work for it.

NM: *Is their class different than the other students or they're taking with everyone else?*

LL: They're integrated. They're completely integrated. They are like everyone else, except they arrive on a bus.

We have other community programs, but the Ballet Bus is my favorite because it's the idea that we're committed to creating a pipeline into the company from the community.

NM: *That's great. So, as you know—and you've talked about Miami City Ballet as being one of the most diverse mainstream ballet companies—in my research, I noticed a couple of trends, not in this company in particular but in the field. I was curious to see if they were things that you might have noticed or that don't jive with your experience. I noticed that Patricia and Jeanette Delgado (two Miami City Ballet dancers) were born in Miami, but overall there's a scarcity of Latina ballerinas, ballet dancers born in the U.S. When I look at women, in particular, who are born in the U.S.A., lot of the Latinx dancers come from other countries. I was wondering if that speaks to the resources available for training Latinx students in the United States. What is that about? And I noticed this, similarly, with Asian students. There are some, but most of them came from countries outside the U.S.*

LL: As opposed to coming from the United States?

NM: *Yes. The diversity that's homegrown is not as prevalent as the international diversity. Globally, ballet is amazing, and it's networking people throughout the world. But what is the United States doing in terms of diversity in ballet?*

LL: You know, it's really an interesting question, and it's one that I haven't really thought too much about. I think it ... you know, ballet, here in America, in the U.S., is fairly young and at this point not necessarily considered a career. How many master dance programs are offered at universities? Also, the arts aren't as integrated in our everyday lives as I feel we would love them to be, as I feel they should be. They're also no government subsidization, which may be a good thing, I don't know. Certainly, the arts in Europe are everywhere and much more embedded in everyday life. Also, there's a lack of arts education and appreciation in our public school systems, certainly in comparison to sports. Sports are taught in school, and if you're gifted in a specific sport you can get a scholarship at a university and play Division One and get a degree. Dance, specifically ballet, does not have that appeal nor recognition, at least not here in the U.S.

For the question you're asking, the answers are what I was lucky enough to have found early on, which is access to the art form at the highest level and an infrastructure around the student and parents throughout the student's years of training that includes financial support among other support in other ways. We tend to forget that it takes 10 to 12 years to train a ballet dancer. If you find the talent and give them what I've outlined above, you then have a young dancer from any community that can compete at the highest level for the best-paying contracts in ballet. You have a dancer who is making a living in their chosen art form.

NM: And this differs from South America or Latin American...
LL: I think that has something to do with it. How many parents think, whether of male or female, say "Let's go to the ballet." They want to do something after school. Instead of hockey or soccer, we're going to put them in ballet? I don't think so—and I'm not putting down the United States, I'm just making a kind of gross observation. So, I think that has something to do with it, access and education, because it's how your parents and how your community see and respond to the art form.

NM: Because you have to start so young, you can't pick it up at 20.
LL: Exactly, because you start so young. So, parents want their kids to do tennis or golf, and for the most part kids want to do sports; it's a community they find during their academic years. I think that's why you find these lower numbers in the arts. You can offer the child the scholarship, but if the parents don't have an understanding of what it takes for their child to succeed in ballet and don't have the support system financially and otherwise, it won't be possible. For the most part both parents here in America now work. Both my parents worked. So, the parents don't have the resources to be able to pick up that child after school, transport them to the ballet class, stay there for the two hours, and then transport them back home. They have other children at home to worry about, in different schools, different ages. It is a commitment from the parents to do this, and the parents need to be part of the equation for success if we want to broaden the margins of success for these children.

The Delgados were very lucky; they were talented and their parents loved ballet. And they both did it. I'm sure it was still very difficult, but having both at the same ballet school might have made it easier for the parents to fully support what their daughters wanted to do. Parents or guardians play a critical role in their children's success.

NM: And it helps when one sibling isn't doing something else.
LL: Yes. Right.

NM: That really makes it challenging when ballet companies are asked to be more diverse, because it's an issue of training. Does that have a connection to the 10-year commitment? Because one is speaking to the other.

LL: Yes, that's exactly why I said, "10-year commitment," because I'm very interested in keeping Miami City Ballet as diverse as possible. And it's somewhat easy for us, because most of our dancers come from Latin and South America, because Miami is the gateway. If I can get these kids from the community that I consider a mosaic, if I can get them in and train them and they want to be here…. If I think of the company 10 years from now with those kids, that's how you start.

This brings me to another goal or dream of mine. I'd like to put in place a similar support system that I was lucky enough to have found through my early years and that is very similar to Ballet Bus but in Latin America. My hope is to create an initiative where we identify five to six cities in that region and then identify ballet schools in those cities. Those schools then choose three of their most talented students between the ages of 11 and 13. We then give these students year-round scholarships, paying for all that they need to dance in their local ballet school. Every summer we then bring them to MCB with a full scholarship to be part of the summer intensive. This support system continues until they are emotionally, mentally, and technically ready to come and study full-time, staying in our dorms. The second part of this initiative is inviting their teachers to MCBS summer intensive to watch the classes, learn our pedagogue and syllabus so that the training of the child continues year-round when they're home. This gives support but also consistency. It helps young students and teachers in a region that needs our focus and help as much as possible. It also gives the student the tools and high-level training so they can then go out into the dance world and compete for the best-paying contracts in the best companies and support themselves. It continues the diversity of MCB and its school. I see multiple benefits.

NM: Do you audition dancers from South America? Do you go there? Do you audition here?

LL: Yes, we audition there. Our school artistic director, Arantxa Ochoa, goes, and she also sends faculty and faculty who speak both Spanish and Portuguese. So, we go to Colombia, we go to Venezuela, we've done Argentina, Brazil, Rio, São Paolo. And we have a wonderful relationship with Alice Arja, who heads one of the largest ballet schools there in Brazil and is Nathalia Arja's mom. She's a magnet; they all come from these different countries to take class there. In these last five years, she has really connected us to other schools in South America. Now, we go there and audition and offer them scholarships, and we also have a Brazilian summer program that we've put in place. We do what we can to connect with them and the region.

NM: I'm curious what your connections would be to Cuba. Because I know you're Cuban American, and I know you can't just go there. But I know that cultural exchanges happen, and sometimes when travel does happen, it can happen through the arts. Has that been a…

LL: I've been to Cuba several times. The first time I went to Cuba was with WNBC/Channel 4 as a cultural arts correspondent and one of the great things about working for television at the time. I went during Pope John Paul II's visit. That kind of integrated me into the arts there because I interviewed artists, singers, and painters. When I came back, I was so touched by really being back home for the first time, in the place I was born, that along with two friends of mine, both who are Cuban American, we started a foundation called the Cuban Artists Fund. It's been more than 20 years now, helping Cuban artists on the island and off the island—at first it was very small—with resources, materials, information, things like that, networking. It has grown since then. Through this foundation, Cuban Artists Fund, I've been able to make trips back to Cuba through OFAC (Office of Foreign Assets Control). The trips need to have a humanitarian or cultural component to get a license. We've brought Merrill Ashley down to set *Ballo della Regina* and to teach class at the Ballet Nacional de Cuba. My trips to Cuba have always had some type of cultural aspect to them. I also recently went with the Ford Foundation and the National Endowment for the Arts and Humanities. It was three days of meeting with individuals and brainstorming on what could be done to further open U.S. and Cuban relations. I can't say what this last trip accomplished. The relationship between the two countries continues to be fraught. I think Cuba's an interesting place. We have not seen where that's going to go. It functions like no other place at this point, and it's been under communist rule for so long, for over 60 years now, that I think any infrastructure is most likely gone as well as a moral structure that a community has, or an individual has, is gone, because every day they wake up thinking "how do we get through this day?"

NM: Do you feel like the arts are protected there?
    LL: I think it depends on which arts. They are producing some wonderful male dancers, but they haven't had any exposure to the West. Zero. However, I think their new AD Viengsay Valdés is really moving things along and doing some wonderful things. I know she has a big vision to really demonstrate what is possible with the company. It takes time.

NM: And you still have this organization that connects artists there?
    LL: We do, we still have it. And we do a lot of work with the visual artists, mostly supplying them with materials that are hard to come by in Cuba, paint, canvas, brushes, materials we take for granted here in the U.S.

NM: And so, how do you feel about the opportunities for Latinx dancers in the United States today? Do you feel like we're doing better? It's the same? It's not an issue in terms of representation.
    LL: We can always be better at everything. We can always better represent the Black community, the Hispanic community, the Asian community. We can always be more inclusive. We can always be more diverse; we can always be more open. There's always room for improvement. It should not be like you've done enough because you filled a quota or one has a few dancers that represent a specific

community or race. For me, it continues to be about providing the access, the opportunity for high-level training and the infrastructure to broaden the margins of success for these dancers, specifically of Color. To compete for the positions, you need the training. There are enough barriers for them already. I feel, or should I say I hope, we've moved away from whether a dancer of Color can do *Giselle* or *Swan Lake* or be a prince or princess. That conversation I hope is over. Now, it's how do we get more dancers of Color into programs or schools that will give them what they need to succeed in ballet.

NM: Do you feel like if they want to, the doors are wide open, or do you feel like there are still challenges in terms of race barriers?

LL: I think the barriers are a result of how difficult access is into the dance world. One reason one may feel they don't belong is because there's only one of you. If there were more it would feel different, and if when you walked into a studio you held your own, despite your race, it's empowering. However, so many things still need to change, because in ballet you need to start young. Someone needs to find you and then bring you to the ballet. Then someone needs to convince your parents it's worthwhile for the child to dance and support the child and the parents for the next 10 to 12 years. Someone needs to trust that the most important thing is that the child will be happy pursuing a career in dance, and someone needs to trust that the art form will open other doors for the student and that pursuing ballet training provides the student with so much more than just a possible career in dance. It prepares you for life, whether you dance or not.

NM: But that can be a good thing.

LL: That can be a good thing. You can end up with two, three careers after dance. I've had unbelievable gifts in my life, unbelievable. The greatest, when I die, the greatest thing about Lourdes Lopez is that I have always done what I've loved to do. As long as I can remember, from the day I was 5. Things might have happened that were unexpected and tragic or simply things didn't turn out the way I had hoped. But in the back of my mind I was always in dance, and I was always happy to be in dance. I wasn't like, oh my god, I'm in a law firm, or oh my god, I really hate what I'm doing and I need to pursue something else. Never. I felt fulfilled, but that didn't mean everything went according to schedule or how I wanted it, not at all. It only means that I was fulfilled doing what I was doing, whether I was successful or not. So, that's a huge gift. There are challenges, yes, for Latinas and for Black dancers. There are challenges, but we need to provide opportunities, access, training and infrastructure support. It's about providing full scholarships. It's about providing the infrastructure, the resources, providing the transportation, the information, and the education on how to do this, and then you create mentors and then you're not the only one in class that is different. We also have to go to them, I think. That's how I feel, which is why Ballet Bus is such a special program, and hopefully this Latin American initiative will be as well. We can't expect them to come to us, you know? We're the anomaly; we're not the norm. It's not like hockey or tennis where everybody knows about it and wants to be part of it. Dance is very different that way. Classical dance is a conservative calling. We're selling ice in the winter. Not everyone wants it or wants to do it or is called to do it.

NM: I have one last question. You've kind of spoken to it in different ways, and I'm kind of interested in it because there's a lot of ways in which you infuse culture, and the repertory has changed and is very contemporary. But when people think of ballet as a white or a Eurocentric dance form, do you look at it differently? Or you see the opportunity to transform it?

LL: And elitist, yeah…

NM: It's an elitist form. But there are some people who feel like ballet has so much opportunity in terms of culture to transform it into a form that can reflect diversity.

LL: It is elitist, number one. I mean, I totally accept it. You know, it was the Sun King; it came from manners and posture and how you stand, how you present yourself. So, all those social norms, protocol and manners, and social graces are part of the beginning of the art form. And yes, as it expanded past the 17th-century courts it maintained those protocols and manners. Now, what we have is what I call the foundation, the ABCs of ballet. We have the vocabulary. The vocabulary was founded on those initial protocols, but those ABCs (foundation block "letters"); letters now are being put together in different ways. Right? Before it was very formal and elitist and spoke to one sector, one specific social group. Now artists are expanding past that and using their backgrounds and creativity, and maybe because more diverse students have access to the art form there's more diversity being created onstage. Maybe because of the opportunities … someone gave Alvin Ailey the opportunity to study. Someone gave Martha Graham the opportunity. You know, all of a sudden opportunity gives rise to artists who are using those same ABCs but in different ways. Ailey and Graham are not ballet dancers, but it's the same concept.

NM: And one of the things I hear you saying is "I don't really look at the challenge. I just find the opportunity."

LL: You're absolutely right! I can't change history. I can't change the past, but I can influence the future. I can't change that this started in Europe and then moved to Russia. I can't. I can't change that we have *Swan Lake*. And frankly, I don't want to change it because it's part of our history. Why should we? It still has a lot to teach us about humanity, about who we are and who we are not. What I can do is look towards the future. Can we impact the future in a manner that is lasting? Not me, because I'm not a choreographer. But how do I give others the opportunity to use our history and move it forward so that it speaks to today's generation and to the community in the audience?

NM: Preserving history and creating the future.

LL: Yes, for me, absolutely. For example, *Giselle*, because it is a 19th-century work and it's about an aesthetic, everybody has to ... the Wilis ... you know *Giselle*, right?

NM: Yes.

LL: (*Here L. Lopez is speaking to how you can take a classical 19th-century ballet and re-present it for the 21st century.*) The Wilis all have to be white, and they all have to look alike. Because that's an aesthetic. Why? Wasn't the vision originally that they're all ghosts? Well, you can't have Black people and Asian people and Hispanic people be ghosts? Of course you can! And they can still be Wilis. It's still a 19th-century ballet. They're still doing the same steps. But it's reflective of a community. So, I'm not changing.... I don't know if I'm explaining myself.

NM: I understand. I think everybody comes to it in a different way, but I understand what you mean. Because I can see it here.

LL: You know, the reimagining with Virginia (Johnson), we were talking about ... oh my god, Frederick Franklin, the reimagined *Giselle*, and it was a *Creole Giselle* that took place in...

NM: New Orleans.

LL: New Orleans. Virginia Johnson was just talking about it, and I remember seeing it a long, long time ago. I had just gotten into City Ballet, and it was great. It was great. And it was still the same steps, still the same moves, but reflected another community, and it allowed classical ballet to speak to that community.

NM: (It's done a lot more in theater) where you would change the time period and keep the story, or whatever.

Lourdes Lopez in George Balanchine's *Theme & Variations*, ca. 1990 (photograph © Steven Caras, all rights reserved; choreography © The George Balanchine Trust).

LL: Yes, we have a long way to go. A very long way to go, but I think we're moving in that direction. And the next step is to create new narratives, using the same ABCs of ballet, that can tell the stories of today, of today's multicultural communities in a manner that connects us all, despite where we come from.

Lourdes Lopez Glossary

> Brief bio-notes of artists and places mentioned in the chapter. This is not intended to be comprehensive but instead to offer a small amount of information to spark more thorough research if readers are interested.

Ailey, Alvin—Founded Alvin Ailey American Dance Theater in 1958. Choreographer and activist.
American Ballet Theatre—American Ballet Theatre. Founded in 1939 by Lucia Chase and Richard Pleasant. Known for presenting classical ballet repertory in contrast to New York's City Ballet, known for presenting and preserving Balanchine repertory.
Arja, Alice—Owner of Escola de Dança Alice Arja in Rio de Janeiro, Brazil. Mother of Nathalia Arja.
Arja, Nathalia—Principal dancer with Miami City Ballet. Daughter of Alice Arja.
Ashley, Merrill—Formed Merrill Ashley and Dancers. Teacher for New York City Ballet.
Ashton, Frederick—Born in England. Choreographer and director for the Royal Ballet.
Balanchine, George—Born in St. Petersburg, Russia. Cofounder and for over three decades artistic director of New York City Ballet. Balanchine died in 1983.
Ballet Nacional de Cuba—Classical ballet company based at the Great Theatre of Havana in Havana, Cuba, cofounded by Alicia Alonso, Fernando Alonso, and Alberto Alonso in 1948.
Boal, Peter—Artistic director at Pacific Northwest Ballet. Retired from New York City Ballet after 22 years.
Creole Giselle—A romantic story about the doomed love of a peasant girl and a deceitful nobleman.
d'Addario, Edith—Director of the Joffrey Ballet School. Died in 2007.
Danilova, Alexandra—Born in St. Petersburg, Russia. Prima ballerina who brought the training and traditions of both the classical Russian and the modern Diaghilev repertoires to the United States.
Delgado, Jeannette—Former principal dancer with Miami City Ballet. Left MCB in 2017.
Delgado, Patricia—Former principal dancer with Miami City Ballet. On faculty at American Ballet Theatre.
Dulzaides, Felipe—Cuban-born visual and performing artist. Pianist, arranger, and composer.
Forsythe, William "Bill"—Choreographer. Founded the Forsythe Company, based in Germany, in 2005; directed the company from 2005 to 2015.
Franklin, Frederic "Freddie"—Born in Liverpool, England. Principal dancer for Ballet Russe de Monte Carlo. Cofounder of the Slanvenska-Franklin Ballet; also founding director of the National Ballet of Washington. Died in 2013.
Gleboff, Nathalie—Born in Russia to Romanian parents. Director of the School of American Ballet. Died in 2007.
Goudie, Sylvia M.—Founded the Sylvia M. Goudie dance studio, in Havana, in 1949. Died in 1997.
Graham, Martha—Founder of the Martha Graham School of Contemporary Dance in New York. Died in 1991.
Hübbe, Nikolaj—Former principal dancer with New York City Ballet. Artistic director, Royal Danish Ballet, 2007–present.
Joffrey Ballet—Founded by Robert Joffrey and Gerald Arpino in 1956.
Johnson, Virginia—Founding member and principal dancer for Dance Theatre of Harlem. Founder and former editor in chief of *Pointe Magazine* and former artistic director of Dance Theatre of Harlem.

Kent, Allegra—Dancer, teacher, and writer. Danced with New York City Ballet under George Balanchine for 30 years.

Kosmovska, Irina—Born in Moscow. Soloist with Ballet Russe de Monte Carlo.

Lichine, David—Choreographer, born in Russia. His many ballets included *Francesca* in 1937, *Prodigal Son* in 1938 and *Graduation Ball* in 1940.

Lubovitch, La—Choreographer. Created the Lar Lubovotich Company in 1968.

Mahr, Martha—Dance teacher. Founded the Martha Mahr School of Ballet in Coral Gabes, Florida.

Mariinsky Theatre—Established in 1860 in St. Petersburg, Russia. Historical theater of opera and ballet.

Martins, Peter—Born in Copenhagen, Denmark. Principal dancer with the Royal Danish Ballet and New York City Ballet. Artistic director for New York City Ballet from 1990 to 2018.

Massine, Leonide—Born in Moscow, Russia. Actor, dancer, and choreographer. Died in 1979.

Miami City Ballet—Founded in 1985 by Toby Lerner Ansin and founding artistic director Edward Villella. The company was built on the repertory of George Balanchine and continues in this tradition today under the artistic leadership of Lourdes Lopez.

Mitchell, Arthur—Cofounder of Dance Theatre of Harlem in 1969. First African American to become a principal dancer at New York City Ballet. Mitchell died in 2018.

Molnar, Marika—Physical therapist, founder of Westside Dance Physical Therapy.

New York City Ballet—Founded in 1948 by George Balanchine and Lincoln Kirstein. Known for presenting Balanchine repertory, in contrast to the American Ballet Theatre, which is known for presenting classical ballets. Also "City Ballet."

Nigodoff, Alexander—Founder of the Alexander Nigodoff Ballet Company, established in Miami, Florida, in 1972.

Ochoa, Arantxa—Director of faculty and curriculum at Miami City Ballet.

Riabouchinska, Tatiana—Born in Moscow, Russia. Prima ballerina and teacher famous for being one of the three "Baby Ballerinas" of the legendary George Balanchine's Ballet Russe de Monte Carlo in the 1930s.

Robbins, Jerome (Jerry)–Tony award winning choreographer. Famous for choreographing on Broadway, including "West Side Story" and "Fiddler on the Roof." Became the ballet master for New York City Ballet in 1972.

School of American Ballet—Founded in 1934, one of the most renowned ballet schools in the United States. Also known as the official school of New York City Ballet.

Taylor-Corbett, Lynne—Choreographer.

Tharp, Twyla—Choreographer. Founded Twyla Tharp Dance in 1965.

Title I—A status given to public schools in the United States that have more than 40 percent of students enrollment identified as low-income. These schools receive additional federal funding.

Tudor, Antony—Born in England. Choreographer. Founded the London Ballet and the Philadelphia Ballet Guild.

Una beca—Spanish word for a scholarship, a grant.

Valdes, Viengsay—The first ballerina of Ballet Nacional de Cuba to become artistic director of the company.

Villella, Edward—Founding artistic director at Miami City Ballet from 1986 to 2016.

Whelan, Wendy—Associate artistic director of New York City Ballet after a 30-year dancing career with the company.

Caridad Martinez

Past affiliations: National Ballet de Cuba (1968–1987) and Havana Ballet Theater (1987–1992)
Affiliations as ballet master teacher: American Ballet Theater, The Ailey School, Brooklyn Ballet, Ballet Hispánico, and Peridance
Country of birth: Cuba
Current residence: New York, New York

Excerpts from a September 2016 interview with Caridad Martinez. This interview was conducted in person in a conference room at Ballet Hispánico in New York, New York. She came into the space with great interest in the process and vibrant energy.

Note: Caridad Martinez is a native Spanish speaker. Because the interview was conducted in English, some of the phrasing has been edited to align with the English-language presentation of this text.

NM: *Tell me about how you began dancing.*

CM: I'm from Cuba, and I always wanted to dance. My mother always took me to cultural events. At some point I saw the movie *The Red Shoes*, and that impressed me a lot. I always wanted to dance, but I liked sports too and drama. I love movies. I loved to express myself and do things. I was quiet, I didn't talk that much, but I was always moving and expressing myself. That's what my mother said.

NM: *How old were you when you saw The Red Shoes?*

CM: I'm guessing maybe 9? … And then, when I was 10, there was a huge audition in Cuba for Escuela Nacional de Arte de Ballet, so my mother took me to that. Before, my mother took me to another conservatory and I was accepted, but it was so unorganized. The first day I was supposed to start the ballet class, they rejected me. They said that I wasn't on the list. So, that was a shock and disappointing. But it was good for me,

Caridad Martinez (photograph by Alberto Ferreras; courtesy Caridad Martinez).

because the Escuela Nacional de Arte audition (came along). I went to that audition—it was long ... three auditions, I think.

The people in charge were Alicia Alonso, Fernando Alonso, Joaquin Banegas, Josefina Mendez, all the big people in Cuban dance. I wouldn't have known who they were, but they were conducting the audition, picking kids for the Escuela Nacional de Arte. I passed the first audition. Before that I think my mother took me to some flamenco classes because that was what she found in my area. She wanted to take me to another dance class after I was rejected from the conservatory. It was so funny (how things worked out).

There are some very famous singers that were from my neighborhood in Havana. It was a very popular neighborhood. Cayo Hueso, Pueblo Nuevo, it's a neighborhood with a lot of musicians and artists that used to live in Havana. There were some famous singers who connected with my mother: Omara Portuondo, the Cuban singer, she's very famous, and Elena Burke, she passed away. These women were amazing singers. These singers met my mother, and they were trying to help me to get (connected to people doing ballet on television). Around that time, the announcement came out for the Escuela Nacional de Arte de Ballet audition. I passed the first one (audition), and then the second time when I went, it was the first time that I faced a problem with race.

It was very interesting because the person at the desk was a Black woman and she said to my mother, "Oh, did she pass the audition?" And my mother said, "Yes!" My mother was a belle, and she talked a lot [smiles with delight as she remembers her mother and gestures to express the cheerfully animated personality of her mother]. At that time, the company that the school fed into was the Alicia Alonso Ballet Company, and they didn't have Black dancers. The woman continued with my mother: "So, you know, I don't think she's going to make it." She said that to my mother [in a tone of appall, such a thing to a child's mother]. But I didn't hear.

My mother walked past the woman, and then she stopped, and I remember that. She turned around with me, and she faced the woman and she said to the woman, "Look at her. She is going to be the first one." Yeah. And that was the only thing that I heard, and I didn't understand why. Years later my mother explained that situation to me, and I made the connection. I said, "Oh, I remember, I heard that. But I didn't know why you said that at the time." And I made it. I got into the school.

NM: Could you explain how race operates differently in Cuba than in the U.S.? When people say Afro-Cuban, is that indicating race or culture? Is it different?

CM: When I lived in Cuba, the Afro-Cuban terminology didn't exist. We were all Cubans. They always said Cuba had race problems. Because I heard those conversations. I remember. I was younger, I didn't totally understand, but I knew they were talking about—race, politics, these things. But we all were Cubans. For example, I'm Black because I'm mulatta in Cuba. My skin is light, but I'm Black, I'm more Black, because of my hair and my nose. If you are light and you have straight hair, you could be light skin; you probably are white. You define yourself as a white person even if maybe half of your family is Black. In Cuba, you can understand how those things work. You know, if you could be white, it's better. It was always better. And it was easier. I want to be clear about that. Everything was easier if you were white.

NM: Like here.

CM: No, here (U.S.) it's stronger, the race problem, because the people have more consciousness about race than in Cuba. In Cuba, I grew up listening to a lot of race jokes that I didn't like. I remember, I never laughed at those jokes about Black people, and I didn't like it. I didn't feel offended, but I didn't like it. Even if it was natural (a norm in the culture) for everyone. Because they laugh at everybody, they make jokes about everyone—white, about Gallegos (a minority group from Spain), some Spaniards that came to Cuba, about the Chinese that came to Cuba. They made fun of them, they made fun of Black people, they made fun of everyone.

But I don't know, it just wasn't funny to me. Then, after the revolution, they said we were supposed to stop the race problems (we are all one nation); it's true. In school, we grew up all together and we were all on the same page, Black, Brown, no differences. But, deep [down], unfortunately, it didn't work out. Even though we were raised and educated in that way, I see people my age and the younger people now being racist in Cuba. And they're starting to say "Oh, I'm white." Or "All my family is from Spain." Or "I don't have Black [people] in my family." Those things never happened before, because before, I remember, the Cubans used to quote Nicolás Guillén, a Cuban poet. He said in one of his poems, "Él que no tiene de Congo, tiene de Carabalí," "If you don't have the Congo, you know the country in Africa, you don't have Caribe (the essence of the Caribbean)."

NM: From the Caribbean?

CM: It's, how do you say, … a tribe.

We were all very proud to be Cuban. When I was young, I never heard that terminology (referring to Afro-Cuban). Then I came back to Cuba, and after 20 years I heard it: "Oh, you are Afro-Cuban. Oh, she's Afro-Cuban. Oh, she's white." Those things never happened before. So (teaching people not to be racist) didn't work out.

NM: So, you passed these three auditions.

CM: I passed, and I started in the school. It was a boarding school. The school was in some houses that the government pulled out from the rich people. They prepared those houses as residences for the students and built some ballet studios in some of those houses as well. And we lived there. We went to school from Monday to Saturday at noon, and we took everything there. Academic, ballet, folklore, character dance, French, music, history of dance. So, it was a complete education, academics and the arts.

NM: So, you stayed at the school from the time you were 9 or 10?

CM: I was 10. The teachers were Fernando Alonso, Joaquin Banegas, Ramona de Saa. There is this story that the director of the Cuban School in Havana, Fernando Alonso told us. The teachers were very young, and he was talking about the process of putting the school together. Fernando had a meeting with them, Loipa Araújo, Josefina Mendes, Joaquin Banegas, her sister Margarita de Saa, and I don't know if I'm forgetting someone. He said, "You are going to be teachers." Now, they were very young; Fernando was preparing them. Fernando Alonso prepared them to teach us—it was a huge responsibility. He said that they (the teachers) were part of how the Cuban mythology was developed.

Fernando worked with Cuban teachers, with Russian teachers, and they were working in the program and at some point they said, "No, we don't want that Russian methodology, Vaganova; no, we will do it (another way)." They were developing what would work for our bodies, for our characteristics. (Vaganova) didn't work for us because we are not Russian. We don't have that type of body; we are totally different. Fernando was very, very clear about what he wanted for the Cuban dancers. He wanted the combination of the African rhythm with the sensuality of the Spanish dance. You know, the Cubans, the way that we move, he wanted to keep that. He wanted us to keep what is in our blood.

NM: That's beautiful. So, you were away from your family during...?

CM: For a week. And I was with my family half of the Saturday and Sunday. And Sunday before 10:00 p.m., I would have to be back at the school.

I was in the school a little less than eight years, because I started late—I was very lucky, very, very lucky. I started working with the company as an apprentice when I was 14. When I was in the school, in the afternoons they would bring us to company rehearsals, or sometimes we got to watch classes.

I remember the first thing we did was in *Swan Lake*, the third act. They took students from the school, I guess the best dancers (were selected to be in the production). I think we were six girls, six boys—the Napolitanos. There is a dance, Napolitanos from Naples; it is a character dance in the third act, so we danced that part with the company in the productions. And it was amazing, because we were watching all those dancers—they were like gods to us.

NM: And they were also your teachers.

CM: Exactly, they were our teachers. And then we were in the third act, after sitting and watching all of them dancing the Spaniard dance, the chair dance, mazurkas. We could watch the second act, since all the girls participated in the third act. Then we started doing some of these dances. So, for us to start working with the company was very smooth and very natural. We were understanding how the dancing (and company life) feels.

NM: Now, would you say this Cuban methodology was Fernando's inspiration, or was it from Alicia Alonso? Was this development directed by her...?

CM: No, Fernando and Alicia worked together. They were a power couple. And they had the same teachers, because Fernando Alonso's mother was the director of one of the important culture associations in Cuba. Not only for dance, for music, and everything. Cuba was a country; I don't know if you know, because of the geographic position, everybody who came from Europe passed through Cuba to America. So, they could see all the big artists, you know? All the singers, Anna Pavlova, Fanny Elssler, everybody passed through Cuba. So, Russian teachers, Italian teachers came to Cuba, and they started the ballet. Alicia and Fernando were students of theirs, and their teachers told them to "go to America to have the varying experiences and finish, to polish you as a professional dancer." So they came to America, and in America they started working; they did everything, musical theater; they started working with Ballet Caravan. And I don't remember right now the name of the teacher, but he was a Russian teacher. At the time, Fernando started (noticing) that Alicia was very special. The way that she moved, the way she executed movement, the way she expressed herself. I remember Alicia telling me that sometimes they were controlling her, because she was often being compared with the other dancers. She was very, very expressive, and she was very fast—the way she moved the arms and upper body. So, Fernando saw the difference and he started analyzing how the American people move, how the Russian…

NM: The national cultural embodiment?

CM: Being fluid in that way. So, they wanted from the beginning to have a school and a company in Cuba. Even (though) they were in the Ballet Caravan, which later became American Ballet, they wanted to have their own school and provide a good dance location in Cuba, because they saw the talent in Cuba.

NM: Why did you dance? What made you enjoy the movement? Did you enjoy seeing what you could become? What was is it that made you want to be connected to dancing?

CM: To express. The movement was the way I loved to express myself. When I was younger, I didn't talk. It was so hard for me to put my thoughts into words. I remember when I was in meetings or conversation and people were talking to me, if they said something silly or I disagreed, I didn't have a quick response. It was hard for me to put my ideas into words. So, I'm guessing that was one of the things that made me want to dance since I was a little girl. My way was moving and jumping.

I remember my mother (she remembers a story from her childhood and calls it a fantasy).… You know, I busted my head trying to fly when I was maybe four? I walked to the stairs when I was three or four, and I was trying to jump but not in the vertical position. I was trying to jump like a bird and then take off into flight. This was before I had dance experience, but I was trying to explore movement. And then I had another one (fantasy). I broke my elbow in another.…

NM: Exploration in jumping.

CM: Exploration in how to fly. So, when my mother saw that possibility, she said, "Oh, no, she has to dance, because no more elbows or head injuries, she needs the technique to understand how to fly." So, I always loved to dance, to be different characters, ... it was so beautiful.

I remember Fernando Alonso, and now when I teach, I talk a lot about him. When he was teaching us *Les Sylphides* he tried to make us understand that *Les Sylphides* takes places in a different environment, a different culture. He explained that *Les Sylphides* had a forest; it was different than our palm trees and the hot sun. He said, "No, no, no, you don't feel this" (referring to the heat), because it was hot. We didn't have air conditioning in the studios. So, he said, "No, no, no, no. You feel how hot it is? No, it's not hot, you don't feel the heat. You feel the winds, and the light, it's not so bright; the light is different." So, he made us believe that we were dancing in a different environment. He did that to create and feel the style as something natural. "Not imposed on our style."

NM: Right. When you tell me about that, it reminds me of how Arthur Mitchell's Creole Giselle *re-created that space for Giselle to be something that would really work culturally.*

CM: Oh. I didn't see it. I read about it when I was in Cuba. And to me, it was something very strong because they didn't want to give me *Giselle* in Cuba. Yeah, they didn't let me dance *Giselle*. So, to me, the possibility of being Black and performing that role.... You know, I danced *Pas de Quatre*, I danced *Les Sylphides*. I was, you know, well reviewed....

NM: I've done some research on color-casting in the U.S., where the dancers are cast if they could pass for white or powdering up to be white or lighter skinned dancers getting parts. Did that happen in Cuba?

CM: Yeah, but we all did it. Not just because you are not white people. We did it because we wanted the skin to look all ... because *Les Sylphides* is not natural. It's not a human being. The same in *Giselle*, it's a ghost; the Wilis are ghosts. Giselle is a human being, but the second act, they are ghosts. So, I like that idea. And also in *Swan Lake*. I was comfortable with that. I didn't use white; white—it looks good on some people—but, for some reason, with my hair color, it was not the best for me. I used a kind of pink color with some yellow, and it blended together to make my skin all the same color. Because in *Swan Lake*, in the Cuban version, you become the swan. So, it's not a kind of human, it's a fantasy.

NM: Do you fantasize that they're Brown or Black?

CM: No, it's okay. Because, any way you use the makeup, you see that the people are Black.... I want to share with you, I have a picture where I am wearing the pink makeup, doing *Les Sylphides*, and I'm Black. You can see that I'm Black, because it's me [gestures to her face and body].

You know something? Here (in the U.S.), I understand what happens here with color. Because here, the problem is the color. I understand that. We didn't have that problem, because the problem in Cuba was not that much … it was the color, but also how you…

NM: The [facial and hair] features.

CM: The features, exactly. The features. But we were all … it was all about creating art, creating the fantasy. So, that's why the white people used white. I didn't use white makeup on my body because I didn't like it that much. And the Black girls, they used … they mixed (colors). Sometimes they used a pink one, because everybody wore makeup, starting from Alicia; she is very white. Her skin is very, very white. She used the most makeup [gestures to covering the whole body with makeup], everything, so if she did it, everybody did it.

NM: It's just part of the performance experience. Can you tell me a little bit about your performance career? You apprenticed from 14 until 18, and then you joined the company?

CM: No, no, I started in the company doing things before. I did the corps de ballet, *Les Sylphides,* and *Swan Lake* corps de ballet, and *Giselle* corps de ballet before I graduated. So, then when I graduated, the first opportunity that I had … was in *Coppélia*. Six of the girls danced with boys, and I was one of them. And you have a lot of lifts and pirouettes; it was challenging; partner work is challenging. I loved it. Back then … to me, that was a big opportunity. Then I was a *coryphée* (a dancer typically dancing in a small group or as a soloist). I don't know in English the terminology; it's when you have the most important part in the corps de ballet, in *Les Sylphides*. So, it's two girls that they worked with the corps de ballet, but sometimes you're a little bit more in the front. So, that was huge for me, because I loved the style. And I didn't have any conflict with interpreting those roles. Actually, it was something I felt very into. All the classical ballets, all of this was easy for me.

NM: So, for a timeline, when did you enter the company?

CM: I got into the company in '69? I think so, or '68. I toured all over the world. Everybody wanted to know about Cuba. Remember, in Europe they were in shock when they saw the company so diverse. Black, Yellow, Brown, tall, short. In Paris and in Italy they said, "What beautiful work Fernando and Alicia and her teams have done. They made it possible for all of those people to interpret and see the classical and romantic styles so pure."

NM: You mentioned the diversity in the color.

CM: *Sí.*

NM: But you also said that you could not dance Giselle.

CM: Okay. Because the beginning of the company, when Fernando was in the company, I remember, for example, that he took care of us, and me, a lot. About my hair, because I was in the school, I didn't know … you have to think about Cuba. In Cuba we didn't have products for the hair, we didn't have anything, so it was hard for me to manage my hair at that moment. And I didn't have my mother with me, because I was in boarding school. Then I went to the company. So, when I (was promoted) to the company, he personally, with another woman that was Black, brought me to the salon to see what they can do with my hair to help me to manage my hair easily. I mean, I was okay, but I understood later that they had plans for me. Traveling, roles with the company, soloist roles. So, they were preparing me to make all those things easy. Fernando did my makeup. You know, he took a lot of care about me and care of the boys that came from orphanages. Most of the boys came from orphanages. So, he took care of them.

But then, when he left the company, things changed. All the people were getting positions other than Alicia Alonso. She worked with me a lot. She coached me a lot. She created, in *Nutcracker*, a piece for me and Lazaro Carreño, one of the principal dancers of the National Ballet of Cuba too. But then she was saying things about, you know, casting us, casting me in contemporary pieces, most of the time (this was a change and I felt it was racially motivated).

I had good reviews, and I was told by her (Alicia Alonso) that I was one of the people who most understood the style and the way that the Cubans wanted to do the classical and the romantic dances. All that was lost. Unfortunately, some of my teachers passed away. Others left the company because the people surrounding Alicia didn't allow them to participate and bring their full knowledge to the company. The people surrounding Alicia were getting more control and influence. This was when the problems with race started to take form. So the company, when they came to the U.S., practically everybody was white. That was the opposite when we came the first time and we have the seasons on the Metropolitan, Kennedy Center. It was an amazing season—our performances were sold out.

We were performing the whole week, Tuesday–Sunday, sold out. And *The New York Times* was writing practically daily about the company. And the reviews were, in general, very good. And what they said … their opinion was very important to us, because it was a different perspective for them to see us, you know? To watch our artistry. So, I don't understand why those changes occurred, why the need to create a company that looks more European than we are.

NM: You noticed it and you saw this happening, but you never really knew why it happened?

CM: No, no, no. We knew what was happening, and we said that. Straight to them.

NM: But why? They just made that choice?

CM: Oh, *sí*.

NM: Is it about money? Funders?

CM: No. No, no, no. In Cuba, they don't need funders. The government gives the money. You know, everything comes from a center.

NM: What motivated the change?

CM: They are racist. So simple. One person with power, got power, besides

Alicia Alonso. Racist people. That's it. They are like that. And right now, for example, I heard that dancers right now are living in Europe and here in the U.S., they said, "No, we don't want Black people in this piece. Just one." Because we just want Othello Black; the others have to be white. I was there when Brian MacDonald created the piece *Prólogo para Una Tragedia*, based on *Othello*. I was there, and in the corps de ballet it was Black and Brown people. Not just Othello. He never said that, never. That never happened before. Always, there were Black and Brown people in the cast.

NM: And what made you want to leave the company, or did you?

CM: I left the company in 1987 because the company lost…. I felt, that it was losing (on race).

NM: 'Cause you were there 20 years.

CM: Yeah. The company is still doing good things. And it was all Loipa Araújo, Josefina Méndez, they were pushing good things. But when older people left…. I don't want to talk for them about why they left. But they left, and those people were supposed to be directing the company right now. Not Alicia Alonso, that is one person that, she doesn't see [referring to her legally blind status], and she's almost 90 years old. So, a person with such experiences like Loipa Araújo, now associate director of the English National Ballet. She could be director of (Cuban National Ballet), besides Alicia, why not? So, things should be totally different. If you see the English National Ballet, go, take a look and see how diverse the company is.

NM: Now, the school is more diverse than the company, I am guessing, because I know that some South African ballet companies have gotten dancers from Cuba in efforts to diversify the company. Because they do not have many Black ballet dancers in South Africa, they are mostly white South Africans. So, are they in the school?

CM: Correct, in the school they don't have those problems.

NM: Okay, so you could find Black dancers attending the school.

CM: Yes, in the school you see people from all over. The school is wonderful. It's wonderful. And it's incredible how they have to struggle to keep the level of the school. It's not easy. It's not easy in a country … they try, and they build their pointe shoes. But ballet is a very expensive career, and you need, you have to be updating.

NM: Can you tell me a little bit about the culture of the company? The Ballet Nacional de Cuba, was it very tied to national identity? Cultural identity? You talk about doing the classics, and you also talk about the Cuban culture coming through the dance. Would they come through the dance in the classics, or would that be the contemporary works that they would do?

CM: Yes, this is another point. There are three features that create the Ballet Nacional de Cuba. Fernando Alonso, he was the brain of the school. He was also an amazing dancer. But he was focused on the school and the vision of the company. Alicia was the ballerina, and Alberto Alonso the choreographer. I have to say that Alicia was a choreographer too of the classical, but Alberto Alonso was the main person among the three of them. That's why it's so sad, what's happening. Since the beginning, all Cuban artists, in all different disciplines, not always in ballet, they wanted to explore the African culture in the performing arts using an international language, like in the ballet. All the first pieces, choreographic works that Fernando, also Alicia, made, and Luis; there's another important person, I don't remember his name, they used our African roots in the choreography. The stories, the themes were all about our roots, and that was incredible. So, the contemporary pieces have a lot of that. They used the Cuban way to move. Actually, in the contemporary company, they used the Graham technique as a pattern, but they all use the Caribbean way to move like Cuba. This was Patterson, Arnoldo Patterson, with the contemporary company.... I don't remember now the name of this other person.

NM: *Is it a separate company? The contemporary company?*

CM: Separate. But even though they were separate, all of us—classical, contemporary, painters, music, poets, writers, we were so interested in our African roots and Spaniard roots too.

NM: *Even people who would be considered white?*

CM: Yes, white people. Actually, all of them are white people. Alejo Carpentier, the writer, if you read Alejo Carpentier, he's all about it. So amazing. About the Cuban roots, you know, the African. What is Cuba? That was who we are. How we become Cuban with the African and the Spanish together, the criollo. That is still in our music. But, in the ballet, it was, to me, something very special, because I don't know other countries (that had) the opportunity to (have that kind of exposure and history) to develop in the arts. How Cuba (exposed these artists), Alicia Alonso, Alberto Alonso, all these artists. But Alberto Alonso's contemporary works in the company were incredible. Then, the younger people came, and they use Cecilia Valdes—you know Cecilia Valdes is a story—so, they created a ballet about Cecilia Valdes. They created a ballet about our histories, literature, and that is not happening anymore. In Cuba they love it, but when we went to perform out of Cuba, it was something very important. Because it was totally new for Europeans.

NM: *Can you tell me about some of your best memories with the company? Like, your favorite moment to think about?*

CM: I have so many. But not only in the company, because I left the company and I had my own company—contemporary company, Havana Ballet Theater. It was a company integrated for actors, contemporary dancers, and ballet dancers.

NM: Was that in Cuba?

CM: In Havana, yes. That was a great experience for me. It was important, because we need to express ourselves in different ways. And that was one of the reasons that I left the company. It's true that Alicia Alonso gave me the opportunity to choreograph for the National Ballet, my first choreography I did for the company. But I didn't find the time to explore and study and develop what I wanted in the company. The reason I left the company is because I saw that the company was changing, and they were not ... it was becoming so bizarre. So bizarre. And I thought, in my opinion, that the company was losing its identity. I think that so many people, they stay in the company a long time, they fight for that (identity). But then, over time the identity is lost ... like right now, they don't have contemporary repertory. It's a white company, practically white company. But it's about color, because we (Cubans) are a rainbow of colors. So, we have to be represented in the company. If you want to see the identity of the company, you have to be there. Because when we were (there) before, and when you see the videos before and after, you can see the difference. I have to say that they have an amazing technique, amazing technique. It's unbelievable how Cuba has developed that. But that is about the school. When dancers finish the school, they are ready to do anything, because the school also is now performing *La Bayadère* and *Giselle*. So, by the time those students get into the company, they have performed a lot.

NM: Do you use that Cuban technique and methodology here at Ballet Hispánico (where Caridad was teaching at the time of the interview)?

CM: Yes. Yes I use it, we have a lot of Cuban teachers here. I use it (the Cuban method), and of course, I see a lot and you take from here and there. But I always remember Fernando and I try to filter and use what works. The other things I keep, I acknowledge it, when it's necessary, but I try to bring my methodology.

NM: Can you tell me a little bit about how the cultures of your students are different and/or similar to the Cuban culture you were taught in? What changes do you implement to make it relevant for this community and these students?

CM: I did not understand your question, but I'm going to say what is interesting for me and then if I didn't answer, let me know.

To me, what is interesting here is that when you get into the studio, you have an Asian person, and Black, and white. (Bodies range from) long European with completely flat, to arching back from Caribbean people, Latino people, African American people—we have arched backs. Our spine is more flexible. So, you have to put all of these together. I love that. How to use my knowledge, the Cuban methodology, to put everything together without draining their identity. Because that was the way that Fernando and my teachers always taught us. You know, go straight, but keep the personality. Then when they're older, they can manage the personality for different roles. But don't touch that [personality]. Don't drain this from them. When I get into a studio and I have a diverse group of students, it's important to make them aware of their accents. Their … what is bright on them. What is beautiful on their identity, what they have to use that is a good thing for them. It could be a good thing for them as a performer. So, beside the technique, that is one of the things that I love to do.

NM: So, when talking about the Ballet Hispánico here, there's a focus on Latin American culture, but the students are diverse. And so, they're not all Latinos?

CM: Actually, I don't know the percentage, but we have a huge number of non-Latinos. And they come because they love the culture, and they love (the opportunity for) their children to grow with different people.

NM: When I look for Latinos in New York City Ballet, or American Ballet Theatre, or San Francisco Ballet or some of the mainstream companies, it's hard to find Latino representation.

CM: Well, if you see San Francisco Ballet, most of the Latino representation is Cuban.

NM: Do you see that as a problem, or have you noticed it, or…?

CM: It wasn't for me.

NM: For the children you teach, do you see their color being a barrier?

CM: I don't know. Because it's different at the moment. Because I hear lot of Black and Brown dancers say how important it is for them to see…

NM: Someone that looks like them.

CM: Someone who looks like them. Some of my students have said to me how important it was that I was their teacher, that it was someone who had a career as a performer, as a choreographer, and now is a teacher. So, it's important. It wasn't for me. Why? I don't know … maybe because of the support that I had from my teachers and Fernando Alonso.

NM: And your mother?

CM: Oh, yeah, my mother, my father…. When I went to the boarding school, my mother told me, clearly, and my father, but my mother, I remember what she said to me: "Listen. You're going to go to boarding school and we won't be there." And I was an only child, so everything was around me, me, me, me. So, they said, "If someone smells bad, they will think the smell is from you. If someone steals something, they will think that you stole it. If something is wrong, they will point to you. So, you have to be very correct. You have to work three times harder than the other students if you want to get the same recognition and to get the same score in the class. Do you understand that?" I said, "Yes." She said, "So now, please, forget it." Because, she said, "If you are all the time thinking about race, you won't go as fast as you can. If you are all the time worried about that." And I totally agree. Not only for race, also with problem that happens sometimes in companies, you have to be like that. You go and you have to be aware, because you have to defend yourself, but if you are all the time thinking about this, it's going to be hard. You have to work, work, work, work.

I think the idea was be correct, work harder. If something happens, be aware of that, but just do what you have to do very well. You don't have to be thinking of that (race) all the time, but be aware.

NM: *What was your favorite performance role?*
   CM: *Don Q., Don Quixote.*

NM: *Why was that one of your favorites?*
   CM: It was…

NM: *The attitude and energy?*
   CM: Uh-huh [nodding yes]. And I loved the prelude in *Les Sylphides*.

NM: *And you liked that one because…?*
   CM: I love the music. I love Chopin, you know, when I hear percussion—ba ba-babaa ba-babaa ba-babaa—in my skin…. I feel it deeply. When I hear people dancing flamenco, when I see good dancers, and, you know, the percussion in the flamenco, *la caja* (a percussion musical instrument), the singing, do you know? When I listen to Chopin, when I listen to Tchaikovsky, I feel the same. So, you know, all this is a part of it.

NM: *Can you talk a little bit about how the field of ballet has changed in the past 30 years and how the opportunities for Latinos have changed, either better or…?*
   CM: In general, there are more opportunities because there are more companies; directors are more sensitive about diversity … and also, the ballet's becoming very athletic. The people that are coaching have to be very careful where there is use of athleticism … and where it is not, because it's technique. It's not tricks. No, you have to have good ballet technique to be able to do that. Art is the way to communicate, to express; that's what I see.

NM: *Your experiences are with companies that are connected to Latino heritage in some way. Either in Mexico or Cuba or here at Ballet Hispánico. Is that important for you to be connected to an organization that has those kinds of cultural ties? Or are you open to working…?*
   CM: No, I work with…. I was invited to work with the concert group at Joffrey. In Alvin Ailey, for example, the diversity is full of European students and African American, Latino.

   I enjoy working with all kinds of people. I have worked with so many artists, I have so much knowledge that I would like to share, because my experience in the classical repertory is huge.

NM: *How do you feel about ballet being described as Eurocentric or white? When people look at ballet as a white dance form, do you push against that idea? Do you understand that idea?*
   CM: It's like to say rock 'n' roll is white music. Go back and see how many Black people did rock 'n' roll. Because Elvis Presley was in that moment, when America

was very, very racist, you know, he was the name put in front. But, if you go back, you find how many good singers and good people were the performers for the rock 'n' roll; looking back, this moment, the story could be different. So, why? Because for so many years, the Black dancers didn't have the opportunity to get the positions.

NM: Can you tell me about some of the community work you do?

CM: At Brooklyn Ballet, yes. The outreach program has developed beautiful performers. Two of the students that came from the outreach program, I brought them to JKO (American Ballet Theatre Jacqueline Kennedy Onassis School) because at that moment, we (Ballet Hispánico) did not have the level for them. They had to work by themselves. And I really thought that JKO would be the best place for them to develop their career—and it was. I have been supporting them strongly for years, because they felt they were "the Blacks." They (JKO) loved them. But the dancers didn't feel comfortable.

You know, it's important for Black people, for African Americans, and Latinos to see people like them teaching them, performing. They came every single weekend to me. And I realized that the problem was that they were surrounded by white people. That's why they came. "We want to stay with you. We want to take classes with you." But they have the good teachers. They have good teachers, right now they are in Houston Ballet, second company.

From left to right, Shaakir Muhammad, Caridad Martinez, and Naazir Muhammad (courtesy Caridad Martinez).

NM: *I understand that need for connection and being able to relate. Is there anything that I haven't asked you that you want to share or talk about and have people know about?*

CM: I think it is important to realize that we all have a right to art. Art education is a right; it's not all business and how much money you make. There is a necessity for people to see art; it is so important. And it's sad when I go to the theater and I see the people in the theater, and I don't see the people that I saw in the subway. They cannot pay $75, $100, or $200 for a ticket.

NM: *Some people will never see the ballet.*

CM: You see. It's important to understand that has to change. People are very smart. They can find a way to have several types of tickets with different prices, and they can still make money. That's possible. And maybe they can deduct from the taxes. But something must be done.

Caridad Martinez in *Tarde en la Siesta*, choreographed by Alberto Mendez, Cuban National Ballet (courtesy Caridad Martinez).

The same thing with dance education. Because it's not enough, a program for diversity, and a program for a scholarship—no. Talented people, if they are talented, they should have free education in art. Free education. If there is someone dedicated and talented who has the determination, the passion, and is completely focused, those people need to have free education. Parents and students cannot be left to worry that "I cannot afford that." Sometimes teachers cannot give particular assignments to students that they should have, because students do not have the budget to pay for so many classes or the materials or tickets to see other artists. Because a dance student should take music, French language, art, all these things work to inform a well-versed artist. From where does that budget come? We need education and art for everyone. Professional education, not just educational outreach. Prepro-fessional and professional education. It should be free for talented students.

NM: Yes. I am so appreciative of your time.
　　CM: No, thank you so much.

Caridad Martinez Glossary

> Brief bio-notes of artists and places mentioned in the chapter. This is not intended to be comprehensive but instead to offer a small amount of information to spark more thorough research if readers are interested.

Alonso, Alberto—Cofounder of Ballet Alicia Alonzso (later to become the Cuban National Ballet) and served as its first artistic director and choreographer. Danced with Ballet Theater (later to become the American Ballet Theatre) and Ballet Russe de Colonel W. de Basil. Choreographed for companies such as Ballet Hispánico, the Cuban National Ballet, and the Bolshoi Ballet. Alberto Alonso died in 2007.

Alonso, Alicia—Cuban-born prima ballerina. Cofounder of the National Ballet of Cuba and the Cuban National Ballet School in the late 1940s. Danced with Ballet Russe de Monte Carlo, founding member of the Ballet Theater (later to be named the American Ballet Theatre), and appeared in several Broadway musicals. Suffered from visual impairment for most of her career. Alicia Alonso died in 2019.

Alonso, Fernando—Cuban-born ballet dancer. Cofounder of the National Ballet of Cuba and the Cuban National Ballet School in the late 1940s. Performed with Mordkin Ballet, Lincoln Kirsten's Ballet Caravan, and the Ballet Theater (later to be named the American Ballet Theater) and danced in several Broadway musicals. Fernando Alonso died in 2013.

Alonso, Laura—Daughter of Fernando and Alicia Alonso. Teacher, coach, and restager for classical ballets. Member of the Cuban National Ballet for 25 years and artistic adviser for the Canton Ballet since 1990.

American Ballet Theatre—Founded in 1939 by Lucia Chase and Richard Pleasant. Known for presenting classical ballet repertory in contrast to the New York "City Ballet," known for presenting and preserving Balanchine repertory.

Araújo, Loipa—Cuban-born ballet master. Principal dancer with the Cuban National Ballet. Became the associate artistic director of the English National Ballet in 2012.

Ballet Caravan—Founded by Lincoln Kirsten in 1936, later merged with American Ballet and then disbanded (not to be confused with the American Ballet Theatre). Lincoln Kirstein went on to create New York City Ballet with George Balanchine in 1948.

Ballet Hispánico—Latinx/Latine/Hispanic cultural organization, founded by Tina Ramirez in 1970 in New York.

Bangeas, Joaquín—A student of Fernando Alonso. Joined the Ballet Alicia Alonso in 1953 and later became a member of the Cuban National Ballet. Former deputy director of the Provincial Ballet School of Havana in 1962, former director of the Cuban National Ballet, and general director of the Camagüey Ballet.

Burke, Elena—Cuban singer, died in 2002.

Carpentier, Alejo—Cuban novelist.

Carreño, Lázaro—Principal dancer with the Cuban National Ballet. Dance partner to Alicia Alonso.

Elssler, Fanny—Austrian-born ballet dancer from the Romantic period (1810–1884).

Escuela Nacional de Arte—Art school in Cuba. Founded in 1962.

Graham Technique—Modern dance technique created by Martha Graham.

Havana Ballet Theater—Multidisciplinary contemporary company. Caridad Martinez, founder and artistic director.

Houston Ballet—Founded in 1969. Developed from a ballet school and foundation into a ballet company, established through a state charter in 1955.
Jacqueline Kennedy Onassis School—The ballet school connected to the American Ballet Theatre.
Macdonald, Brian—Canadian-born dancer and choreographer. Founding member of the National Ballet of Canada. Served as artistic director of the Royal Swedish Ballet, the Harkness Ballet, the Batsheva Dance Theatre, and Les Grands Ballets Canadiens.
Méndez, Josefina—Principal dancer with the Cuban National Ballet until her retirement in 1996. Died in 2007.
Mitchell, Arthur—Cofounder of Dance Theatre of Harlem in 1969. First African American promoted to principal dancer at New York City Ballet. Died in 2018.
Moreno, Karemia—Graduate of the Bolshoi Ballet Academy in Moscow, dancer with the Cuban National Ballet, and later served as a ballet master for the company. Also worked as a ballet master and guest teacher at the Compañía Nacional de Danza in Spain, Ballet Estable del Teatro Colón in Argentina, and Béjart Ballet Laussane in Switzerland.
Parés, José—Born in Puerto Rico, member of the Cuban National Ballet. Founded the Dance Theater of José Parés in Puerto Rico.
Patterson, Arnoldo—Founding member of Cuban Contemporary Dance. As a choreographer and teacher, he led the way in Afro-Cuban dance training and performance.
Pavlova, Anna—Born in Russia. Principal dancer with the Imperial Russian Ballet and Ballets Russes. Originated many classical ballet roles but most widely known for *The Dying Swan*.
Plisetsky, Azari—Russian-born ballet dancer, teacher, and choreographer. Trained at the Moscow State Academy of Choreography (Bolshoi Ballet Academy) before joining the Bolshoi Ballet and later the Cuban National Ballet, where he was a principal partner with Alicia Alonso.
Portuondo, Omara—Cuban singer and dancer.
Presley, Elvis—Iconic rock-and-roll singer. Presley died in 1977.
Saá, Ramona de—Director of the Cuban National Ballet School and founding member of the Cuban National Ballet. Ramona and her twin sister, Margarita de Saá, were the subjects of the documentary *Mirror Dance* after being separated for years.
Saá White, Margarita de—Student of Fernando and Alicia Alonso. Rose to the rank of principal dancer at the Cuban National Ballet. Cofounded the Pennsylvania Academy of Ballet with her husband, John White. Margarita and her twin sister, Ramona de Saá, were the subjects of the documentary *Mirror Dance* after being separated for years after Castro's revolution. Died in 2017.
Valdés, Cecila—Character in the novel *Cecilia Valdés* and a ballet of the same title about interracial love. The novel was written in 1839 by Cirilo Villaverde.

Crystal Michelle Perkins

Past affiliations: Augusta Ballet (1993–1997) and Dayton Contemporary Dance Company (2001–2010)
Current position: Associate artistic director, Dayton Contemporary Dance Company (2010–present), and associate professor of dance, Ohio State University (2017–present)
Hometown: Augusta, Georgia
Current residence: Dayton, Ohio
Age at the time of the interview: 43

I interviewed Crystal Michelle Perkins on September 27, 2022, via Zoom after many candid personal conversations about her experiences in dance and training at a ballet school in the southern region of the United States. I requested this interview with Crystal toward the completion of this book, as she shared certain lived experience that I believed would further advance the intent of the text. I will be transparent in sharing that Crystal is a friend and colleague, and my prior knowledge of her dance experiences guided me through this interview.

NM: *Tell me what kind of dance professional you are and how you would describe your dance, history, or training.*

CP: I feel like these kinds of questions make me pick.... Currently, I am an associate artistic director and professor and next to that is a choreographer and teacher,

Crystal Michelle Perkins (photograph by Scott Robbins; courtesy Crystal M. Perkins).

a dance artist really, which I think captures all of those things no matter what place or institution, or space. I love making dances. I am talking about the importance of dance, and I'm thinking particularly for me about Black folk dancing through all of those spaces.

NM: *How did you get here? How did you get to these competencies to be able to do those things? What was your entry point into dance? How did you come to understand the structures that got you where you are?*

CP: Well, like a lot of folks who come out of studio practice, my entry was a dance class; very, very young, well not as young as most folks. Now, I was probably seven or eight when I began to take a ballet class, because I was too young for tap at a place my mother found called the Augusta Mini Theater. The Augusta Mini Theater was run by a couple called the Butlers in Augusta, Georgia, and they essentially were focused on Black arts and in the city—piano classes, dance classes, theater classes and all sorts of things like that. That's where my sister and I were introduced to the arts. That was where I took my first ballet class.

The teachers from that space were from the Augusta Ballet. And, I didn't know this until much later, but the folks teaching from Augusta Ballet were also teaching at the (local) Arts Magnet. So, eventually when I was old enough to audition for the Arts Magnet, which was John S. Davidson Fine Arts School, my teachers, in cahoots with my mother, got me over to the audition for the Arts Magnet. Then, after a few years there, the same folks got in cahoots with my mother again and sent me over to the (Augusta) ballet school, and so I was at the ballet school quite late in comparison to the other young women who were dancing.

NM: When you talk about the Arts Magnet, was this a high school?
CP: Yes, it was a middle and high school. I went to that same school from the fifth to 12th grade and studied with the same people. And again, all the dance teachers there were from the Augusta Ballet.

NM: You talked about the Augusta Mini Theater as being culturally affirming, and I'm assuming racially affirming space in relation to Black arts, were those dance teachers from Augusta Ballet Black?
CP: Nope. They were not.

NM: So, when did you enter the ballet school? What was that experience like?
CP: Well by the time I entered the ballet school, I already had this sort of three or four years of on again off again, I'm going to use air quotes, "training." Because at the Magnet School they did the Royal Academy of Dancing syllabus, and so when it was time for me to go over to the Augusta Ballet, I already had an introduction to ballet. I already knew the language there and the people from the ballet school. So, by the time I got there, there wasn't a space of discomfort because I had grown up with these people. These are people who taught me how to dance in studio practice, and for them in our relationship, at every turn they were asking and offering more: "There's a class over at the ballet school," "There's an opportunity to do this" or "an opportunity to do that," and later on it was "You should audition to be an apprentice."

NM: Did you feel that those asks and offers were to Crystal? Or were they to all the kids?
CP: Those were to Crystal.

NM: So, already you're getting special invitations.
CP: Those are special invitations. It wasn't being offered to a group. I was being offered an opportunity in the space, and I was going alone, and I think part of that was my family trying to figure out how to navigate a gift or a talent that we didn't have any family experience in. There was no one in my family structure who understood how to navigate after-school ballet classes at the ballet school and everything that came with the culture of that at all.

But I did have a mother who knew how to recognize an opportunity, and she could kind of trust the space that she put us in, and because the Butlers trusted the

Augusta Ballet in this thing that they had built right for Black kids and Black children in the city. It was easy for my mom to trust that whoever they introduced me to, you know that was credibility, and for her I would be safe enough there.

NM: When you say you knew the people at the ballet school, did that include your peers? Or was that strictly admin and teachers?

CP: That included some of the peers. A lot of the same students at the ballet school also went to the Arts Magnet; we kind of studied together. I didn't always benefit from that sameness. We didn't live in the same neighborhood even though they went to the same Arts Magnet. The Arts Magnet had a kind of interesting set-up. It was 45 percent white and 45 percent Black and 10 percent other. When Beverly Jane Barnhart founded it that was her vision for the cultural demographic of the school, that it would have this sort of equitable approach for that time to creating an arts magnet for the city. Because the city is so small, the folks she went to for dance teachers were at the Augusta Ballet.

When the Augusta Mini Theatre wanted to include dance folks, they went to the Augusta Ballet, and so they were all in the same network. But in terms of the people, I was going to the Ballet School with, they all lived somewhere different. We weren't friends in that way, but I knew them. When I arrived, there were people that I knew.

The first ballet class I took at the ballet school was actually with the company. And that was pretty unusual, because I didn't have enough skill or vocabulary to really do that. But it was the only time my mother could take me because of her work schedule, and there wasn't anyone else at home who could get me to the three o'clock class, or whatever time the earlier class was, quickly enough after school, and I was still a little young to take Augusta public transportation by myself.

It's not like being in New York. It wasn't quick, and everybody's not doing it. You could be alone and standing on the side of the road by yourself for a long time, and so that wasn't an option. But the class she could get me to a couple of days a week was the company class. I think it was at 4:30 p.m. She could get off a little early to do that, and I remember not knowing enough vocabulary or having the speed or skill to take that class, but whatever the directors of the company could see, it was like, just leave her there. It seems like she can follow it. Since this is the only class she can take, it's fine.

So that gap, that I was sort of behind, I always thought I was behind. But I think the years that I took that 4:30 p.m. company class helped me to catch up in a way that maybe if I could have been at the 3:30 p.m. class I would not have been able to. Because it would have been more on par, but I was always sort of chasing the thing, and that's how I ended up as an apprentice with the ballet company. And then I think I was a company member in my senior year, which is kind of standard for a regional company, and the way that they build their corps de ballet out. And then somewhere in my senior year a woman, Rene Tool, who introduced me to ballet through the Royal Academy and dancing syllabus, I had gotten the Southern Recognition

University College application in the mail at the high school. She ran the high school program, and at the end of class I was hanging out in the studio, as I always do, and she just threw the application packet at me. She said, "Here, I think you're the only one interested in this. If you are, have your mother call me."

And I handed this to my mom, and my mom called her. In the spring I auditioned, which was rather late to be looking for colleges in the spring. I auditioned for the program. I got in, and I got a scholarship for Southern Methodist University (SMU), and that's where I went. I think I only auditioned for one school; it was SMU. And then I got into Brenau Woman's College through word of mouth, which I was not going to. They had a really great ballet program at the time, and I was not going there, I even had a full ride to go to Brenau, but I chose to go to Texas because I was running. I was running from the South. I was running from one kind of house to another kind of house, and so I ended up in this ballet program.

NM: I have two questions to rewind on. First, I would imagine that if I made it into a ballet company—I was apprentice, and then in my senior year promoted to the corps—that I would want to stay there and dance for a while before going to college. Because a lot of times people at that age are trying to get into a company. What was the thought process to say "I'm in this company, at entry level, at corps level, and it's a regional ballet company. But now I'm going to leave my company position to go to college."

CP: Oh, they made that offer. They made that suggestion. It was not for me for a lot of reasons. I think now, thinking about it, I had a particular drive. I didn't know that's what it was in the moment, but I knew.... I knew what the company felt like, I know this is on the record, but the company felt small, and I had more to learn.

NM: Oh, that wasn't your dream to dance professionally.

CP: It was my dream to dance as the principal in a ballet company, but I knew I could come back (to that company). I also knew there was much more to learn, and at 18, if I was already there (at Augusta Ballet).... I just sort of knew that inherently there had to be something else. But that plan was talked about. Stay here, go to college, you know, and then we'll send you to New York or whatever the usual plan is, that was one thing. The other thing is, I wanted to get out of my house. I wanted to escape the structure that I was in, not my family. But the idea of a college degree (called me). My mother wasn't a college graduate; my father at the time was a college graduate but postmilitary, and he didn't raise me. I had done lots of precollege programs, upward bound, and college prep.

NM: That was a very important accomplishment to attain.

CP: Yeah, college was a thing. I had been on the Historically Black College and University (HBCU) campus in Augusta, Georgia, Payne College. The magnet school I went to was a college preparatory school; it was a Georgia School of Excellence. So, staying home for college was not the goal. That was not ingrained. And the HBCUs that I was looking at, many of them did not have dance programs, and they definitely didn't have ballet.

NM: So, now I want to rewind a little bit, because you touched on something that I think could be its own book, and that is what were some of the navigations culturally from your family and home life and community to coming into ballet studio culture. And because we've had previous conversations, I got the sense, and you can correct me if I'm wrong, but were there times in which you had to be the translator of norms or customs either from the home to the ballet school or from the ballet school to your family? Can you talk a little bit about those translations and what you were doing as a cultural interpreter?

CP: Oh, I have so many. There are two that really come to mind. The first is my very first *Nutcracker*. My mother dropped me off at rehearsal, as she always does, and you know, when I tell this story, I am always thinking about, you know, my people knew that there was a theater, and that there was a ballet, and there were shows.

But there are some smaller fine details about belonging and understanding how that works that our family just didn't do. Mostly cultural divide but also a culture not just in Black and white but economic status, ability, all of those things that make that complicated. So, I remember sitting with all of the children in this large dressing area [for] *Nutcracker*, and flowers were being delivered to everyone, these sort of gifts and things. I had this strange feeling. First of all, it took me a little while to figure out what was happening, and then when I realized it was coming from the ballet, and it was like a thing the ballet did, and everybody was in on it. You know, it was your merde gift, or your good-luck gift. And I remember the dancer next to me asking had I gotten mine and I was like "No," you know. We went on with rehearsals and the day.

NM: And how old were you at this time?

CP: Oh, my first *Nutcracker*, I played the part of a polichinelle girl. I had to be maybe in the seventh grade, so what is it—12, 13? And I've always had a kind of go-with-the-flow resilience. I'm aware that something is happening. I did not have all the words to articulate it, but I would find them and say them. And so, after the performance and dress rehearsals, I said to my mother, "You know everybody got gifts there. I think that's something we're supposed to do." And she was like "I'm not supposed to do anything," you know, good Black mother rapport [laughing]. "You don't tell me what I need to do" type of stance [laughing]. I don't think it was that year, but in the next year she did start participating in those structures, and that really meant a lot because she started paying attention to what other families were doing to support their children.

There's another example I can think of, sort of the opposite—me explaining my family to the ballet school/company. My family was very proud to see me in *Nutcracker*, and this was some years later. I remember I was wearing pointe shoes by then, and I was doing "Waltz of the Flowers." It's a very lovely old theater and was built with a balcony. My family would sit in the top left balcony, and even when I perform now I still look up there even when there's no one there. They would make so much noise, they were so Black [*laughing*], it was so beautiful, and they would scream midperformance (beaming with joy, pride, appreciation, and smiles). It was my personal standing "O" (ovation). I remember coming off the stage and hearing people say "Who was that yelling like that?" with a sort of an attitude. That's when I realized that Black families celebrate differently, like we do at graduation, because these are firsts, these are milestones. And again, I knew that something important was happening, and I did not at that age have the language, but I had enough wherewithal to say "that's my family, and they're just very excited" to the dancers who were asking. Then, among all the company it went from "Why are they being disruptive?" to, as the years went on, they would take up the answer to that question: "That's Crystal's family."

There's a superinteresting thing that begins to happen, because you're spending so much time with the same folks that if they're good people, they'll take up that charge for you, and you won't [speaking through tears in her voice] ... you won't always have to do it. And so, the conversations about race and ballet are really polarizing for me because I have so many stories of the typical things. The only students, the overheard whispers, the trouble with their hair, and tights, that's basic.... I have tons of those stories. But the ones I remember, the ones that kept me in the field, are those moments, that (in a "hands-off" tone, both defending and affirming Perkins) "A—that's Crystal's family and they're proud, and they should be."

Then there are the troubling moments where you get your first bio and headshot, and your director, who's endeared to your dancing and who is trying to get you to be something in the field, asks you to wear a braided wig, and so it's really a sort of emotional and psychological trip at that age, trying to figure out who and how to trust. And you really need your family unit to pay attention. My mother vetoed that; by then she had been paying enough attention to say "Oh, no, she won't be wearing a braided wig." But I have my first bio, and I'll share it with you. It says something like "Crystal Fuller (maiden name) joins us with her exotic looks" or something like that, because you don't write your first bio. Those things are sobering to try to figure out how do you continue into a craft that you ... recently a DCDC [Dayton Contemporary Dance Company] company dancer asked me: "How did you come to your understanding in ballet?" And I said, "No matter what your structure actually does, whether or not you have a ballet body, whatever that is, there are people who have this inherent understanding of the form and how it's organized and an appreciation for how the steps function and the puzzle pieces together." I always had that. I always understood ballet in that way, and so to be in something that you have a gift for and constantly having these conversations that require cultural shifting (was hard). On one hand, you've got exotic looks, and can you braid your hair? On the other hand, that's Crystal's family; let's make room and space, here's a scholarship, don't forget to audition for that thing. You can see opportunity and also see that things need to be fixed. But that period of time between the seventh, eighth grade through senior year of high school very much felt that way.

It was also a time when this particular company was trying to figure out how to diversify the stage. And so, towards the end of my junior and senior year of high school, the company was creating their versions of community outreach programs at that time, and I remember there being a male Latino dancer and myself; we were the only two dancers that would participate in that community outreach program. And they would bring young African American boys into the studio and we would have a short creative movement class, a really typical program, and then invite them to the show, and I didn't know whether or not they actually made it to the show. But that was my first community teaching at the ballet school, but I mostly remember other folks weren't there, so I couldn't figure out what was happening.

Then, all of a sudden, in the same couple of years, we did a collaborative performance with Wynton Marsalis. That was probably my introduction to the idea of a national stage or national attention. It was sort of another strange out-of-body experience. Augusta Ballet hired a dancer who had just left Garth Fagan. She was a New Orleans native who signed on to the company for a couple of years, and she ended up teaching at the Arts Magnet. This was my first experience with a working Black woman, professional artist. That's when the teachers who I had for a long time started showing things like Garth Fagan videotapes. And then, because you had a Black professional who was likely asking the questions, "You got a lot of Black girls in this Arts Magnet program? What are you sharing with them?" And so, out comes the Ailey tapes and Dance Theatre Harlem tapes, and it's happening at a great time for me, because I am considering majoring.

At the same time, I spent the summer at the Joffrey Ballet School summer program in New York, where there was a small group of Black girls dancing there but not so many. We were dispersed across various levels so we were not together, and we really did not know each other. The feeling while in class was that of being the "only story." The Joffrey program was another reason why I didn't want to stay in Augusta. A New York summer gave me eight weeks to look at and compare the skill set that people really had.

Southern Methodist had an excellent dance program, and I knew it. It was a classical ballet and Graham program; it was a small private school. That's how I ended up at SMU.

NM: I remember you mentioning you knew some of the girls who danced with you, and some of them extended social invitations to you. What were some of your social negotiations like?

CP: Are you talking about the story with Melissa in the foyer of her house?

NM: Yes, tell me about Melissa.

CP: Yes, that's one of my favorite stories. I think it was a Halloween party. Melissa was one of those dancers I went to school with. There are so many times when I felt pretty out of pocket in social situations; one of them is with Melissa. She was a good friend at school at the time, and this was probably one of the last times we had a connection, and after this we sort of went our separate ways. I don't think she remained dancing with the company, so I don't think that this had anything to do with it, but she invited me to this party, and it was in a different area. Most of the girls I went to the ballet school with lived around the ballet school. I lived on the south side of town, which was about 35 minutes away, which is normal for that area; you have to drive where you're going. So, she invited me to this party, and it was fine for me to go. But my mother never let on (that there was anything special or significant about the situation I was walking into); my mother's just not like that. She's very proud of the life that she has built, and she should be. But there was never anything like "When you go, don't be alarmed, it's probably the largest house you've ever been in in your life, and this is how you … [laughing] there's a coat closet and things … but there were things we did not do when you enter a home."

I remember, I came into the house; I was excited about the party. My mother had styled my hair into a beehive that I was pretty proud of, and I came in, Melissa greeted me, and I could not leave the foyer. I was so startled by all of the wealth … that I did not know what to do, and Melissa tried her best to coax me in. I don't even know who else came to the party, and I stood in that foyer and in that doorway until my mother picked me up two and a half, three hours later. I was so embarrassed, but I didn't know what I was embarrassed about.

NM: Do you remember what Melissa was saying to you?

CP: "Do you want to come in?" "Do you want me to take your coat?" "Can I get you something to drink?" You know the typical hosts things. But eventually she just left me alone, and I don't remember seeing her parents. I don't remember an adult intervening to help.

NM: Were you in high school; were you like 12 or 15?

CP: I must have been like 14. This is about this time we were maybe sophomores.

NM: When you look back at that moment, do you think anything would have coaxed you in?

CP: I think a parent? I think an adult would have helped. Someone who could see the world a little bit bigger than I could navigate would have helped make me feel [gets choked up continuing with tears] … a lot more comfortable.

Because by that time I was doing these sorts of cultural leaps all of the time. Whether it was riding the bus to get to the ballet school; it took me from 4:00 to 4:45 to get to the ballet school. Then I would get there and order a pizza, because food doesn't keep all day. Lunch containers were different. I would get there and order a pizza, and I remember my ballet teacher being so upset. Because weight was always the thing, my teacher would say, "You'll gain 10 pounds eating like that everyday after school." But, what else to eat? You know, when you're kind of on your own with the situation. Find something to eat after school, you know. Eat and take class. And so, I was always trying to figure out how to show up and be prepared. And again, it's not like there wasn't a support system, you know. (Crystal was very emotional during this memory, as she remembered the struggle of a child trying to please her teacher and figure out how to get nourishment to push through long days that went from early morning to late at night.)

I got to the dance store somehow. But two pair of tights was it for the year. There weren't gonna be like tights and tights and tights. And so, how did you explain why your tights have runs in then? How do you explain that your shoes are broken? How do you keep navigating all of these things when you're in a household that has lots of love and support but limited income and understanding of the field that you're in?

NM: And pointe shoes cost a lot of money.

CP: Pointe shoes cost 80 dollars at the time. And tights. We had a certain pair; I had one pair of good ones that I would buy and save them for performances. They were D18, I think they were Danskin D18, and they had a seam down the back. That was it for all of our performances for the year. You wore those, you got a hole in them, you sewed them up, and you went on about your business. But that was it. Renee Toole, the woman who had sort of kind of looked after me at the Arts Magnet, she owned the dance store. And so, somehow I would always have everything I needed. Between her and my mom, they really made sure, and a lot of this, as a young woman, I had no idea, what was going on. I can see it clearly now, but I had no idea.

NM: So? You go up to SMU, and it's a good experience. You get your degree, and you're studying Graham and ballet. You get to DCDC and become associate director, so something happened, right?

CP: Oh, yes, something happened. So, the summer before my senior year in college I went to the Ailey school for eight weeks. The only other summer experience I had was in high school at the Joffrey. The same thing happened after both of those eight-week programs. I got really good, really fast, from the way those programs are set up, in such a way that when I could concentrate on dancing, without having to worry about all the other things, I could really lean into my gift. When I got back from the Joffrey program, the question was "When did you get good?" I remember a dancer saying the same thing to me when I got back from the Ailey program. One of my Graham teachers was having me demonstrate something, and another student in the class said to me "When did you get good?" I ignored it and kept sort of managing whatever it was that I was doing. But I just took her insult as "Oh, so I'm good now." What she intended to be an insult was like a signal for me to say "Okay, now you can consider this seriously as a career field," and I'm sure that she didn't mean it to operate that way. But at any rate, that sent me into my senior year quite serious about trying to find a job. And I entered an audition season in the spring, mostly for ballet companies, that went horribly. It went pretty bad.

I think I auditioned for Fort Worth Dallas Ballet and made it pretty far in the cuts, which I always did. And I don't know if the world just was not ready for a Black ballerina. Because of the late start and the sort of access issues I had, I don't know if I had *the* skill people were looking for to hire a Black ballet dancer at the time. Augusta Ballet wanted me to come back there, but I didn't want to go home, and so I was quite frustrated. And even though I made it far—through multiple rounds, I'd been cut at every ballet company I auditioned for. I was auditioning at (a ballet company), and this was sort of the straw that broke the camel's back. The director at the time kept something like maybe six men and six women in the last cut. Everybody walks out of the room. I'm like "whoo" you sort of have that deep breath moment where you're like, okay, now I can really learn whatever it is. And he sat down at the table, and he looked up at me, and I don't know what conversation he had with himself, but he got up from the table, and he said, "Thank you very much." And, I left the room.

I like to think now that he thought, I actually don't know how to do this right now. I want to be able to, but I don't know how to. I don't know that this is going to work. So "thank you." There could have been a lot of reasons, but my gut has always told me that he just couldn't figure out how to make that work, right now. You know, in 2001, at that moment.

So, I was upset, and I went storming into the director's office at SMU, my version of storming, which is very quiet, and I asked him, "What do I do?" And he says what they all say—"Arthur Mitchell hasn't seen you; you should just move to New York"—and I had this big lump in my throat because I thought "Who can afford to move to New York?" I had been to New York twice already, and it was super clear to me that I didn't know how to make that happen. And that's all the advice he had, and so I walked out of his office; I look down on the table, and there's a *Dance Spirit Magazine*. It's Sheri "Sparkle" Williams and De Shona Pepper Robertson on the cover, and they are gorgeous. Their hair was on point, they had this undercut hairstyle, shaved in the back; they had microbraids, which was all the rage at the time. Their leotards are cut up the Dwight Rhoden style, because he was the resident choreographer for Dayton Contemporary Dance Company then, and they were embarking on a new project called *A Fight Project*; this was their publicity in this magazine. Their shoes were brown; their bodies were incredible. I picked that magazine up and turned the corner to Shelley Berg's office. She had just stepped down as the director of the department, and I said, "Shelley, who are these people, and why don't I know about them?"

She had a real conversation with me: what to do and how to go about it. [Verklempt] She was always like that. Shelley always saw me. Let me back up. While I was in college, there was a guest choreographer in the department who was setting a contemporary dance work. I had auditioned for the choreographer, and he didn't pick me. I remember her calling me the morning of his first rehearsal. She said, "Crystal, where are you? Are you coming to the building?" But we didn't have (mobile) phones, so I didn't know why she asked me that. "No. I'm at home. You're calling me at home. I didn't get picked." She said, "Well, listen. He doesn't know who he picked. He likes pretty girls. Put on that purple leotard, the boatneck one, and come on in, and don't say anything. I'll take care of the rest."

She made sure that I had a solo; she ensured it. And the whole time I was "understudying" this part, the solo and duet, she was saying, "Come on up, Crystal." She was trying to teach me. She was really trying to teach me how to take a part, how to kind of come out of my shell a little bit, but she was the same person who talked me through finding a job. So, I found out that DCDC had some auditions, and I went. I didn't get into the company the first round, but it was the best audition I had been to, just because there were so many Brown people and so many welcoming folks. It just felt like I could be there.

I go to the audition for the company, and it's a great audition. But they did not hire me. In fact, there was this sort of out-of-body experience I was having, because I didn't know the vocabulary, and I couldn't quite put the steps together; but it didn't bother me in the same way it would have in a ballet audition, because it was exciting. It was exciting to be working with repertory from so many Black choreographers and for the company to be so welcoming to Black artists, and at the end of that audition several of the company members sort of pulled me aside and said, "Are you coming back? He was watching you. You just need a little bit of work. Here's my number" and "Here's how you get involved or invested." One of the dancers there was a friend and an alum of Southern Methodist University. And so I accepted the offer for second company, unpaid, and not the goal (at that time I was determined to get a paying dance job), and that's how I ended up at DCDC.

NM: So, you were at SMU in Dallas, Texas, and you went up to Dayton for that audition.

CP: I did. I did. By that time, I had a work-study job. You know, you emptied out your bank accounts to go to auditions. I went to two contemporary dance auditions that year. I went to Philadanco and to DCDC. I had to pick. Quite similarly to what dancers are having to do now, I had to pick which auditions, not in the city, that I was going to go to. The Danco (Philadanco) audition went horrible as well, but the DCDC audition, I got second company. So yeah, that's how I ended up here.

But the second company turns over all the time. It's got anywhere from 15 to 25 members. It wasn't set up like second companies are now, and it's unpaid. Largely the education ensemble, so it wasn't a place that you were going to go for a long time, but you could stay for a little bit; you could stay for a year. In that year, in the autumn of that year 9/11 happened. There was a Japanese dancer in the company who was in her senior year at Cincinnati Conservatory of Music, and her student visa didn't get renewed, and so she had to leave the company to go back to Japan. By spring there was a woman's position open, and that's actually how I got my job in the company. One of the things that Aoi Funakoshi had, that they were trying to replace, was a contemporary dancer was a strong ballet aesthetic, and out of the folks who were there at the time I really had that particular, quite frankly, commodity. That's how

I got my job in the company, and then it wasn't very long. I may have been working three-quarters of a year before they asked me to start teaching company class in ballet, which was another sort of "wait a minute" moment, because it didn't make sense to me. I understand, on this end now, you want to have the person with the ballet skill set teaching the thing. And so that was why I was doing it. But for me, it was a lot to have my Eurocentric training privileged and centered in a space where I was a relatively new junior company member, now teaching members senior to me. But it was just another kind of career hurdle.

NM: I want to ask you about your cultural identity and the works that you performed at DCDC. I have assumptions that they are wildly different than the kind of works you would have performed had you pursued a career in a ballet company. Can you talk to me a little bit about specific works that you danced that are treasures to you, or really special, or things that bring you closer to your cultural identity?

CP: I have a theory about Black dance companies, that they're a sort of way of returning us to ourselves, that their repertories hold a set of histories and choreographies that are really about a people, and much of the repertory here at DCDC does that. I can't speak for other companies. That's what I see from the distance. But there's a way of learning about ourselves, particularly as African Americans here. One of the most influential works in doing that was probably *Children of the Passage*, which was choreographed by Ron K. Brown and Donald McKayle in 1999, I think. I might have the wrong year, but in 1999 it was one of the last big projects that the founder of the company wanted to put together. And it's just a mastery of storytelling; it was the first sort of iteration of what we call it now kind of Afro-fusion form and modern dance working together, because both of Mr. McKayle's vocabulary and Ron K. Brown's vocabulary had to come together—dancing that piece over the course of a decade is a thing (special experience). What that piece does has highly informed what I think is possible in the body. And yeah, I think what I found at DCDC is quite different than what I would have found in any ballet company. And in fact, I don't know that I would have found my way to being a choreographer at all at ballet company.

Because the institutional structure here requires everybody to give back and feed back into it. So, artistic leadership starts to identify gifts early. You're a teacher. You're a maker. Try your hand at this. Try your hand at that. And so by the time I was dancing in the repertory, that was a great experience. All the folks, Jawole (Willa Jo Zollar), Bill T. Jones, I mean, who wouldn't want to be a maker? Diane McIntyre, Bebe Miller, Doug Varone, Reggie Wilson, all of these people were in my first two or three seasons, and they had wildly different ways of looking at the world and being Black and putting that on a concert dance stage, which for a Black woman is a pretty powerful place. It's a place where everybody is listening and watching and paying attention to your message, and I learned that through dancing those works.

NM: Just a couple more questions. What have you taken from your relationship with Debbie Blunden-Diggs that you now see in the relationships with you that you have with your young dancers?

CP: I think I do this. And don't tell her, I'm sure I stole this from her. One of the things that she does is identify a gift someone has before they can see it and then make a space, a place, or an opportunity for that (their gift) to happen. I'll do that times 20, share resources, times twentyfold. Here, here's a grant. Here's a performance opportunity, even down to the "I believe that the field is meant for you. We want you here as an artist at DCDC. But if you don't want to be here, where do you want to be? And who can I call?" Because it's more important that Black people are dancing and making and teaching and being successful and that there is a network for that, then that they are here or with me. That has been exciting to watch blossom, you know, to see people end up on Broadway, to see how wide the DCDC network is and how big the DCDC family is. I think that's one thing that I've got from her that's really probably always been a part of me, part of my story, that I like to continue to do. I think the other thing I get from her is just Black woman mentoring, that a lot can be worked out for artists talking about the experiences we're having and what we want to accomplish and understanding that there has to be room and space for mentorship to happen, often. Also, to make any of this work, we have to understand that artists are humans within these organizations—we are not machines or cool objects.

NM: Who would you say inspired you to do your best dancing?

CP: Kevin Ward!

NM: What were the tactics or strategies he used to get you to your best?

CP: Oh, no BS kind of director [laughing], I was just talking about him the other day, something about his leadership of this company as a Black dance company ... the "no playing around" mentality. There can be a shyness to me ... it's a thinking space, but it can feel timid to other people. He always invited me, slash, demanded that I skip over all of that (shyness) and do the thing, because we had a legacy to contend with, and we didn't have time: thank you for your personal story, but the field does not have time for you to play around with such important legacies and history, and that I needed to invite myself to the party. I began to dance with much more rigor, much more knowing, much more importance. There was no hiding. There's a thing in the corps de ballet that there's a hiding. I may not have recognized it until this moment, but in my training, really, if you were not identified as a principal dancer or a soloist, you were really taught to blend. And in Black contemporary dance, it's not about blending; it's about showing out and making a mark. Like in Talley Beatty's *Stack Up*, right? It's a group ensemble number, but the Pink Girl has to be Pink Girl. She has qualities; she has steps she has to hit, and that requires a certain force, a certain kind of Blackness. And Kevin knew that I had it, and demanded it. So, not of tiptoeing around how I had been trained, saying, and I see this a lot, "Oh, you're trained as a ballet dancer, so we're going to expect a particular power or force." He came out of a ballet program as well. He just said, he didn't buy it. He expected me, knowing full well that I didn't come from a Black dance background, to do what was in my bones. I trusted him. So, I tried to produce that for him.

NM: Do you ever use those tactics on your students?

CP: I didn't at first, but now I do! I understand the importance of clarity, pressure, weight in training, making sure they understand what is at risk or at stake. But I try never to remove their participation, their autonomy in training or the dance. But I do invite them to be much more rigorous and to understand what happens if you don't come to the craft with that kind of commitment. First, their investment is at stake if they don't come to it with a particular rigor. But second, and particularly for Black dance students, Black dancers, dancers of Color, we risk not seeing them on stages, playing a kind of game with the field where folks are saying there (are) not enough of us.

NM: I don't hear it as much with Black dance as I do with HBCUs. But with HBCUs, there is an understanding of what we as a society miss out on if HBCUs go away. What would you say to Black dance students that they are missing out if they do not have a Black repertory dance experience, what are they missing out on? And if we don't support our Black dance companies, in terms of the American society, what are we missing out on if Black dance repertories and companies don't thrive, survive, and continue? What does that dancer who never got to perform in a Black dance company miss out on? What do audiences that never witness and experience Black repertory dance miss out on?

CP: That question is complicated. Here's a deal, for the dancer, if they never dance in a Black dance company, I don't know that they're missing out on anything. You know, to be honest, it's personal life path, and it's the experience.

NM: Because they get something else.

CP: Yes, and the field gets something else, and that's important, you have to have people who do that. But what they are not having is the opportunity to experience being seen, and seeing themselves, and all of this sort of uniqueness about who they are, and the families that we come from, and our cultures, the way those things show up in performance. Because if we're artists, if we say that dancers are artists, and art is commenting on our life, or participating in this conversation about our life; I don't know how we do that and not take into account our actual lives. How do you go an entire career and never have the experience of being Black onstage, not being Black and also onstage, but being Black onstage in its fullness, in our stories. I hope that for everybody. I hope that everybody gets to know what that is, and that won't be everybody's tale to tell, but at least once as a Black dancer, you need that moment.

NM: Is there anything else that you want to talk about in terms of your training, career, or teaching?

Crystal Michelle Perkins in Reggie Wilson's *We Ain't Goin' Home but We Finna to Get the Hell Up Outta Here*, 2007 (photograph © Andy Snow; courtesy Crystal Perkins).

CP: No, I want to stop crying so with you. Those are all the things.... I could talk for hours about all of this.... I think if there was one thing more I wanted to share ... I'd say because of the dance environments I've been in outside of DCDC. The education environments, especially the programs, the ballet programs, SMU (where her BFA was earned), OSU (where her MFA was earned). My training spaces that have become commodities in this Black dance space is a particular interesting tension where all the studio things I know about dance are prized in this Black dance space. Not all the culture things I know about dance but all the studio things, the sort of Western things that I know about dance are prized in this Black space. And I am curious about where we are in this conversation, about how we prize more things. How do we do that in both directions so that I'm not always operating in two worlds? There's a sort of white institutional practice where being a Black dancer is a commodity, particularly now. Then, there is a Black dance institutional practice where having classical training and a degree or two is a commodity. I look forward to a time where those things meet centrally, so there's this possibility of being full in both spaces and not valued by the other (ballet or Black dance) community's measure.

NM: *I love that; that truly is a great destination to arrive at.*
Thank you.
CP: Thank you. Okay. And you owe me dinner for all these tears today.

NM: *Oh, yes, dinner on me when we do.*

Crystal Michelle Perkins Glossary

> Brief bio-notes of artists and places mentioned in the chapter. This is not intended to be comprehensive but instead to offer a small amount of information to spark more thorough research if readers are interested.

Ailey, Alvin—Founder of Alvin Ailey American Dance Theater in 1958. He was a choreographer and an activist.
Augusta Ballet—Founded in 1961.
Augusta Mini Theater—Founded in 1975 as the first community arts school focusing on multi-art disciplines.
Barnhart, Beverly Jane—Founding principal at John S. Davidson Fine Arts Magnet School.
Beatty, Talley—Dancer and choreographer. Became principal dancer with the Katherine Dunham Company at age 16.
Berg, Shelley—Professor of dance at Southern Methodist University. Retired.
Blunden-Diggs, Debbie—Artistic director for the Dayton Contemporary Dance Company.
Brenau Women's College—A private university located in Gainesville, Georgia.
Brown, Ron K.—Choreographer. Founding artistic director of Evidence a Dance Company in Brooklyn, New York, in 1985.
Dayton Contemporary Dance Company (DCDC)—Founded in 1968. African American repertory dance company.
Fagan, Garth—Jamaican-born choreographer. Founder and artistic director of Garth Fagan Dance. Choreographer of Broadway's *Lion King*.
Fort Worth Dallas Ballet—Founded in 1961, now known as the Texas Ballet Theater School.
Funakoshi, Aoi—A dancer from Chiba, Japan, currently teaching in Colorado.

HBCU—Historically Black Colleges and Universities
Joffrey Ballet—Founded by Robert Joffrey and Gerald Arpino in 1956.
John S. Davidson Fine Arts School—Founded in 1981 as a fine art's public magnet school.
Jones, Bill T.—American choreographer and dancer. Founder of Bill T. Jones/Arnie Zane Dance Company, 1982.
Marsalis, Wynton—Musician and composer. Artistic director and cofounder of Jazz at Lincoln Center in New York.
McIntyre, Diane—Choreographer. Founder of Sound in Motion and the Sound in Motion School in Harlem, 1972–1988. Created works for companies such as the Alvin Ailey American Dance Theater, Dance Theatre of Harlem, Philadanco, and Dancing Wheels.
McKayle, Donald—Dancer, choreographer, teacher, director, and writer. Known as the first Black man to both direct and choreograph major Broadway musicals.
Miller, Bebe—Founder and artistic director of the Bebe Miller company, 1985–present.
Mitchell, Arthur—Cofounder of Dance Theatre of Harlem in 1969. First African American to become a principal dancer at New York City Ballet. Mitchell died in 2018.
Paine College—Founded in 1883 and located in Augusta, Georgia, a church-related private institution.
Philadanco—Philadelphia dance company founded in 1970 by Joan Myers Brown.
Rhoden, Dwight—Founding artistic director and resident choreographer of Complexions Contemporary Ballet.
Robertson, DeShona Pepper—Former DCDC dancer. Dance director at the Stivers School for the Arts since 2004.
Southern Methodist University—A private university located near Dallas, Texas.
Tool, Renee—Dance teacher at the John S. Davidson Fine Arts School.
Varone, Doug—Choreographer and artistic director for Doug Varone and Dancers in New York City.
Ward, Kevin—Former artistic director of the Dayton Contemporary Dance Company
Williams, Sheri "Sparkle"—A contemporary dancer with the Dayton Contemporary Dance Company.
Wilson, Reggie—Artistic director and choreographer. Founder of the Fist and Heel Performance Group in 1989.
Zollar, Jawole Willa Jo—Founder of Urban Bush Women, a performing ensemble, in 1984.

Stephanie Marie Powell

Past affiliations: Oakland Ballet, 1991–1996; Dance Theatre of Harlem, 1996–1998; Alvin Ailey American Dance Theater, Donald Byrd/The Group, 1998–1999; Las Vegas Contemporary Theater; and the Broadway Show *Lion King*, 2000–2002.
Current Position: *Professor of Dance*, Long Beach City College (2005–present)
Hometown: Bakersfield, California
Current residence: Long Beach, California

Excerpts from May 30, 2014, interview with Stephanie Marie Powell at her home in southern California. At the time she had an infant daughter, whom she held in her arms for most of the interview.

NM: *Can you tell me a little bit about how your dancing began?*

SP: Sure. I started with a woman named Cindy Trueblood in Bakersfield,

California. My cousin was my babysitter, and I was two at the time. We didn't have a studio; she just pulled the cars out of the garage, and we danced in there. I was just sitting on the floor, because (my cousin receiving instruction) was my babysitter. I guess by three I started to stand up and mimic some of the stuff Cindy and my cousin were doing, and (Cindy Trueblood) decided to go ahead and take me. So, I've been with Cindy for the last 38 years. I always go home and contribute to her studio. She was a Caucasian woman from Oklahoma; she never danced professionally. I think she went to San Francisco Ballet for one summer with a girlfriend and ... she taught me everything I know.

In Bakersfield, it's pretty much the top studio as far as ballet is concerned. It's expanded now; it was just ballet and jazz when I was a kid. But now it's modern; it's contemporary, whatever that means, and jazz and tap and, you know, everything under the sun—hip hop. But it was really a ballet studio and jazz and disco back in the day, and she was still dancing then too. She was my ... confidante. She was like a mother to me; still is. She's the godmother of my daughter. I think it's important (to have that kind of mentorship) at that point in my life, as such a young girl that I didn't understand kind of the politics of ballet.

Stephanie Powell (photograph by Jerome Thomas; courtesy Stephanie Powell).

It was just my favorite hobby, my favorite thing to do. I was very active as a child as far as music is concerned, piano and flute and band and orchestra and choir; my mom kept us very busy so we wouldn't get in trouble. And Cindy, I guess, saw something in me and gave me lead roles and things for years and years. I did Clara in *Nutcracker* for four years in a row. And Sugar Plum Fairy for three, four years in a row. I knew there were other mommies that were not happy about it, but she didn't back down, you know, if that's who deserved the role, that's who got the role. I didn't know it was a Black issue. I just know I busted my behind; she saw that, and she worked with me.

NM: Do you think the discontent from other parents was a Black issue?

SP: I think it was "Well, she's done it already, let my daughter do it once, why does she have to do it four years in a row?" (mimicking parents).

NM: Do you think it happens at a lot of studios?

SP: I was the only Black girl, so it was like…

NM: Are you trying to make a point in reference to how the director navigated the situation?

SP: Yeah. And she never said anything to me, to this day.

My mom and dad just adore her. She's that figure in all of our lives. And my cousin stopped dancing. She's like an ER physician. But, you know, I go home and teach master classes, and anything she asks for, you know I do it. Duncan Cooper and I, from DTH, did a *Nutcracker* with her for her 20th anniversary and stuff like that. So, she's dear to my heart. Her mom just passed away a couple weeks ago, and she was like a grandmother to me. It's a very strong sense of dance family in Bakersfield. There are several other schools there, but nobody has the long-standing history. We're the only school that does *Nutcracker* shows to a 3,000-seat house and a full philharmonic. Since I was three we've had the orchestra full, like a 50-piece orchestra. So, she is doing it, she's been doing it, I'm sure she's tired of doing it. She's the reason why I am the way I am, truly.

NM: You talked a little bit about modern and contemporary, and I know you danced both. Do you have a preference?

SP: I like contemporary ballet. I don't like what people call contemporary now. You know, when I say "contemporary ballet" I'm thinking (George) Balanchine, I'm thinking Alonzo King, I'm thinking the shift from romantic ballet, classical ballet, into contemporary ballet; that's what it is. This, like, *So You Think You Can Dance* stuff, that's not contemporary to me. And there is no dance that's 90 seconds long. You know what I mean? Ya'll think you're twirling? No, you need to twirl for half an hour. That's not it. They've got skill, unbelievable skill, you know, and lots of tricks and flips. But, I loved … you know, I love doing choreography by John Lane and of course Balanchine, which we did a lot of (referring to her time dancing with DTH). It was challenging, it was fast, and coming from the West Coast I had never moved that fast. I got injured from it, I got plantar fasciitis from it, but I loved it. I had the opportunity to dance with Lorraine Graves and Charmaine Hunter and some of the divas of DTH that were still dancing in the company and Endalyn (Taylor), you know. So, it was amazing to be a part of that process with those ballerinas at the time (speaking of DTH company members).

NM: You also danced with Ailey and danced with Donald McKayle. Was the shift (to modern) just opportunity and happenstance, or were there employment issues? (Many ballet dancers shift to modern professional company work due to a lack of ballet employment opportunities.)

SP: No, no, it was deliberate. I left DTH and I joined Donald Byrd first, 'cause I didn't get into Ailey. There were four girls left and three spots, and I was the fourth girl when I was 28. Judy (Judith Jamison) called me and she said, "You know, I'd like to have you in the company but there's only three dancers that have left the company. You're my fourth person. I'm going to talk to the board and see if they will allow it." She called me back and said the board said "no" 'cause it was not in the budget. But you know, I said, "You'll see me next year." But at the time, I was with Donald Byrd.

It was an intentional shift for me. I had a bucket list of things that I wanted to do. And it started with Oakland Ballet, those old ballets that had been reconstructed, *Les Sylphides* and *Bolero* and, you know, those dances that you just don't see anymore. I just really wanted to get some of those dances under my belt. And then when I went to DTH to do the Balanchine repertoire, I just didn't have access to that at Oakland Ballet, had never moved like that … and music … just to be in a cast of 52 Black dancers doing Balanchine was fabulous. But I knew that I had modern on my list, and I had musical theater on my list. So, it was just time. I was also suffering from ridiculous corns on my toes and in between my toes for some reason. I was practically bone on bone by then. You know, you use Dr. Scholl's, and you just keep taking a layer off and a layer off. By the time I did several sessions of that, it felt like rocks in my pointe shoes in between my toes, constantly even when there were no corns. I just felt like, "it's time." I also was doing principal work and not getting paid for principal work. I submitted a letter and I got no response, and I submitted another letter and I got no response. And I resigned. You know, I just finished my contract and I said, "It's okay." Like, "You can't just keep putting me out there and not give me the contract that honors the work that I'm doing."

NM: Was that something that happened to a lot of people?

SP: I don't know. I didn't discuss it with other dancers; I was very private. But business is business to me, and I think a lot of people are just, like, "I just want to dance." I've never been that person. I've always been a negotiator. I've always been a major saver, i.e., I bought my own house, by myself, with all dance money. Like, I never worked at the GAP, never did Starbucks, never did anything; I've just been an artist all my life. So, when I didn't get a response, basically telling me we're not going to promote you, we're not going to do this but we're going to abuse you and keep putting you out there and doing *Prodigal Son* and other dances that other corps members were not doing. There was another dancer also, Thaddeus Davis, we both put our letters in the mail at the same time and walked away. So, auditioning for Donald Byrd … was a huge transition, but it was deliberate. It was like "Okay, I'm ready to make, you know…" Even though I did my audition in ballet shoes, I still was like—I never danced barefoot, I'd never really been in a modern class before. I just really liked his movement, and I thought it was … it was also a job at the time, you know. I mean it wasn't a thing like "I don't have a contract, I'm unemployed." I've never been unemployed for longer than 30 days in my life. And I was freaking out those 30 days. But, work has always come my way; I've been very, very blessed—[turning away to comfort her daughter in her arms]—very blessed with not having to struggle and be fearful, and I've had union contracts that have protected me and (I was) given a salary and a per diem and, you know, really lived a pretty good life as a dancer. It wasn't horrible, you know.

NM: What would you say are some of the differences you experienced between dancing in a ballet company and modern company work?

SP: As far as the physical differences, it's all rigorous, it's all painful. I think it's just a different kind of work, different muscles, different techniques. I took two classes with Milton Myers and asked him "What's a bison? How do I do this flat back thing? What's the Horton technique?" I never had low back pain until I went to Ailey. I just, I was constantly dealing with pointe shoes stuff, hamstrings stuff ... but not *Revelations*, that is low back stuff.

NM: Is the energy different, the atmosphere, the approach to the work?

SP: Not for me. I think the repertoire and the touring is different with Ailey, because they are on that road, I mean, nine months. I had never been on the road for nine months, you know, and you just don't get a chance to catch up as far as your injuries are concerned; you're like just constantly nursing, and I didn't feel like that with DTH. I really took advantage of our breaks and went on vacation. If we stayed in Europe and we finished our tour in Athens, I would stay; the rest of the company would get back. But I would stay for seven days and just enjoy the little bit of time that we did have. I mean, you had to run home and get on the unemployment line.

But as far as work ethic, I think everybody was just trying to get through it. It's just rough, and it's not a position where I think a lot of dancers now think "Well, I'm in the company, so I should just be getting all these roles, and it should just be a piece of cake." And there's this sense of entitlement. Where we (when SP was dancing) fought for a role, you auditioned every single time a choreographer walked into the room, and just because they liked you didn't mean Mr. Mitchell thought it was okay. If he wanted somebody else to do it, don't think he didn't say something and have some kind of an influence on their decisions whether they liked you or not. I think there were some great opportunities for some other dancers that he wouldn't have picked, because the other choreographer saw something in them. But as far as the work ethic, everybody busted their tails.

NM: Can you talk a little about the culture that Mr. Mitchell created?

SP: Yeah, that's tender. I think, Mr. Mitchell, he and I have a very interesting relationship. I was not a submissive quiet dancer. I was not a union rep. They asked me to be a union rep, and I didn't want to because I thought it would threaten my career a little bit. But Mr. Mitchell has a very dominant personality. I mean, he's gorgeous to look at; he walks in the room, he's in a suit, he teaches class in a suit. And ... class is a performance; you know there's no relaxed moment. There's no sitting down in the studio; even if he walked in and surprised you when Lorraine (Graves) or Charmaine (Hunter) or somebody was rehearsing, folks got up and started working on tendus or something as soon as he walked in, like there's just always something to work on. I feel like the culture—that I kind of didn't like, was a little bit like … you needed him. "You're a Black dancer and you don't have a whole lot of places you can go" (explaining the atmosphere).

I didn't come from that. I came from a lady in Bakersfield who said I could do anything; I can go anywhere I want to go. And I did come from another company (referring to time in Oakland Ballet before joined DTH). So, it was like "huh, what do you mean? I don't have to be here. I chose to be here," you know, like, Christina Johnson was in Boston Ballet before she came to DTH. And I got the sense that he had some control over those babies that grew up in the school. He got them under his wing to where he made them feel like they couldn't go anywhere else. He wasn't a huge fan of us taking class downtown, did not want you going down there to Steps and stuff like that. We did it anyway. We got a lot of those classes from Willy Burmann. God, I can't think of their names, Allegra Kent and Michael Vernon. Oh, there's another one that's escaping me—people snuck out, you know, people snuck down there. But he wanted to covet us, and I really didn't like that, you know, I didn't like the feeling. (I felt like) whatever you need to do to get better you need to do. But you know, it was just "You need to stay in Harlem; you need to be here." I didn't like that, you know.

NM: You were talking a little bit about his preferences and his choosing for roles. As a company member, in terms of the camaraderie amongst the company, was there a sense of roles being chosen on a whim and not necessarily talent?

SP: I think it's always talent, that's undeniable. But I think that if he had something to say, it would get changed. Like, even Suzanne Farrell came in and set *Serenade*; as soon as she left, he changed choreography. You know what I mean; (he would say), "That's not what we're doing, this is what we're doing." You know, and it's like, we spent two and a half weeks with this woman; she's part of the Balanchine Trust. But your boss says "this is what you're going to do," and he was there, so … we can't really, he was there before her, you know, and that's what he likes. So, I mean there's just that dynamic where what he says goes. I think there was a little too much of that on the administrative side, where he couldn't keep his hand out of every little thing.

And that's a difference from Ailey, that is a machine, and Judy does not, she didn't heckle with those ladies. Predominantly ladies that worked in the office and ran the organization. She was in the studio, or she was going to meetings or being the iconic face. But yeah, I think he (Mitchell) has an air about him, you know. I think we're better now that I'm away from the company than when I was with the company, because I challenged him, you know, I would say something back if he said something crazy. I don't think he liked that; I know he didn't like it at all, but I could dance. So, we got along fine when it came to that. But as far as if there was something he wanted different, for example, *Sasanka*, what was that South African choreographer's name (Vincent Mantsoe).... I can't think of it, anyway, *Sasanka* started barefoot, and we loved it. We had never taken our shoes off, and, you know, it was going to be difficult to go from *Serenade* into *Sasanka*, but it was fun to be barefoot and get your full gang-gang on, and you know, as a ballet company, 'cause he always talked about, we're Dance *Theatre* of Harlem, and we can do anything. And he came in the room, and he was like "All ya'll put your shoes on ... we are a ballet company, put your shoes on." And we were like "Okay." So that's kind of an example, like he's old school, and he walked in and was like "Oh, uh uh, that's not who we are, uh, uh, we're not Ailey, we're not Garth Fagan, put your shoes on, put your ballet slippers on."

NM: *And he was stretched thin, because I know he gave a lot of input into the school too, so he was working intensively....*

SP: I have no idea. I was like trying to get through 10 a.m. to 6 p.m., you know what I mean. I don't know what happened downstairs (at the school). You just got in the elevator, went up to the locker room, put your shoes on, and hit it for eight hours.

NM: *And how many years were you in the company?*

SP: Three and a half. But on the flip side of the culture, the culture as far as answering your question, Judy (Jamison) would never, um, if somebody wanted to do something ... with dancers, she didn't come in and say "oh, you need to put somebody else in"; she just let those choreographers do things. Now, if she didn't like the dance and it didn't do well or reviews didn't go well, it would premiere at City Center and you'd never see it again. So, that's her way, you know what I mean. It's still power, it's still her control, she paid for it, it's still gonna run, and that's it; it'll never go on tour. If it doesn't do well and doesn't get good reviews, she's not just gonna keep putting it out there. You know, and at least a couple of them were very well-known choreographers where you would just think, like, "of course," but they didn't. So, they both have their, I mean, every director has their vision and has their standard, and they have their power, you know, and they will assert that. But it's different; I think Mr. Mitchell was more about Mr. Mitchell and Judy was about her empire that she created.

NM: *When you were with DTH, did Mr. Mitchell see you as extensions of him in a sense? I remember somebody mentioning that the company had to be presented a certain way.*

SP: [Responding with urgent immediacy] Oh, he did, always. We were not allowed to travel in sweats; we had to be in slacks or skirts on the plane because we were often greeted by the press. So, his presentation was flawless always, like, I'm sure he wakes up beautiful, you know what I mean, like he's just a gorgeous man. But, he taught us about, even in class, like, you know, there are no runs in your tights and holes and disheveled hair and, you know, all of that stuff because anybody can walk in the room. We worked with Freddie Franklin, we worked with legendary people, so you just don't have that look that these kids have these days, where they look like they just woke up and you can see the creases on their face. That's just not okay, it's never been okay, and I carry that to this day with my students. Yeah, he had an expectation, and he upheld it himself, and he expected all of us to. Now, those dolls that had been in that company for years, honey, they would show up to JFK (airport) in a full-length mink coat [SP laughs with happy memories]. I have never seen anything like it—I mean, Gucci sunglasses, Prada boots, the whole nine. I mean, they looked like movie stars. I was young and I didn't have that kind of money, and I didn't spend like that, but I was always proud to be around them. Like wow, these ladies are *pulled up*. You know, I mean, somebody like Lorraine who's 5'1" as it is, walking in—we're going to Detroit, so it's gonna be cold, but I was like "Okay, this is fabulous."

So yeah, he expected that, so the ladies and the men, I mean, all the people in the company were beautiful anyway, I mean, everybody was not just physically beautiful; I mean, they were just fabulous from the inside out, but they dressed to the nines. Even just going to Japan on the airplane, you get to sit there that long you'd think you'd be in some sneakers or something comfortable. Uh-uh, you had to be pulled the whole time.

NM: And how was that different from your time at Oakland Ballet?

SP: Oakland Ballet was much more familial. Ronn Guidi, at the time, was my director, and he rode the bus with us. It was the most culturally diverse company I had ever danced for. We had Cubans—Afro-Cubans, we had two Chinese girls that were 5'10", Canadian, Mexican, me, two African Americans, a couple Caucasian girls. It was awesome just to look around the room. I felt like I was in the United Nations in a ballet company. He (Guidi) was about the people. He was about us and making sure we got the work done. But we also enjoyed each other. And some of those girls, and I mean all of my jobs that I've worked with, I have made some really great friends. I'm the godmother to my roommate's child with that company. There's just some serious long-standing friendships that are there. I think maybe because it was my first company and I was there for six years. Those are some of my fondest memories. I think it's 'cause it was also a lot of bus and truck, so you spent some *hours* with these people, and when you finally graduated to getting your own two seats, you know, and you could stretch out and sleep, and you weren't just by yourself or sitting with somebody else in a single seat for 12 hours on a bus, 'cause that's what we do. And Ailey and DTH, your union, you don't have to deal with that kind of stuff as much. But yeah, I love those Oakland Ballet folks—yeah.

NM: What were some of the roles that were really special to you, your favorite roles that you found yourself working for?

SP: Oh, there's so many…

NM: Top three.

SP: Okay, so, Oakland Ballet. I think one of the most rigorous audition processes for a choreographer was *The Green Table*; that was a four-day-long audition process for "the woman in red." And it was my, I have a white twin—she's like my sister—and we literally have the exact same dimensions, like our legs were the same length, same size shoe, everything. She was just white; everything else was identical. And we were always up for the same stuff. Either she would get first cast or I would get first cast. Or she would get second cast. But we were very, very close friends; there was never that bitchy ballerina hateration–type thing, never even to this day.

I got first cast, but it took four days for them to decide. For a role for just one person, the audition just went on for hours. You can only do so much with one person. But four days of that, it just kept going and going and going. So, that one is dear to me because I fought for it. We still love each other, and she would coach me and I would coach her. But it was like, I want it bad, and she wanted it bad too. That one is—it was just a process to get it, it wasn't like they watch class and your name goes up on a wall. This was like you're going to have to prove yourself over and over and over, unlike a cattle call audition where you just put the number on your chest and you get picked.

Bolero was another one; it was a Nijinska *Bolero*. We did a lot of old ballets that had been put to rest, Ronn (Guidi) would always bring these old ballets back. So, that's the *Bolero* with the table on the stage; it's like the size of the stage, and there's men and women around the table and then there's a solo dancer on top of the table. The whole piece. So, I did that. That was rigorous just because you're on a table for 20 minutes in character shoes. And it's just a lot of pressure to maintain an audience for 20 minutes and people just doing kind of rhythmic things, seated, around the table. So, that was a big one.

Always Sugar Plum. I don't care what anyone has to say about *Nutcracker*. It was a special day. I don't know if you're interviewing her, but Judy Tyrus is from DTH. Judy was from Oakland Ballet, and she went to DTH before I went to DTH. Judy came back to do a performance as a guest, so she did Plum and I was doing Flowers, I was doing Rose Queen. And I remember walking out, and there's a little pas de quatre, right before Plum goes out, or pas de trois, but it's Snow Queen, Rose Queen, and Sugar Plum, so he (Ronn) does a prelude-type thing right before; it's different than any other *Nutcracker* I do, and it's a full little section of dancing. Well, I walked out and (Judy Tyrus) walked out, and I looked across the stage and I was like "oh my God, I've never been onstage with another Black ballerina, hmmmmm"—that did it, that was kind of my impetus to get to DTH. I thought, "There's another one like meeee right now." [speaking with emotion in her throat] It had never happened, ever, in my whole life.

As far as Donald Byrd is concerned, you know Donald was crazy. I mean he still is, but he's calmed down, I hear, a lot. He created work when I was there, so that was nice. *Harlem Nutcracker* is one of his; I think it's a masterpiece. I think he didn't nearly get the attention and credit he deserved, 'cause it is phenomenal. Loved dancing that piece, just fun, fun, fun, stuff.

Bristle is another just beast of a piece to get through. Donald was about dancing as fast as you possibly could. I'd never had to do that. He wasn't interested in dancing on the beat. He said everybody dances on the beat, don't dance on the beat, just go as fast as you can. He would blink his eyes [she blinks her eyes] like that. And you know those picture books, those Disney picture books, that just flip and it's like a cartoon? That's what we were supposed to look like, so if you stopped dancing in the frame of his blink you were going too slow. I had never moved like that, and *Bristle* was a piece that was just ridiculous.

The other one would be *Jazz Train*. Max Roach was the lead drummer; we had a live band that played for that, and Max Roach was an old musician who was just phenomenal. Everybody had a solo in that piece, and that's how the piece kind of finished, and my solo was last, and Max stopped playing on my solo. It was kind of this moment where everybody else got this crazy, crazy drum stuff, and then mine came, and he just let me go. So, it was just sweet little moments like that, artistic choices.

(With) Ailey, of course you have your *Revelations*. There was another piece called *Letras de Amor*, that was my first duet with Bernard Gaddis, who is her godfather [gestures towards her daughter in her arms]. And it got horrible reviews, and I absolutely loved it. It stunk because it didn't stay much in the rep, but I loved that ballet; it's by Retta, *Letras de Amor*. The men wore coats that looked like capes down to the floor. It was just superdramatic. It was my first time doing improvisation onstage, so that one's special to me.

NM: Is that part always improvised?

SP: There's a section of it that's improvised; it was really cool. I use it as a classroom exercise now. Let's say there was a past lover in your life or a memory or something. The improv was kind of around that motif, but Bernard would blow on me, and that would initiate my movement. So, I literally did it with my eyes closed and just let him take me wherever it was. If he blew on my neck, that would take me to the side, and then he would pick me up and turn me around and blow on my hip, and oh my God, yeah, yeah, that was a highlight moment.

NM: And then with DTH?

SP: I love *Concerto Barocco*, entrechat six to the knee at the end. I've never felt more accomplished—like, this dance is gonna kill me. And it's a corps de ballet dance; the principals are right with the corps the whole 20 minutes. I think there's even a YouTube thing about a corps ballet dancer at City Ballet (Ashley Laracey) that talks about it right now, where it's just, you just gotta push, you just gotta push to get through that bad boy, and it finishes with six, you know.

I got to do *Prodigal Son*, and I was a siren, and I got a nice review in the *New York Times*, so that was special, another Balanchine work. And *Firebird*, of course. I wasn't the Firebird, but I love the music, love Stravinsky. Oh, and *Dougla! Dougla* is like the closest to African I had ever danced. And Geoffrey Holder came, and you know, those ballets are just. I think anybody that was a DTH dancer will say something about *Dougla*.

NM: *What were some of the things Mr. Mitchell would talk about when rehearsing/creating?*

SP: I did a lot of Balanchine. (Mitchell) would say that Balanchine gave him the entire repertoire. We got all of that for free; nobody else has that.

NM: *Did he make mention of the African American influences on Balanchine's aesthetic?*

Are you familiar with Brenda Dixon Gottschild's Digging the Africanist Aesthetic, *how she talks about Balanchine's work being influenced. Does that make sense to you?*

SP: Yeah, (Balanchine) loved jazz, he loved Black people, he loved the way we moved too. I just don't think the funders were trying to have that, but that still was a preference of his. And you see it in the movement, you see how the pelvis is all over the place and the music is almost like a jazz musician would play, especially with speed. Like it's just, some of it is just ridiculous. Maybe because I was focused so much on learning, always, I just felt like even if I wasn't cast, I would go and sit in the back and just watch rehearsals, and it worked to my advantage a couple of times, where somebody didn't show up for work, and Mr. Mitchell would come in and be like, "So-and-so is sick; does anyone know this part?" And it was quiet, and I just kind of put my hand up. And he was like, "Miss Miss, let me see it." He knew your name, but he would just call you "Miss." And I would always have something smart like "it's Stephanie." And then I got cast. I don't remember it being about the Black experience so much. I just know that you just had work to do, you had a legacy to maintain, you had an expectation to represent Black dance and Black ballet in particular with him, and just do ballet well.

NM: *Did he ever mention the Negro Ballet Company or Black ballet companies before that didn't make it in terms of building a legacy in the way that DTH did?*

SP: Not in a historical sense. We were so focused on work, it was just work, and everything was fast, everything was, you gotta get this done, and you gotta get these dances up—and they were long, they weren't just these four-minute dances—and casting changes. You've got new choreographers constantly coming in.

I didn't grow up in the school. I'm sure he came and did little lessons in history. I'm sure other ballerinas who were there longer remember him: "well, in my day…" It was all getting the work done and the quality of the work and just precision.

NM: *What do you think of the field of ballet in terms of the changes over the last 20 years, in terms of opportunities for employment, and seeing Black ballerinas dancing when you go to the theater or feeling like it's possible for your students or other young aspiring dancers?*

SP: I think it's gotten minimally better. I mean, you saw the most recent *Pointe* magazine with the three ladies, and Misty's book just got launched, and Misty got promoted, and Lauren's been that figure for a long time. I think it's just sad that it's still just one or two. I don't know what it is, because there's so many beautiful girls now. You really can't even say anything. When I was doing my research, I called (New York City Ballet) and asked if I could just inquire because I knew Andrea. Andrea Long and I danced in the company together (DTH). And I asked if there had ever been in *Swan Lake* an African American lead performer, and I remember the receptionist was like, "Oh no, oh no, there's never been," and I was like, "I was just confirming my research."

NM: *Did you ever feel like you were pushing harder because you were Black, or did you feel you were just pushing harder to be the best anyway?*

SP: In my career, in my companies ... with Oakland Ballet it didn't matter, at my school it didn't matter. So, I got some of those lead roles, I pushed anyway, I worked hard anyway.

NM: *Do you think Oakland Ballet was unaffected by social constructions of race?*

SP: Sure, sure, you're talking about me, as far as the way that I felt. I didn't feel like "oh, we can't give Stephanie Snow Queen." That doesn't negate the fact that when we did do *La Sylphide* the ballet mistress asked me to powder down. So, it's still there. But as far as the roles and casting that I got, I got to do everything that I wanted to do.

Then I went straight to a Black ballet company. But I still think even at DTH, and I wrote about this as well, there were skin tone preferences. And you see this with roles like Medea, which was Charmaine, always, you always had a Brown-skin figure that was doing those ... there's just certain roles. Like Virginia was never going to do Medea; Virginia (a lighter-skinned woman) was going to do *Creole Giselle*. There's just certain things, so (Mitchell) even fell into that trap of what is expected of a Black swan. Almost maintaining the stereotype of this music, which is very robust and strong, so that was Karen Brown (a darker-skinned woman fit the description of that strong music) versus the sylph and all these ethereal creatures, the lighter-skinned girls; it happened at DTH. Some of them will not admit it. But if you look at the videos and the casting, it's clearly there. But for me, personally, I felt like I got to do everything I wanted to do. It may have been color-specific, but I still got to dance everything I wanted.

NM: *Can you tell me a little bit about how you feel about ballet as an art form and what you enjoy about it today, either when you are taking class, performing, or watching?*

SP: Ballet is my first love. I grew up with classical music in the house along with Motown; in my house we played everything, in the car, driving to L.A. We used to come to L.A. every weekend. And my child has music that plays Baby Einstein

Classical; she loves it. I think there's two different dance forms that make me feel the most feminine, and I think ballet's the first and the second would be Latin dance, like salsa, bachata, or merengue—that kind of music is where I just feel fabulous. There's something to be said for being in a tiara and feeling like a princess and a queen and having jewels on and a tutu and pointe shoes. I think it's "high art" as they say. But it's just something I think I was born to do, since I was two, just sitting in the garage, just listening to classical music on a reel to reel.

I worry about it a little bit, in the way that it's shifting now with this contemporary ballet. I feel like we're losing some stuff. Things are getting a little crazy. It's very difficult as an instructor to bring people back to the basics. They see what they see on TV and they think that that's how you start. And it's just not humanly possible to start like that; there's no foundation, there's no base there. They get injured; they really do.

NM: Does the shift cause you to shift the way you teach?

SP: No, I refuse, I absolutely refuse, and I get criticized for it, but I don't care; I have a huge following. I stuck to it. These are some of the basics; it's been around for a very long time. This new stuff that you see, it's been for the last maybe 15 or 20 years, and it's awesome, it's fun, it's difficult to do, and I respect it. Same thing in the modern world and contemporary. There's a reason that Horton technique and that Dunham technique and that Limon technique and that Cunningham technique makes you strong. You don't get injured. Like friends from Cirque (de Soleil), 26 years old, having a hip replacement. A hip replacement? Like what kind of tilt are you doing? If you work correctly, you can have a career like Renee Robinson at Ailey for how many years and no surgery. If you're getting injured, that tells me you're not getting something; oh, it's called "class," like they don't have class. Like there's this shift where it's just about how high you can kick your leg. And trust me, Judy wanted our legs up. There was no 90 degrees, there was no 100 degrees; it was up, as high you can get it. To whatever extent, make it happen. But we knew how, and I just don't feel like these dancers really know how to dance until they get hurt, and then they come back and they're like "I just need a beginning ballet class and the basics," and it's like, "Boo, this is what you needed from the gate" because that is … it's like your house, it's the foundation of a house; you can't just paint with no frame. You have to have those basic techniques. Here you have even some prominent figures in dance who are not teaching the basic techniques anymore and just offering contemporary with no clear definition as to what that is and getting rid of codified techniques. Just getting rid of it completely, it's old. I just see it as very functional and efficient for the dancer to have some longevity, because some people think it's already a short-lived career as it is.

NM: Are there any other topics or ideas that you would like to comment on?

SP: I think if there's an advice section in your book, I could share a couple things. As far as etiquette is concerned, I don't think it's really being taught—some of the things that you do and some of the things that you just never do. Sometimes you should just keep your mouth shut; not that it's shut up and dance, but I do think that sometimes dancers have this expectation.

NM: What do you mean by that? I'm curious, because you spoke of your personal nature to push back.

SP: I did, I did. Some of that was inappropriate because I was young. For example, a friend of mine has a company, and a dancer auditioned for the company, and you think that if you're auditioning you want the job. This dancer went up to him and said, "Well, I'm going to audition for a couple other companies, so I'll check back and see." It's like, what? Why are you telling me you're looking somewhere else, and then you're going to let me know if you choose me? It doesn't work like that; that puts a director off—right away.

In academia, I feel like students are not clear on what is expected from them as outlined in the syllabus. If they forget or miss an assignment or an exam, they request a favor or expect the instructor to cut them a break. Every student is given a syllabus that serves as a contract between the instructor and student, which is comparable to the artistic director's contact with a dancer. Students need to follow their syllabus deadlines closely and submit coursework on time without excuses. If an emergency comes up, it's important to communicate with the instructor—be it COVID, an injury, or whatever. Most instructors are compassionate, but that does not take away the responsibility for the work. I have students who have stated, "I missed the deadline; is there anything I can do?" And my answer is, depending on the circumstances, there may be an adjustment to an exam date, but that is not regular practice. I give students an agreement where all expectations are outlined, and students initial each point; that indicates that they understand the outlined guidelines, and they are expected to follow them, as I am.

I think physically, body maintenance and self-care are not something that dancers are focused on as much as they should be. I remember at Oakland Ballet we had ice parties. We would go on the road; everybody would bring two trash cans into the room (to fill with ice), we'd all pitch in three dollars, we'd get the movie and order pizza, and do a contrast bath to reduce inflammation. Like that was our family. There were six of us on the bed, on the couch, sitting, watching TV, taking care of our bodies as maintenance. Not from injury, just being proactive, if we had a difficult week or just regular maintenance, we needed to take care of our ankles and get this swelling down, we're gonna fly (on a plane) tomorrow, and we're gonna be swollen, and we're gonna get back on the box (pointe shoe). We did it with each other, and we made it fun. I feel like dancers ignore signals from their bodies; where they feel the twinge or have pain, they ignore it, and they put some Tiger Balm, BioFreeze, or CBD on it and keep hitting it and not warming up properly, and then they're unable to rehearse or perform. They don't realize the magnitude and stress that it puts on their fellow castmates, the artistic director, and the crew.

Now we have to have an emergency rehearsal, get the floor mopped, rearrange spacing, and that is added stress to an already pressured environment where dancers want to perform at their best. Had the student (dancer) taken care of their body and injuries at the onset, nurtured it before it turns into tendonitis, the impact of the whole situation could have been far less. If you don't take care of your body, the consequences impact not just you and your career but all the members of the production and your dance family. Some students feel they're resilient and they'll bounce back 'cause "I'm young and I'll be fine, I'll just take some Advil." I just think self-care needs to be a daily regimen just like brushing your teeth and washing your face. As dancers, we have to massage, ice, and get enough rest to rejuvenate the body and the mind.

After the pandemic, I lost the range in my first metatarsal on my right foot. I was simply not able to go all the way up on relevé without pain, and I never had that before. So, I had an X-ray and learned I have bone spurs on both the bunion and the first metatarsal, and they are like daggers—they are like two little hooks.

You know those little toe spacers you wear when you are on pointe? Turns out even after I was out of the pointe shoes for years, I probably should have kept the toe spaces in my regular shoes. And that is the self-care that I'm really pushing now, the somatic practice, the Bartenieff Fundamentals, those things that they call "old," you know, technique. But there's a reason that you're on your back to start the class; it's in preparation to get you into verticality without the same weight bearing pressure on those joints. It really saddens me to see gifted and talented dancers being operated on so young. And some of them jump back in there. It's amazing, you know, but some of them are done. If it was just a little bit of self-care that you could learn or physically go to the doctor.

I had one student that just would not go (to the doctor). She'd say "Oh, I have shin splints, I've shin splints." Then it was "Oh, I iced last night" or "I put some CBD cream on it, and it's better now." Next day she's in pain again, saying "I can't dance. It hurts, and I'm going to sit out today. Okay, is that all right?"

Then finally I just said, "No, no, you can't. You can't be in the show; you have to go to the doctor, you have to GO." And sure enough she shows up in a cast with crutches, and I was like, "Yay! you went." Now we know what's been going on. I'd been begging her to go, and it was two years later, and we learned there were stress fractures in the tibia.

When you have bone damage you have to stop. But had it been treated before it became bone damage, maybe you could still be going and you wouldn't have those pins and those screws and those rods.

I try to look out for dancers, because I'm retired and want to share what I've learned. I'm starting to see the effects of all the pounding and all the mileage. I mean, even something like my bunion joint, you could not have told me that this was going to be reality, because I didn't have pain. But once I saw the X-ray I was like, "What is that!?" It's a huge hook (in my foot), and two of them.

I think dancers also need to be taught about finances very early—especially those babies that sign their first contracts in commercial work, concert dance, or working on Broadway. While I encourage dancers treating themselves to a nice meal or a beautiful dress or a pair of shoes, I strongly believe that investing in a retirement fund like a Roth IRA so that one day they can use that money tax-free and purchase their first home, like I did, would be empowering.

NM: What was helpful for you in that aspect?

SP: My parents. I watched my mom. My mom managed the finances in my house and wrote checks. She would pull out her card table once a month and had a ledger, like a handwritten excel spreadsheet, and wrote checks by hand. I watched that growing up, and I still do it, by hand, 'cause my computer crashed and documents were lost, and I was devastated. Electronics and devices can be temperamental, so I still do my finances by hand. But more importantly, seeing it in a hard copy made me more accountable to what I was spending. I made it a hobby on tour. Because the money that I did save, I would then treat myself to a trip home for a holiday or a massage or a weekend getaway.

About saving, this was back in the day when we used to cook in the hotel room. That is no longer legal; you can't do that anymore. But we used to have hot plates. We would see the big Super Target from the side of the road, and we would yell out "pull over," asking the driver to pull the bus over. We loved buying groceries to cook our own food. One of the dancers would buy chicken, another dancer would buy onions and bell peppers, we'd all bring in a little skillet from our theater case. And we'd make fajitas, and that would save us money. We'd buy oatmeal. When I got my per diem, I didn't spend it all. And I knew what I was eating, what was in the food, instead of pizza and buffalo wings, and just unhealthy fast food on the road that doesn't serve your body for the extreme activity that we require of it. Eating healthy, together, created this communal sense within the company and brought us closer together as friends. After performances, we would have ice parties and cook.

And DTH has that (family structure), where senior dancers adopt incoming dancers. Endalyn Taylor and Eddie Shellman were my parents at DTH. I don't know any other companies that did this. My parents helped me by making sure that I was on the bus on time and that I had my passport, or if I had any questions about being on the road or I needed somebody to help me with choreography, they were there for me.

NM: And how do you model that at Long Beach?

SP: I do a similar practice of new students being adopted by a big brother, big sister, for the performance course during the first week of introducing the cast and the pieces. They can assist with new students who need to go to costume fitting. New students have no idea where the costume shop is; it's across campus and in the basement. So, you're going to be assigned to this person, who's been here for two years and who's going to go with you. Do you know where the registration building is? Have you ever been to the bookstore?

Stephanie Powell in Donald McKayle's *Angelitos Negros*, ca. 2006 (photograph by John Crawford).

You need somebody to show you around. You need somebody to handhold you and at least just expose you. They are not going to stay for your fitting. They're just going to walk you down the stairs, show you the back door, show you a stage door, and just kind of talk to you along the way, become a friend. And that I think really changed the face of the program when I came, made it more familial—a tight-knit community. Now you've got students in the other studio before classes start, and they're all playing in the studio with hip hop music and bringing their lunch, and that's like their second home. As a commuter college program, some of our students are still living at home, but the studio is a safe place for them to be themselves. I think that's important.

Stephanie Powell Glossary

> Brief bio-notes of artists and places mentioned in the chapter. This is not intended to be comprehensive but instead to offer a small amount of information to spark more thorough research if readers are interested.

Alvin Ailey American Dance Theater—Internationally recognized dance company founded by Alvin Ailey in 1958. "Using the beauty and humanity of the African-American heritage and other cultures to unite people of all races, ages and backgrounds" (Alvin Ailey American Dance Theater 2023).

American Negro Ballet Company—Formed by Eugene Von Grona in 1934.
Balanchine, George—Cofounder of New York City Ballet and artistic director for the company for over three decades. Balanchine died in 1983.
Bartenieff Fundamentals—A movement system developed by Irmgard Bartenieff to support movement function, efficiency, and expression.
Brown, Karen—Former longtime principal ballerina for Dance Theatre of Harlem, former artistic director for Oakland Ballet, and assistant professor of Dance at the University of Missouri–Kansas City.
Burmann, Wilhelm "Willy"—Well-known ballet teacher based in New York. Former principal ballet dancer with the Frankfurt Ballet, the Pennsylvania Ballet, and numerous other companies. He died in 2020.
Byrd, Donald—Internationally recognized choreographer. Artistic director of Spectrum Dance Theater and former artistic director of Donald Byrd/The Group.
Cirque de Soleil—Canadian-based high-quality production company that creates and executes artistic productions throughout the world.
Cooper, Duncan—Choreographer and dancer. Previous affiliations: San Francisco Ballet and Dance Theater of Harlem.
Copeland, Misty—First African American female principal dancer with American Ballet Theatre in 2015.
Dunham Technique—Modern dance technique, created by dance pioneer Katherine Dunham, rooted in the movement and cultural traditions of Haitian folk dances and Afro-Caribbean movement vocabularies.
Guidi, Ronn—Founding director of the Oakland Ballet Company. Guidi died in 2021.
Fagan, Garth—Jamaican-born internationally acclaimed choreographer. Founder and artistic director of Garth Fagan Dance. Choreographer of Broadway's *Lion King*.
Farrell, Suzanne—Former principal dancer with New York City Ballet. A collaborator of Balanchine's. Founded Suzanne Farrell Ballet in 2000, housed in Kennedy Center, Washington, D.C.
Franklin, Frederic "Freddie"—Born in Liverpool, England. Principal dancer for Ballet Russe de Monte Carlo. Cofounder of the Slanvenska-Franklin Ballet; also founding director of the National Ballet of Washington. Died in 2013.
Gaddis, Bernard—Founding artistic director for Contemporary West Theatre.
Gottschild, Brenda Dixon—Internationally acclaimed dance and cultural historian. Professor emerita of dance studies, Temple University.
Graves, Lorraine—Former dancer. Theatre of Harlem principal ballerina and ballet mistress.
Holder, Geoffrey—Born in Port of Spain, Trinidad. Principal dancer with Metropolitan Ballet. Choreographed works for companies such as Alvin Ailey American Dance Theater and Dance Theatre of Harlem.
Horton Technique—Modern dance technique created by Lester Horton in the 1920–1940s based on Native American dances (Alvin Ailey American Dance Theater website).
Hunter, Charmaine—Former dancer for Dance Theatre of Harlem. Currently the director of community enrichment for the Orlando Ballet.
Johnson, Christina—Formerly a principal dancer with Dance Theatre of Harlem. Extensive history and experience coaching and teaching throughout many dance and ballet schools, such as the Ailey School, the Joffrey Ballet, Cedar Lake Contemporary Ballet, Complexions Contemporary Ballet, and many others.
Johnson, Virginia—Founding member and principal dancer for Dance Theatre of Harlem. Founder and editor in chief of *Pointe Magazine* and former artistic director of Dance Theatre of Harlem.
Kent, Allegra—Ballet dancer, teacher, and writer. Danced with New York City Ballet under George Balanchine for 30 years.
King, Alonzo—Founding artistic director of Alonzo King Lines Ballet (1982).
Laracey, Ashley—New York City Ballet dancer.

Limón Technique—Modern dance technique created by José Limón.
Long-Naidu, Andrea—Former principal dancer with Dance Theatre of Harlem; on faculty at the Boston Ballet School.
Mantsoe, Vincent—South African–born choreographer.
McKayle, Donald—Choreographer. Died in 2018.
Mitchell, Arthur—Cofounder of Dance Theatre of Harlem in 1969. First African American to become a principal dancer at New York City Ballet. Mitchell died in 2018.
New York City Center "City Center"—A theater, known for presenting dance, founded in 1943 by Fiorello La Guardia.
Nijinska, Bronislava—Russian ballet dancer and choreographer.
Oakland Ballet—Oakland, California, ballet company founded in 1965 by Ronn Guidi.
Roach, Max—Jazz drummer and composer.
Robinson, Renee—Member of the Alvin Ailey American Dance Theater from 1981 to 2012.
Stravinsky, Igor—Russian composer. Composed music for classical ballets such as *The Rite of Spring, Petrushka*, and *The Firebird*.
Sugar Plum Fairy—Featured principal female role in the *Nutcracker* ballet.
Taylor, Endalyn—Former principal dancer with Dance Theatre of Harlem. Former director of the DTH School. Currently dean of dance, School of Dance, North Carolina School of the Arts.
Trueblood, Cindy—Founder and teacher for the Civic Dance Center in Bakersfield, California.
Tyrus, Judy—Former principal dancer for Dance Theatre of Harlem, 1977–1999.
Vernon, Michael—Company teacher for Dance Theatre of Harlem, American Ballet Theatre, Alvin Ailey American Dance Teacher, and numerous other companies. Currently professor of music (dance) at the University of Indiana.

Endalyn Taylor

Past affiliations: Dance Theatre of Harlem (1984–2007)
Current position: Dean of Dance, School of Dance, North Carolina School of the Arts
Hometown: Chicago, Illinois
Current residence: Winston-Salem, North Carolina
Age at time of interview: 47

Excerpts from a July 2014 interview with Endalyn Taylor, in person, at the Dance Theatre of Harlem School in New York, New York. Upon meeting, Endalyn offered me a tour of the building, including studios, the costume shop, the archives, and administrative offices. Taylor's energy was warm and generous. It was apparent that she welcomed people into the DTH building often and was comfortable sharing about its rich history.

ET: (Endalyn began by leading me down a hallway to a display case featuring skin-colored pointe shoes.) We love these displays, you know, because one of the unique things about DTH are the flesh-toned tights. Although more companies are doing that now, at least matching the shoes to their skin.

NM: *Can you tell me more about that?*

ET: I know at Complexions, the dancers often don't wear tights; they wear bare legs, and then they color their shoes to match their skin tone.

NM: *I am thinking too.... Ballethnic also matches skin tone with the tights and the shoes. And since they are second-generation DTH, it makes sense.*

ET: They are a second generation, exactly. And I think Fabian Barnes, who doesn't have a company but has a nice school in D.C., they do it as well. But this originated at Dance Theatre of Harlem. And by the time I came along and was in the company, we were so spoiled; we had a team of wardrobe people who really studied and made sure that we had exact matches. They dyed our tights for us, so we didn't have to worry about them.

Endalyn Taylor (photograph by Peter Mueller; courtesy Endalyn Taylor).

NM: *That's so nice.*

ET: Yeah. I'm sure you've heard Mr. Mitchell's ideology around why (to extend the line of the leg through to the toe). It's funny; it's such a part of me now that whenever I see pink tights on brown legs, I have to get used to it, you know. It's shocking to me.

NM: *Yes.*

ET: So, this was the only stairwell leading up and down to the basement and the second floor. When I came as a student, the second floor held such mystery because it was where the company rehearsed and took classes. Once I got into the company, I felt like, oh my god, I'm in Studio 3. You know, that's a big, big deal. So, all of this was here.

NM: *How long were you at the school before you joined the company? Did you apprentice for a while?*

ET: Yeah, but as an apprentice back then you were dancing full-time. I joined the school in the summer of 1983. I was asked to stay for the fall because they were getting ready to do *Giselle* and they needed a corps de ballet. They hired a number of us. I think there were four or five of us who got in that year, mostly from the summer intensive. I think Augustus Van Heerden and Christina Johnson also came in that year. I was a baby. I was 16 or 17 at the time, the youngest one in the company at that point—and very green. You know, very naive about a lot of things, but the beautiful thing about DTH was, someone immediately took you in, as family, and mentored you. Charmaine Hunter was my mother in the company, and that very first day she was like, "Girl, we've gotta work on this. Your hair, that's not right. I'm going to show you how to do makeup."

NM: Was it a formal mentoring? I mean, was it an assignment, or...?

ET: It was informal, but people took it very seriously, and, you know, when it was my time to do it, when I saw someone, it was just like, I'm going to mentor you. No one assigned them to you, it was much more organic, which in many ways was great.

NM: But there was nobody who didn't get one?

ET: There was no one who didn't get one. Everyone had someone. Somebody would take someone under their wing. This [pointing to the office door while walking down the hallway] Mr. Mitchell's office, now Virginia's.

NM: With any change in administration or artistic direction, there are felt changes. What would be the most felt change since Virginia has transitioned into leadership?

ET: It's a good question. I mean, since ... I guess, I worked for Mr. Mitchell as a performer. Some of the things that I know he implemented, stood for, and instilled in us may be different, only because it's a different generation and the mission is not exactly as prominent. Back when we were dancing, one of the things he made us realize—when we got here, there was this real sense of unity and this sense of purpose, you know; we're representing something larger than ourselves. That was a message that he delivered over and over and we truly felt. I think it happened quite naturally for many of us, having trained in places where we quite often were one of few or the only (Black dancer). We were much less about self and more about the goal, the cause, the overall projection of what DTH looked like and what we put out there. And I think, nowadays, dance is more of an immediate gratification, and there's even the ability for ballet and ballerinas to brand themselves. There's more of an individual goal-oriented group that's here. That's not necessarily a negative thing.

NM: It's different.

ET: It's just different. Some of us were almost too self-sacrificing; we didn't fight for things that we maybe should have—that we deserved because we put in the work. So, this group is that way (self-advocates), not necessarily because of Virginia's leadership but the changing times.

NM: [pointing to a picture on the wall] That's Lydia Abarca Mitchell, right?

ET: Yes. Lydia Abarca Mitchell. And that's Virginia, Arthur Mitchell, and Homer Bryant. That's Paul Russell. [We walk into the library, where Judy Tyrus and Robert Garland are working.] This is the library. Some of the wonderful work that Judy Tyrus is doing is making our library comprehensive, where the videos, everything on DTH, the articles, are cataloged and easy for us to come in and do research should we need to. At some point, the students will be able to use the archives as well.

NM: That's a lot of work [looking at the room full of documents, programs, posters, and photos].

ET: Yeah. It is a lot of work because she's also digitizing it for online documentation.

NM: I am thinking when I see them in their costumes [pointing to older DTH posters hanging on the wall, in contrast to newer posters] that that's very generational. Would you agree? I feel like the older pictures of DTH were more conservative in appearance.

ET: Yeah, a little more conservative, right. Probably our most risqué or revealing costume was *Dougla*.

NM: I love Dougla.

ET: A great piece. We wore long skirts with sheer tops and flesh-colored bras underneath—our bellies were out. But yeah, this is much more a sign of the times [pointing to a newer poster]. Those costumes are from a piece that Robert (Garland) choreographed; it's a cool piece because it uses the music of James Brown and Aretha Franklin. It is a modern twist on a pointe shoe ballet. The classical idiom is there, but he funks it up brilliantly.

NM: So, African American vernacular dance? Contemporary?

ET: Yes, he funks it up with some African American vernacular dance. You know, he's from Philly; every once in a while, it pops out.

All of our Firebirds are in pictures [pointing at more photos]. Bethania Gomes is from Brazil. She's actually coming in to do master classes. It's funny, because she's got a little boy who is about seven or eight; we all have families now. My son was the first company baby that actually toured with us.

NM: Oh, wow!

ET: Yeah, he's 23. Because my ex-husband was in the company as well. So, my son took his first steps onstage.

NM: That's so awesome! Does he like dance?

ET: He's a break dancer. He dances with a crew. He stopped dancing for a while but backed his way back into his parents' profession. But where we try to balance this way [upright], he's upside down (referring to breakdancing's head spins).

NM: That's wonderful. So, continually, the space has been growing even though, historically, companies have so many financial challenges just to exist. And yet, there's been so much growth throughout those decades, where just staying above water is a challenge.

ET: Staying above has been very, very challenging. Improvements in the building came through a grant from the city as part of a project of Scott Stringer's; we got money to update the studios.

For years Zelda Wynn was our designer. She was amazing, and it was a luxury to have our designer on hand like that. We've been really lucky with our wardrobe people. I think they are kind of underestimated, they are so important to a company with a range of body types. Because of our aesthetic, there were things that they did that really highlighted and maximized our sinew—our shapeliness.

Pamela Allen, our most recent designer, designed when I was in the company and designs costumes even today. You can spot her work anywhere, because I guarantee you, there's never any pucker. They fit your body like a glove. And so, what we have (in terms of our body/shape) is highlighted, never in the negative but in a flattering way because of the way she drapes it on your body. You know, finding costume designers today is not easy. I would call them artisans and craftsmen really … but the work is deliberately done from Mr. Mitchell to Virginia (Johnson). She carries that tradition of being very particular about who does costumes and why they are designed the way they are.

NM: What's the relationship between the school and the company? Is it a feeder?

ET: Well, that's one thing that we've tried to work on a lot in recent years, and it's a huge desire of Virginia's. We work really closely together now to develop our programming and the syllabus so that, hopefully, there will be that actual feed into the company. Our professional training program actually has fed into the company. Two years ago, two of our dancers went into the company when it returned. But, you know, the company was on hiatus for eight years. So, there was a period where we just had to hold the school down and keep it going without the shiny apple at the top. There was nowhere to really go; then the ensemble started to develop more and started touring.

NM: How much of the ensemble was able to move into the company when the company came back?

ET: About half. Half of them. Half of the ensemble and two professional training program students moved in, and the other ones have gone on to either dance in other places or shifted to going to school and doing other things. That was a tough transition. A very tough transition. The company now has 18 members. I believe the largest it got was about 50 dancers.

NM: Can you tell me about how you began dancing?

ET: I started dancing when I was seven, in Chicago. Really, kind of a funny story. I was just an outrageous child, where I think I probably existed 50 percent in some make-believe world and 50 percent in the real world. I would answer the door draped in sheets and go "Welcome to my wedding. Are you here for the bride or the groom?" My mom's bed was my gymnastic arena, and I always won the gold medal. So, my mom had her hands full, basically. We were visiting a friend of my mom's one day; she saw me just start to dance throughout the house as "Tiptoe through the Tulips" came on. I was doing movement that neither of them was sure what it was, but her friend said, "You should put her in ballet or something," you know, because obviously there's some creativity there. And that was the beginning. I started at Mayfair Academy on the south side of Chicago, which was founded by a tap dancer, Tommy Sutton. My first teacher, her name was Ms. Lodi—not sure of the spelling myself—carried a cane like so many of the others back then and was not afraid to poke or hit you with it, you know, which nowadays is just unthinkable. But yeah, those were my early beginnings.

NM: *Do you still dance today? Do you ever take class?*

ET: I don't take class. I will demonstrate a combination pretty full out on one side. Every once in a while, I'll…

NM: *The right?*

ET: Normally the right side, yes. And every once in a while, I'll do a combination full out in the center; I'll throw a double tour in or something. I kind of was known for my jump, so every once in a while I'll just do it so that they know I can still do a thing or two. But there's all sorts of myths and legends around my jumping now, that I did double tours in pumps and so on and so forth. I will confess to having taught in pumps a few times. But never did I perform a double tour in them.

NM: *Legendary indeed. Do you know, one of my dance teachers used to talk about your jumps, Reginald Savage, all the way across the country in Oakland, California. He said you would get competitive in class with Mikhail Baryshnikov [I said in an inquisitive tone] and you would challenge him and try to outjump him, so the story goes. [Taylor looked at me and smiled widely with an affirming expression].*

Can you tell me about your performance career?

ET: My performance career was … pretty incredible. I think the journey from a student in Chicago, wondering if I would ever fit in anywhere because of *Nutcrackers* where I had to put baby powder on so I would not look so brown in the snow scene, to knowing that roles were made for me and that I was as strong as the other people getting to perform them but not getting them, to coming here and being amongst dancers who looked like me and teachers who looked like me, worked with me, and registered no surprised at my presence. Still, even within that, learning that ballet is a competitive art form, in which you can't sit back, be a sweetheart, and wait for things to happen, was challenging and crucial. You know, I had to develop some grit.

I'm the baby of my family; I was loved, and just thought that's the way everything in my life would be. There were tough lessons learned on the road to becoming a ballerina. I remember when I performed my first role with DTH; I was a Crab Girl in Balanchine's *Four Temperaments*. We performed it in Boston at the Wang Theatre. I was so excited to tour with the company and be in that piece! The toughness started almost immediately, with Mr. Mitchell saying afterwards "Okay, you've got to lose weight; you've got to do this…"; he was always on you, on you, on you. At the time, the only kind of love that I'd received was an encouraging kind of love. Even when my parents reprimanded me, I knew love undergirded the discipline. I didn't realize that Mr. Mitchell saw something in me, wanted me to get to a certain place, and maybe didn't think I'd get there quickly enough if he led with kindness. He was insistent—he would see me walking down the stairs of the hotel at which company stayed, I could hear him coming after me, saying "And another thing…" There was a period where me and a young man named Stephen, who was a bit of a carbon copy of the young Mr. Mitchell; whenever he (Mr. Mitchell) saw us, he would have something to say. We got to the point of asking other people to look out for him; if he was around, we would go the other way.

At the time, I didn't realize the value of that iconic person taking an interest in me. But once I did, once I got my own grit and self-determination, that's when I started to blossom and grow as a dancer and as an artist. That's when the roles started coming in, and I went from an apprentice to a soloist to a principal, still having to work and fight my way through all of it, but, you know, having an opportunity to dance ballets that I didn't think I'd ever get to do.

NM: *You mentioned having to use baby power in* Nutcracker. *Can you talk a little bit more about that experience?*

ET: Yeah. I had gone from Mayfair Academy to Ruth Page School of Dance. I had gotten a scholarship. My mom realized I was serious about dance and that it was more than a creative outlet, that there was real talent there and real opportunity. And so, I auditioned for Ruth Page. I auditioned for their *Nutcracker* and simultaneously for their school. I got accepted into both. And in my first year I did Arabian, as opposed to the party scene. I was so disappointed, because the party scene had the beautiful dresses, the fun music, and the long section of dancing. There were four of us in Arabian, and the girls who weren't Black—everybody but me—had to wear this oily, shiny brown grease paint—basically blackface, which was so politically incorrect, you know, even back then. And even though I was young, I wouldn't have known what to categorize it as, but it felt wrong to me that they were putting on this grease paint, you know, to look like me, and that's the role that I was cast in. So, that early lesson was hard, although I couldn't put my finger on why it felt so uncomfortable. Because nothing was ever spoken. You know how that is, it's all the things that are not said that rankle later in life, once you realize what you were going through. But as I got older and continued at Ruth Page, Mr. Long—I love him dearly—certainly pushed me, encouraged me, and taught me many of the things I know. But when *Nutcracker* came around and I finally got to do Snow, Ruth Page was still alive and she, herself, told me "You know, you're a lovely dancer but you need to powder down." And I didn't understand what she was talking about. I put on makeup, and I put on the compressed powder, but they meant baby powder; she said, "You don't look like snow, you look like slush." That was an early memory for me and a strong one.

NM: How long were you at that school?
ET: Gosh, I was at Ruth Page for quite a while. I was there at least … four or five years….

NM: It's interesting; I hear a story like that, I always think "And then you left!"
ET: Right, no, I stayed.

NM: Right, but that's what you would do in the '80s, right?
ET: Yes. That was what you would do because what other choice was there? I mean, there weren't a bunch of Dance Theatre of Harlems out there where you could get quality training. I was grateful for Mayfair Academy because it gave me my early ballet foundation. But I knew I needed more and had the potential to do more in the discipline. And so, you look for a school with a reputation for quality training, and that's what my mom did. It was either Ruth Page School of Dance or Ellis-DuBoulay. But I didn't feel like I was mistreated all of the time. In class, like I said, Mr. Long gave me tons of attention. Patti Klekovic also gave me tons of attention. All of the teachers gave lots of attention and loved me. When it came down to roles, however, I wasn't cast. I was an understudy or, you know, third from the last girl.

NM: What do you attribute that to, that they could love you sincerely as a person and also have this construct of race that didn't fit for them in terms of the stage? Do you attribute that to ballet, the ideology of classical ballet? Or do you think it's the U.S. and racial constructs in the U.S.? Or both working together?
ET: I think initially I just thought of it as ballet and those confines of the European aesthetic and not fitting that aesthetic because I am obviously a Brown girl, not even a fair African American, with muscularity and strong ethnic features. There would be no way for me to slide in and pass as it's been rumored they asked people to do in the past. I attributed it to that initially. But thinking about it now and thinking about it from the perspective of an adult and as someone who does programming and considers what the public's response to something will be, I'm more inclined to attribute it to the U.S. They were probably worried about what the audience would think. Just because they were accepting, they didn't want it to affect the bottom line.

NM: How long were you a company member here (DTH)?
ET: I got into the company in 1983 and, once I had my son, left for a brief stint to perform on Broadway. And that was in … when I did *Carousel*? I think that was '90 … I don't remember, maybe '91 or '92. And then I came back once *Carousel* closed, and I stayed until 1997 before leaving to do *The Lion King*. I came back in 2004 as a teacher and then in 2005 was surreptitiously announced to be the school director.

There was no applying for the position; Mr. Mitchell literally put it in my lap in a meeting. But that was his way.

NM: Now, you mentioned that your son was the first company baby. What was that like?

ET: It was great. I mean, I know other people had children, but he was the first one to actually tour with the company. He traveled with us. He had his first birthday in Cleveland, and everybody came to his birthday party backstage in between shows. He had this giant extended family who taught him a lot of amazing things. The costume people would make Halloween costumes for him. He had the best costumes. He always won competitions.

NM: And both of you (Taylor and husband at the time) were dancing in all of the shows?

ET: Both of us were dancing in every performance, not necessarily the same pieces, and it was literally "You're not on now; here, you hold the baby." And sometimes it wasn't just the two of us. It was very extended, and everyone was willing to help and pitch in. Even Mr. Mitchell's sister, Shirley Mills, who traveled with us, would watch him during the day many times at the hotel, and then she would bring him to the theater in the evening. My parents would tour with us every once in a while. I looked at it as an opportunity for them to travel and experience what I was experiencing and also know that my child was in really good hands. My sisters went a couple of times. So, for him, I think it definitely created a love and a passion for the arts. He's very much that way now.

NM: How long did you tour with him?

ET: Until he was five years old. It was a nice stint of time. And it definitely skewed his perspective on women too. When he was in high school, I remember him telling me about this girl that he liked, and he was like, "She has this beautiful neck." And I'm like, what boy even looks at a neck? Someone who's been around a bunch of ballerinas all his life.

NM: You mentioned being in a meeting where Mr. Mitchell asked you to be the school director.

ET: Yes, he told me that I was the school director. There was a meeting with a panel of men and me for some new collaboration. And he told them, "If you have any other questions, speak to the school director, Endalyn Taylor." That was how I found out. And just kind of like, oh, good, okay. Yeah.

NM: You have worked with other companies and collaborated with other programs in schools and institutions in ballet. What would you say is unique about the culture here at Dance Theatre of Harlem? Certainly, they have a different mission, but beyond skin color, what do you feel is a difference here that you have experienced?

ET: One of the things I always say to people is that Dance Theatre of Harlem is reminiscent of a mom-and-pop organization. It feels like a family, even though we have this huge legacy, and it is a world-acclaimed organization. There's always a sister, brother, mother or a father, someone there to nurture and give you support. I've felt that way from the moment I got here, and I've heard it from students who have been at other schools, who come here for the summer or who come here from another place, that there is a sense of nurturing and support. And a genuine sense of finding their identity and being able to feel comfortable in their skin. That everything they come here with is absolutely enough. What you do with that then becomes up to you, your hard work and what you're willing to put in. It doesn't guarantee that you're going to be a dancer, but I think it guarantees that your life is going to be enriched by the experience. That you will walk out of here knowing something more about yourself. I think there's learning to dance, and I think there's learning about yourself through dance. I would say that's probably the biggest difference.

NM: Now, you've talked a little bit about the influence Mr. Mitchell had in shaping you at a young age. Did you have a teacher or advocate that helped you get to where you are today? Mr. Mitchell or someone else?

ET: I learned a lot of my technical skills, cleanliness, and attention to details from Larry Long, who taught at Ruth Page. He was the director of Ruth Page's school. He was great in that sense of making you understand the importance of transitions and connecting your movements. Mr. Mitchell, more so than anybody, emphasized the need to be an artist at all times, that from pliés on, you should be thinking about a story, a purpose, a throughline. So, I really attribute the idea of being a thinking dancer, whether you're doing something abstract, a story ballet or not, for you, there is always a story. There's always a reason why you're doing something. You're never moving because someone has told you to move.

NM: Can you share a challenge that you experienced in your dancing, in terms of ballet, that was monumental to you or that stands out as really hard to get through?

ET: Oh, gosh. Probably so many. I think, for me, while there were certain things that I had naturally that immediately got me attention, like my jump, I was reasonably flexible—at one point I was extremely flexible. I actually have something called a spina bifida, where part of my back is underdeveloped, the spine. My back was hypermobile but weak. I got injured one day and had to learn how to rework my muscles to gain strength around that area because it was vulnerable. I lost flexibility there, particularly in arabesque.

My biggest challenge, dance-wise, was improving my feet, which I worked on tirelessly to create a more beautiful line aesthetic. They were always strong, but the look of things was the big challenge. I felt at times that my leg line was the reason I was rarely cast in adagio roles. I spent the bulk of my career moving really fast, jumping, turning; I was a pyrotechnical dancer. So, when I crossed that threshold and Glen Tetley came in and chose me to do a pas de deux from *Dialogues*, I was so excited because I would get to slow down and luxuriate in the movement. I was cast in two pas de deux in that piece. Both were lyrical supported with jumps and turns.

Performing those pieces was a welcome challenge, crossing over into roles that kept me on the ground and extended lines, where maybe they would get a photograph for a change.

NM: Yeah, I can imagine. Would that be the high point, the peak? Would it be those adagio roles? In terms of achievements that you attained in ballet that stand out?

ET: Gosh, that's hard to say. Those were probably personal peaks that stood out to me. Roles that were high points because they were encompassing of artistic and technical prowess would be more like performing Myrtha in *Giselle* or doing Medea; both were dramatic, driven, and demanding roles that pushed my abilities. Really developing and honing that artistry where I knew I could tell a story with just my movement as opposed to wowing them with a big trick. Connecting to audience in that way and losing myself and becoming something else. I loved working on Medea, and I loved doing Myrtha. Myrtha was a real highlight and challenge because somehow the casting failed to go up until the week before I was to do the role. I was still transitioning out of the corps and had very little time to prepare. Fortunately, my ex-husband—at that point he was my boyfriend—rehearsed and coached me well into the night until they kicked us out of the building. Mr. Mitchell was not going to be happy hearing "Oh, I didn't know I was cast until the week before the performance." His response would have been "Well, why didn't you know about it?" The blame wouldn't have lain with whoever neglected to post it on the callboard; it would have rested with me. Ultimately, if you're the one out there, you have to be responsible. You have to be accountable.

NM: So, how would you learn a role like that if you hadn't danced it before, if you had been in the corps? Would you use videotapes? Would a person coach you? How would that happen?

ET: Combination of both. You would use a videotape if it was a role that was already in the rep and built, and then someone would coach you. The ballet master or mistress arranged rehearsal schedules and things of that nature. For Myrtha, I got one or two legitimate rehearsals, one of them being the onstage dress rehearsal. I was an understudy, and they usually rehearse far less than the first cast. You could always ask somebody to help you. Maybe the person for whose role you understudied or someone you trusted to work with you. Thankfully, there were people willing to do that. My ex was already a principal, so that was helpful, and he played Albrecht.

NM: What do you think of color-casting?

ET: Oh, the brown paper bag test casting? It happened here sometimes, whether intentional or not. Certain roles appeared to go to dancers because of their coloring. I mean, I always played strong roles. Myrtha, who's ice cold, Medea, who killed her children and convinced them to kill someone else. It wasn't until the birth of my child that roles switched for me. I got to portray romantic roles and the femme fatale; I was the flirtatious one. Mr. Mitchell saw me in a different light. I can only speculate that in his eyes maternity softened me, made me more feminine. But certainly, you know…

NM: Did you notice it and identify it at the time? Or do you reflect on it in hindsight and say "Oh."

ET: I reflect on it in hindsight, actually. Other people pointed out the color-casting. We were questioned as to why there were so many light dancers and so few dark dancers. These questions were directed towards Mr. Mitchell at times. We would hear it in conversation from people who came backstage for autographs. They were like "Wow, you are brown. There aren't that many." It was noticed, and sometimes you attributed that to some people are always going to look for the negative side of things. Other people, not so much. Was it there? Yes, it was there.

NM: Was it something that brought animosity, or was it something that felt like it's not fair? Or was it just accepted?

ET: It probably varied for different people. You know, I looked at it with some humor. There was a group of us in the company known as the Károlyi kids—Károlyi was the coach for the gymnastics team that won the gold—because we danced all the time. We were in every ballet, every night. Even when we started to get lead roles, somehow we were on the stage all the time. For us, we figured whether we were light or dark, it didn't matter; we were out there and happy to be out there. Though not always doing the roles we wanted to do, we certainly got our share of time onstage. So, we came up with skin tone–specific nicknames for groups. There was the Coffee Club, the Brown Girls, and the Butterscotch Girls; they were the lighter ones. And so, we laughed about it and got on with our day. I imagine for some, color-casting was harder to deal with, particularly if they weren't getting many opportunities to perform and fulfill that passion within them.

NM: As somebody who has the opportunity to make decisions in terms of marketing and things of that nature and sometimes casting, I imagine, with the school and students, do you ever think about skin color impacting your marketing decisions?

ET: You know, that's a good question. For the most part, it doesn't really come into play because the students are so beautifully hued, I enjoy them all. And the casting … if I am thinking about those decisions, those are impacted more by aesthetics—a linear look. But even that is diverse. We celebrate individuality here, and I admit to wanting to make sure to represent the spectrum of colors that we have.

Endalyn Taylor Glossary

Brief bio-notes of artists and places mentioned in the chapter. This is not intended to be comprehensive but instead to offer a small amount of information to spark more thorough research if readers are interested.

Allen-Cummings, Pamela—Longtime costume mistress and designer for Dance Theatre of Harlem.

Baryshnikov, Mikhail—Director, choreographer. Former principal dancer with American Ballet Theatre and New York City Ballet.

Bryant, Homer—Born in the Virgin Islands. Director. Former company member with Dance Theatre of Harlem and Donald McKayle's Company. Performed on Broadway. Ballet master for Joel Hall Dancers and Dance Chicago.

Ellis-DuBoulay School of Ballet—Ballet school in Chicago, Illinois, founded in 1952 by Richard Ellis and Christine DuBoulay Ellis.

Garland, Robert—Dance Theatre of Harlem artistic director. Former principal dancer for Dance Theatre of Harlem. Choreographer who created works for New York City Ballet, Britain's Royal Ballet, and Oakland Ballet.

Gomes, Bethania—Born in Brazil. Choreographer, ballet coach. Danced with Dance Theatre of Harlem.

Hunter, Charmaine—Former principal dancer for Dance Theatre of Harlem. Currently the director of community enrichment for Orlando Ballet.

Johnson, Christina—Former principal dancer with Dance Theatre of Harlem. Extensive history and experience coaching and teaching throughout many schools including, among others, the Ailey School, Joffrey Ballet, Cedar Lake Contemporary Ballet, and Complexions Contemporary Ballet.

Johnson, Virginia—Founding member and principal dancer for Dance Theatre of Harlem. Founder and editor in chief of *Pointe Magazine* and former artistic director of Dance Theatre of Harlem.

Károlyi, Béla—Olympic gymnastic coach.

Klekovic, Patricia "Patti"—Principal dancer with Chicago Opera Ballet.

Long, Larry—Director of the Ruth Page Foundation School of Dance and co-artistic director of Civic Ballet of Chicago. Died in 2009.

Mayfair Academy—A dance school, founded by Tommy Sutton in 1957, on the South Side of Chicago to give Black children opportunities in dance.

Mitchell, Arthur—Cofounder of Dance Theatre of Harlem in 1969. First African American to become a principal dancer at New York City Ballet. Mitchell died in 2018.

Mitchell, Lydia Abarca—First prima ballerina of Dance Theatre of Harlem. Ballet coach at Ballethnic in Atlanta, Georgia.

Mitchell-Mills, Shirley—Arthur Mitchell's sister, valuable supporting member of the DTH organization for decades.

Myrtha—Queen Myrtha of the Willis, a featured role in the ballet *Giselle*.

Page, Ruth—Chicago-based choreographer, dancer, and director. Founder of the Ruth Page Foundation School of Dance. Page died in 1991.

Russell, Paul—Principal dancer with Dance Theatre of Harlem and San Francisco Ballet. Russell died in 1991.

Savage, Reginald—Founding director of the Savage Jazz Dance Company in Oakland, California.

Stringer, Scott—New York City comptroller.

Sutton, Tommy—Founder of the Mayfair Academy in Chicago, Illinois, in 1957.

Tetley, Glenford—Choreographer. Former artistic director for Netherlands Dance Theatre and Stuttgart Ballet. Tetley died in 2007.

Tyrus, Judy—Former principal dancer for Dance Theatre of Harlem, 1977–1999.

Van Heerden, Augustus—South African-born principal dancer for Boston Ballet. Also danced with Dance Theatre of Harlem and Wisconsin Ballet. Dance Theatre of Harlem associate director of the Lower/Upper school.

Valdes, Zelda Wynn—Costuming designer for Dance Theatre of Harlem. Valdes died in 2001.

Wang Theatre (Boch Center)—Historic theater in Boston, Massachusetts.

Set II—
Dancers Who Are Still Performing or Recently Retired

Shelby Colona • Monike Cristina •
Yinet Fernandez • Kristie Latham • Claudia Monja •
Margaret Severin-Hansen • Melissa Verdecia

Shelby Colona

Past affiliation: Ballet Hispánico (2014–2022)
Hometown: Houston, Texas
Current residence: Olympia, Washington
Age at time of interview: 24

Excerpts from a December 5, 2017, interview with Shelby Colona in person. The interview was arranged by Ballet Hispánico and conducted in a conference room at Ballet Hispánico Studios in New York, New York. Shelby entered the conference room with bright energy and enthusiasm. Her youthful energy set the tone in the space of "ready to get to it."

NM: *Tell me how you began dancing.*
　　SC: I started when I was three years old. My older sister actually danced first. I went to see a recital of hers. My mom brought me, and I got really intrigued with the fact that my sister was onstage in costume and doing everything. And she was kind of the center of attention. I was really jealous, because I like being the center of attention. So, I told my mom that's what I wanted to do. She put me into dance class, and I just haven't stopped since.

NM: *Can you tell me about your performance career? How long has that been? When did you make the transition from prepro training to the company?*
　　SC: Right after high school, I went to the Ailey School certificate program ... a

three-year program, but I did it in two. I met all my requirements early and graduated with the class above the class I entered with. From there, I had time off. I was really young. I was 20 when I graduated, so every audition I went to, everyone was like, "You're too young. You don't have any experience." And I was like, "How am I supposed to get the experience if you won't give it to me?"

So, I got certified in Pilates and then I ran into Nicholas Villeneuve, who used to be the rehearsal director of the second company here. I had met him when I was 15 at Perry Mansfield Performing Arts Camp in Steamboat Springs, Colorado, and I was in his piece. I ran into him at Ailey, and he said, "Shelby! Hi." I was like, "Hi." He goes, "What are you up to?" And I said, "Nothing. I graduated. I'm just here watching a friend's show." He said, "We have an audition for BH Dos (Ballet Hispánico, second company) this weekend; can you come in and audition?" He was like, "I remember you; I'd like to see you." So, I said, what do I have to lose at that point? One of the worst auditions I felt I ever did, but I did end up getting the job, and I was in the second company, a transition between school and professional.

Then, I had a meeting with Michelle Manzanales, who used to be the rehearsal director of the first company, and Nicholas, and they said, "Well, where do you see yourself going after you're done with BH Dos?" And I told them—which was really aggressive for me at the time, because I'm not the kind of person who likes to just put myself out there. I figured with hard work, people kind of come to you. But I said to her, "I see myself in the first company." And they were like, "Oh! Okay." And I was like, "I know that I'm really young, but …" Technically, I wasn't really the right fit, because I didn't feel like I was Latin enough. I'm not Latin at all, you know? And then I auditioned—they still made me go to the audition. I got in, though. Right there, and I was kind of double-teaming on BH Dos and the first company. Someone got injured, and they needed someone immediately. Luckily I was able to pick up fast, and they threw me in halfway through the season. They brought me in slowly into certain things.

NM: You mentioned it just a minute ago, but I wanted to ask you a little bit about your cultural and ethnic background.

SC: I am a ton of different things. I am Japanese, which shows, a quarter. I'm a quarter German, I'm a quarter Irish, and I'm quarter British. But I ended up in this Latin dance company. I haven't dived much into the DNA testing, because I'm probably a thousand other things.

NM: So, what's it like for you to be part of a Latin American dance company?

SC: It definitely was interesting and a little bit … it's a little hard, I think. I mean, from stage my look is very vague.

NM: Some call it ethnically ambiguous.

SC: Yes, ethnically ambiguous is basically what I am. So, I fit in when I was at Ailey, and I come here and I fit in here, but I'm really Asian and most people don't know that. Especially when I'm traveling with Ballet Hispánico.

I think it's a little difficult being in Ballet Hispánico, not being Latina, only because there's a lot of things that I want to do with the company to represent them. However, I'm not the best representation of the company because of my background and my heritage. That being said, they are very inclusive; their whole mentality here in the company is community. This Latin American company, they're into diversity and how we all come together in a community and how we can teach each other about our different cultures. But really, I am learning more about the Latin culture. I feel like I'm more Latin than Asian over these past four years, so…

NM: Does it ever cross your mind, what would it be like to be in an Asian company?
SC: I've thought about it. But I haven't really seen many, like, kind of Asian-based companies. I know there's Nai-Ni Chen, and you see all the advertisements for Shen Yun. But I've never really been … I think their aesthetic is, or from what I've seen, their aesthetic is very different from what I'm interested in. I love that there's a lot of flavors, a lot of flair, a lot of intensity here in what we do. And then, very grounded and earthy. We also do salsa and, you know, I feel like there's a lot more learning here for me.

NM: Do you have a teacher or advocate in your life who helped you get where you are today in dance as a woman of Color?
SC: Yes. I have a lot, but who was the most? I think Peter Chu. He went to Juilliard and worked with Crystal Pite and Kidd Pivot. He became the guest rehearsal director for Netherlands Dance Theatre. He's also Asian, he's Chinese—he helped me be okay with who I am and embrace who I am as an Asian woman but also telling me that I can do any and everything that I want. I have known him since I was probably nine years old, and I was really the only girl of Color at my studio.… I danced competitively at a studio; there was a big group of us, like a company, a jazz company.

NM: Where are you from?
SC: I'm from Houston, Texas.

NM: There is a prominent ballet dancer of Color there.
SC: Yeah, Lauren Anderson. I actually saw her last performance as Sugar Plum Fairy, and I was, like, over the moon. Lauren Anderson, I mean, she broke a huge barrier as the first principal.

I lived in a very cookie-cutter, white suburban neighborhood where everything and everyone is, like, kind of perfect. We called it "the bubble." So, I always felt like I was like everyone else. Peter and also Eduardo, our artistic director here, told me to embrace being me. When I joined, Eduardo said, "I know that you're not Latin. However, a lot of us Latinos come from Asia." He was like, "I myself am part Chinese.… I think that you need to dive more into your own culture to be able to stand out and understand more about what we're doing here." Which was a really interesting thing, because I think when I joined I was like, oh, I need to be more Latin,

I need to have that flair. And really, it was just like, I need to find myself and be comfortable with myself and understand that before I can even start to go off in another direction, which was something that Peter had also mentioned to me too. He was like, "Embrace who you are, because who you are is superspecial. And, you know, you stand out. You have a look different than everyone else. It's intriguing, it's unique." And, so I learned to embrace that slowly. It took a second, but I got there.

NM: What challenges and achievements stand out the most?

SC: Challenges…. I have always trained classically in ballet. However, I am not your classical ballerina. Most of the women here, especially when I started, were all trained with a classical ballet aesthetic. They were all movers, they could all still move, but I felt a little out of the box. Because I was like, wow, I'm not as technical, I don't have … they all had great facility, really pretty feet, extensions like out the ceiling. And I think when I joined, I was like, okay, number one, I'm the youngest girl here, so this is really awkward. Number two, I'm nothing like any of these girls. Like, they are all Latin, have been here for a really long time, and are technically, to me, perfect. So, I was kind of feeling out of place, and it was really hard, and I started second-guessing a lot of things I was doing, because I was like, oh, that's not right, I don't look like them, and it's not right. And one of my friends, who's now the rehearsal director of the first company, was in the company with me, and he said, "You need to stop worrying about what anyone else thinks and you need to embrace yourself, because you're now starting to hinder your ability to improve. Because you're now starting to worry about so many other things, you're not really being you." So, I took that. I was a little bitter about it, because, you know, hearing that from your friend is a little hard, but it was helpful. Because no one else was going to say that to me. They were waiting for me to figure it out on my own. So, I finally started embracing that I was hired for a reason. You were probably hired because you don't dance like any of these other girls, and that's maybe what they're looking for. So, I started to take ballet a different way. I was not trying to be so classical and perfect anymore. I was doing what looked good on me and what worked well for me. Every contemporary thing, I started to embrace what I was really good at. Get deeper into the ground on certain things that they maybe can't go as deep into the ground as I can. But then, I was challenged with other things. Like when we do a piece called *Havana*, it's all heels, it's all technical, it's all ballet. And I learned how to make it technical but make it work for me, which actually ended up going in my favor. You know, so, those were the challenges I felt like I had when I first joined.

Now, as I'm getting older, I've been here for almost four years, and I'm close to one of the senior girls. There's one girl who's been here longer, Melissa (Verdecia); she's been here longer than me. And slowly but surely, I found myself improving steadily every year. And as long as I haven't hit a plateau, I'm achieving something. Every year, I started at the bottom where everyone else does, and slowly, roles started to get better. What I worked for and what I wanted started happening, and people started to notice; choreographers started to notice. A woman from *Dance Magazine* noticed. And so, there's all these little things, which ultimately, to me, are really big things, but I find that I'm achieving more every year. And, you know, at this point, there's nowhere to go but up, and they encourage that here too. They're like, "Keep going, keep going, keep going. What else can you bring?" And they'll put you into roles that normally wouldn't be for you, you know. Melissa was first cast for one of Annabelle Lopez Ochoa's pieces, and they put me as the understudy, and then they gave me the opportunity to do it, actually. And I was like, this isn't my work. Like, this isn't my piece; I don't do it like her. It was a challenge and a way to break me out of my shell and what I'm comfortable doing. So, I find that when I take on a role that I don't think is for me, when I finally feel comfortable doing it, then I can stop worrying about everything else. That's a big achievement for me.

NM: How would you describe the culture of Ballet Hispánico?
    SC: Family-oriented. Trusting. I think it's definitely diverse. But there's a lot of trust here. You know, we're not your typical company where everything needs to be the same. There are certain ballet companies where the corps needs to all look the same, this is what it looks like, and your finger needs to be bent at this point. We're definitely an ensemble, and we definitely dance in unison, but they're all about individuality. We come from different cultures; none of us are the same. You know, there might be two Cubans, but they're not just Cuban, they're something else. Or Puerto Rican, but they're not just Puerto Rican, you know? So, when we're in that space and we're working together, they allow you to make choices that are right for you, which is basically the trust that I'm talking about. They are like, okay, well … you know, sometimes we'd run things and it'd go completely bad and wrong and not any of the corrections were put into it; it's just a disaster. And they'd be like, "You know what? We don't need to run this again. We trust you. We trust that you know what it is because we've seen it, and we don't need to tell you again because you know what it is." So, I think that's a huge thing, because, you know, it's kind of like your family. Your family trusts you the most, and they're like, okay, we know you won't do that again. Because we trust you. That's kind of how I feel like it relates in Ballet Hispánico.

NM: Can you think of a piece that you were in—either the role, or the ballet, or the evening—where the works correlated to the social climate and it meant something more because of that?
    SC: There's been one piece that we're working on now that maybe isn't so much socially in my culture but definitely personal. It's personal, as in I relate very much in my personal life to what … so, the story of Carmen. We're doing that piece by Gustavo Ramirez Sansano; he choreographed the work *Carmen*, a more contemporary version. And when we first did it, I actually wasn't even in it because I was in BH Dos, but they brought it back, and this year, luckily and thankfully, I get to be Carmen.

NM: Congratulations!

SC: Thank you. It's an achievement. Ever since I saw the role, I was like, that's the role I want to do. How can I get there?

NM: That's awesome.

SC: But, yeah, I don't know, it really hits home. Obviously, I'm not murdered or anything, but, you know, Don José comes in and falls in love with Carmen and she falls in love with someone else, and she gets killed at the end. I mean, obviously I'm dead, but that was a big … it hits really close to home for me because I've been through something like that, where you're kind of torn between these two lovers and how do you make this conscious decision … yeah.

Other than that, we've been getting more abstract for certain things. I think it's hard for me to relate to a lot of the pieces, only because some of them are really specific and narrowed towards, like, Mexican-Americans, but I guess Michelle Manzanales did a piece called *Con Brazo Abiertos*, which is basically a battle of being an American … she's Mexican. Her family is Mexican. They speak Spanish, but she says that she was kind of torn between these two worlds when she grew up in Houston, Texas, as well, so "When I was in Texas, I was the really ethnic girl. But then when I went to Mexico, I was the gringo." You know, everyone was like, "You don't speak Spanish, you speak like a white girl"; there's this kind of torn reality. She's like, well, where do I fit in? I don't fit in anywhere. I don't know if I belong here. And I think I related to that a little bit in the way of how I grew up. I mean, we both grew up in Houston, Texas. Although it's a very diverse city, where we grew up is very suburban. So, the greater area of Houston is supersuburban.

I guess I never really realized…. I always thought of myself as a white girl, you know, because I grew up around all these other people who, I mean, didn't look the same, but they all come from the same kind of mentality. And then I would go to an event and they'd be like, "You're super exotic. You're really ethnic." And I'm like, "Really? You think so?" I just never saw it; I was blind to it. And then I went to the performing arts high school downtown. No one batted an eyelash, because we were all Jewish and white and Black and Asian, you know, we're all different kinds of cultures. And I just never really understood why…. I felt really off. Sometimes people would say really offensive things, like "Oh, those Japs in World War II," and I was like, do people not know that that's really offensive, or do they not realize that I am Asian? They notice it sometimes and wouldn't notice it other times when they decided to disregard it. So, I started to brush things off like that, until recently when we did this piece, and it was like, you can't just let people slide and say things like that. You know, if I were to say something derogatory about white people, they'd probably get on me immediately and say, "You can't say that." I related to her piece in that way, because it's hard growing up in … I don't want to say white America, because it's not, but in the area I grew up in, it was. So, I think it was difficult growing up there. No one ever treated me mean or awkward, but I always felt a little out of place. I didn't feel like everyone else, you know? And that's kind of what her piece portrays.

NM: Was that amplified in ballet, or was that just part of your life?

SC: It was just part of my life. It never really … whenever I went to dance, I could be exactly who I was. You know? And I never felt slighted or different. Actually, when I was in the ballet company.… I was in a youth ballet company in my hometown growing up, and I was Clara. Like, my parents in *Nutcracker* were white as can be and I was an Asian Clara, and I happened to have a Filipino Fritz, so it worked out. We looked like adopted kids, but no one ever…

NM: Questioned it.

SC: Yeah. The director was never like, "Ah, this doesn't work, we need to find …" It was never like that. So, I thought that was always great, because there was like this one world of everyday people that didn't understand. And then there was the dance world, where I felt everyone was accepting of any and everything. It changed a little bit when I got older. When you're younger things happen the way that they happen, along the lines of either you're a good dancer or not. But when you grow up, everyone's a good dancer. So, it starts to become typecasted. Not in a way of you're not good enough, but … at the time I joined, there was an Asian dancer in the company. I think that if I looked any more Asian, maybe I wouldn't be here (as if to say they could only have so many members that did not fit the aesthetic mission of this Latin-focused company). And not because they don't want me to, or they feel like they're denying it, but there's something that they need to fulfill in every company, and there's typecasting, and there's all this other stuff. So, I just kind of feel like it happened at the right time.

NM: One of the things that's been interesting for me in my research is the scarcity of Asians in ballet in terms of, like, American Ballet Theatre, New York City Ballet, and San Francisco Ballet, companies with larger-scale operations. When I've looked for them, I tend to find dancers that are not born in the U.S. And I just found that perplexing and pondered it. I was wondering if you'd ever thought about that or if you felt there was a lack of Asian women as role models. Was it an issue for you?

SC: I've actually noticed it as I got older. So, obviously, everyone's like, you see all these videos on YouTube and everyone's like, "Wow, these Asians are so fierce! They can do crazy things with their bodies and they're so incredible." But I agree, I feel like there's not a lot of Asian women in dance in general. I mean, obviously, I know a few but none that really stand out, that get attention. I never had really … my Asian role model was my mentor.

NM: Peter (Chu)? Who is a man.

SC: Yeah. Who is a man, which … maybe that's why I dance a little bit more masculine. I don't know. I mean, I've definitely been told that. I'm a little more grounded, I'm not as feminine, I have a lot of power in my movement. So, that's also a challenge, making the movement a little more flirty. But, yeah ... I guess, especially in pop culture. It's really beautiful and inspiring that Lauren Anderson, Misty Copeland—although there's still not many of them, they're now on this pedestal. You know, she gets so much attention for who she is, because she's so beautiful and she's worked so hard to get where she is.

NM: There's a lot more (African American ballet dancers) and largely, probably, because of DTH, right?

SC: Yeah, but there's also more in Asian culture, and I feel like ... I mean, Shen Wei is really big here (in New York), or, I guess not really big, not many people know about it; I have always loved that company. But I guess there was never really any role model, you know, how every girl is like "Oh, that girl looks like me and I could aspire to be her." I never had that. And still, to this day, I don't see it often. You know, you look at all these movies; there was one movie that came out with, you know, they wanted all these Polynesians and Hawaiians, and they ended up casting some white girls, and that's how it is. I wish they would be more true, and I wish that there was more attention or more…. I don't know, maybe there just aren't a lot of Asians in dance, or maybe they're just not getting much attention. But I haven't really seen much or had a role model besides Peter.

NM: And I think one of the suggestions that's been made as to cause is an issue of cultural values that steer dancers away from the arts. Obviously, that wasn't your experience.

SC: Meaning, like…?

NM: Family doesn't encourage dance as much as, like, maybe science or STEM or something.

SC: Yeah, I mean, that's absolutely true. I mean, you think about how successful in certain areas—music, engineering, science, math, all of that stuff, they are encouraged to do that, because that's their culture. That's how they grew up; that's what their family went into. And a lot of people, I think, feel the need or the want to do the same thing that their parents and grandparents and generations have done before. I think there's that inspiration of these are my parents, and I'm inspired by them, and I want to do what they did, or something that they support, right?

So, I was really lucky to be supported in that way of doing whatever I wanted to do that was going to make me happy. My parents wanted me to go to college. Hands down, wasn't a question, I was going to college. By the time it rolled around, they were like, "You don't really need college. Unless you're going to go teach at a high school or another college, do you need a BFA?" I can always go back and get a degree in something else. I can always learn, but I can't always dance. And that was something my parents encouraged. When, on the other route, my brother became an engineer like my dad. You know, my sister became a schoolteacher.

NM: You trained a lot in classical ballet. How do you think your relationship to ballet changed as a student and now as a contemporary dancer? How do you relate to ballet differently now than you used to?

SC: I did not like ballet when I was younger. But I knew that it was the foundation, so I had to do it, and I knew where I kind of wanted to go. But actually, the more that I'm doing contemporary work, now more than ever, the more I appreciate my ballet classes. We take ballet everyday. I used to take ballet class at school, ballet at the studio after school, and pointe class. I think now I've fallen in love with ballet even more. So, you need the juxtaposition of the two: really grounded and really lifted. But also, ballet can be really grounded and contemporary can be very lifted. I find that I've fallen more in love with it over the past few years because I need it.

NM: How do company officials, like PR, marketing, maybe the company artistic director, talk about art for the Latino community? I know they do a lot with the community, so how do they frame the work that's being created here in terms of serving the community?

SC: Serving the community has a lot to do—a lot—with our performances. We don't think of them as just performances; we think of them (as) serving our community, which is something that was big with our Apollo season this year, we had themes of migration, immigration, and how people are relating to that to this day. I think that Eduardo (Vilaro) and the staff here like to keep things very human and very real-life. You know, a lot of dance is this fantasy world, like these princesses and fairies and mystical creatures, which is really beautiful because it's an escape from this reality that people fall in love with because they're kind of drawn into this different world.

Lately at Ballet Hispánico, we've been keeping things very real and very raw, and that's something that we bring to the community as well. We go out to California, and I think they've done it in some other areas as well, but we go in, and how do we bring dance to an all-boys incarcerated youth camp?

NM: How do you?

SC: How do you relate? Exactly. I was like, oh my gosh, how are we going to do this? We went in and we talked to them about.... Eduardo does an exercise with them. "Okay, dancers come out. Boys, give me what you want this couple to do. Do you want them to be low, medium, or high?" They're like, "We want them to be low!" "Okay, do you want them to be in a forest, space, or whatever?" So, he kind of gives … it's interactive and he gives them the opportunity. He's like, "Look at that. Now, you just made choreographic choices." And so, now we're dancing in the choices that they made. This is a very specific case in what we do community-wise, but it gives them some worth, these kids who have been in whatever situation that they've been caught in and what they did, and they now get to be a choreographer. And they get to experience other things, to know that dance is enjoyment. They had a lot of fun. You know, these boys, they come in sitting like this [crossing arms with a mean or blank expression on her face] and we leave with them smiling and excited. You didn't think that these boys wanted to dance—but they do.

NM: I think you might have answered the next questions in a way, but if you want to say any more about them…. Dance is competitive, so you compete all the time. But, did you ever feel there was an issue around race, where you had to be better than white dancers, students?

SC: I guess I'm just really competitive in general, so I think maybe yes, in different ways. But actually, I felt it more, which may seem interesting, I felt it more at Ailey. I felt like I had to be competitive with the other Black people that I was surrounded by. Only because that's the school that I went to. It could have been different if I went to SUNY Purchase or NYU (New York University) or Marymount. You know, just depending on how it was.

NM: Sure. But you were the different person, and so you had to … establish your value.

SC: Yeah, so I had to (demonstrate) … what makes me unique, what can I do to stand out. Not that I'm not a great dancer, but how can I get them to want me? Same thing here.

NM: Right. Now, do you feel that you've been color-cast at times because of your ethnicity?

SC: Yeah.

NM: Because your ethnic background played a role in your work, your being hired.

SC: Yeah.

NM: Would you say that that happened on more than one occasion, or would that be an isolated incident?

SC: I wouldn't say that it denied me work.

NM: No, I mean, got you work or denied you work, either way.

SC: I think that I've definitely been—people view Asian women, I think they sexualize them in a way. Because we have almond-shaped eyes and we're kind of this like … this is what I've perceived over the years. People scoff or laugh at it, but I feel like Asians have been kind of sexualized in this sexy, innocent, sultry type of way. And I think that I've been cast in certain things because of that, absolutely.

NM: Even though that's not true to your character, as you've already described.

SC: Yeah, I'm more like, haah! You know, ready to fight.

NM: I know that you've trained in a lot of places: Ailey, Lines, Complexions, all led by African American artists. And some having more full casts than others. How important is it to you at this time in your life to be in a company with people of Color? Is it just, I want to be dancing and I want to be working? Or is there a draw to be around people of Color?

SC: I don't know. I think maybe there is a subconscious, or maybe it's just what I'm interested in, you know, those companies … because I've always been a mover.

Shelby Colona (photograph by Lee Grumbs Photography; courtesy Shelby Colona).

When I chose to go to the summer program for Lines, I wanted to go there because I loved the way they did ballet, because it wasn't like your Sugar Plum Fairy. You know what I mean? Same with Complexions. More contemporary, sliding on pointe, doing … what everyone is trying to do now. You know, they're trying to add that into their repertory. I find … there's just a different kind of passion and a different way that some of these ethnic companies operate. And I think that there's a part of me that relates to them, and that's why I'm so drawn to them.

NM: It's not an accident.

SC: Yeah, I mean, it's just the feeling that I get. They understand what I understand. And we can all relate to each other, because we're all kind of in the same storybook. Different chapters, but same book. I felt the same way about Cedar Lake … I mean, that is a company that I wanted to be a part of really bad. Very culturally diverse, so many different choreographers, and I was attracted to that too. There's something about the companies that stick to their true self and their original mission that I think is really inspiring.

Shelby Colona (photograph by James Diaz Photography; courtesy Shelby Colona).

With Ailey, although not all the Ailey classics are my favorites, and I think everyone has their own opinion, but I love that they're still doing Alvin's original work. On top of it, they're adding in this new European flair. But they still have this mission of here's where we started, this is where we're going, but we're not forgetting where we came from. Same here. We're doing flamenco-based pieces, we have like four of them, but they're more contemporary. So, we have *Bury Me Standing* from the '80s, and then we have *Linea Recta* from 2016. You know, so they're maintaining the culture. They're maintaining it and preserving it, which I think is really exciting, and you don't see that everywhere.

NM: Awesome. Shelby, that's all I have. Thank you so much!
    SC: Of course! I hope I gave you something to write about.

Shelby Colona Glossary

> Brief bio-notes of artists and places mentioned in the chapter. This is not intended to be comprehensive but instead to offer a small amount of information to spark more thorough research if readers are interested.

Alonzo King Lines Ballet—Contemporary dance company, founded by artistic director Alonzo King in 1982.

Alvin Ailey American Dance Theater—Internationally recognized dance company founded by Alvin Ailey in 1958, "using the beauty and humanity of the African-American heritage and other cultures to unite people of all races, ages and backgrounds" (Ailey website).

Anderson, Lauren—First African American principal dancer with a mainstream ballet company in the United States, Houston Ballet.

Ballet Hispánico—Latinx/Latine/Hispanic cultural organization founded by Tina Ramirez in 1970.

Cedar Lake Contemporary Ballet—Founded in 2003 by Nancy Walton Laurie. The company closed in 2015.

Chu, Peter—Dance teacher, affiliated with the Broadway Dance Center and the University of Southern California Glorya Kaufman School of Dance.

Complexions Contemporary Ballet—Founded in 1994 by choreographers Dwight Rhoden and Desmond Richardson.

Copeland, Misty—Became the first African American female principal dancer with the American Ballet Theatre in 2015.

Kidd Pivot—Contemporary Dance Company based in Canada.

Manzanales, Michelle—Ballet Hispánico, director of the school.

Nai-Ni Chen—Dance company led by an Asian American woman, Nai-Ni Chen, with a mission to provide innovative cultural dance performance. Chen died in 2021.

Ochoa, Annabelle Lopez—Belgian-born choreographer. Director of the Contemporary Classical Summer Program of the School at Jacob's Pillow.

Pite, Crystal—Canadian choreographer.

Sansano, Gustavo Ramirez—Choreographer. Former artistic director of the Chicago-based Latino-focused contemporary dance company Luna Negra Dance Theater.

Shen Yun—Classical Chinese dance and music company.

Sugar Plum Fairy—Featured principal female role in the *Nutcracker* ballet.

Verdecia, Melissa—Former dancer with Ballet Hispánico.

Vilaro, Eduardo—Artistic director and CEO of Ballet Hispánico.

Villeneuve, Nicholas—Canadian-born dancer for Ballet Hispánico.

Wei, Shen—China-born director and choreographer. Founded Shen Wei Dance Arts in 2000.

Monike Cristina

Affiliations: Cia Estável de Dança and Joburg Ballet (2016–present)
Country of birth: Brazil
Current residence: Johannesburg, South Africa
Age at time of interview: 26

Excerpts from March 10, 2017, interview with Monike Cristina, in person. This interview was conducted at the Joburg Ballet in Johannesburg, South Africa. The

Monike Cristina in *Don Quixote* (photograph by Lauge Sorensen; courtesy Joburg Ballet).

interview was in person, but video recording was not permitted by the company. I was allowed to record the interview by audio device. Translator Michal Lee was present and translated the questions to Monike and her responses back to me. One limitation of this interview was the language barrier that impacted the extent that Monike and I were able to develop a connection in a short amount of time. I got the sense that the location of the interview, right outside rehearsal studios between rehearsals, arranged by the company, did not put Monike at ease, although she was pleasant and willing to interview with me.

NM: Can you tell me about how you began dancing?

MC: I started when I was six years old, in my city. I am from Piracicaba, in São Paulo.

This passion I have for dancing comes from my childhood, because my grandfather used to listen to classical music; he would put me to sleep with it. My grandmother used to sing (*música erudita* in Portuguese) just classical music. So, this comes from family; my mom danced for a while, my uncle and my aunt. And then after a while, I went to dance in São Paulo, the capital of the state.

NM: Is classical music the typical genre or unusual where you are from?

MC: No, it's not typical. But for my family, yes, it was always like this.

NM: Where in Brazil did you study ballet?

MC: I started in a school called Criação Ballet (Ballet Creation). After that I went to the capital, in São Paulo, and then I danced in a school that is called Eda.

NM: Is the Joburg Ballet the first company you've worked with?

MC: No, I started my professional work at Eda.

NM: And how old were you?

MC: I was 16. I traveled for dance a lot. I went to Berlin in Germany for a competition. After Berlin, I went to New York City Ballet for another competition, YAGP (Youth America Grand Prix, a large student ballet competition). And then I went to the Bolshoi—you know Bolshoi—because, in Brazil we have the Bolshoi. I was dancing professionally with the Bolshoi company. While I was with the Bolshoi, I went to Switzerland, then Zurich, Russia, and Ukraine. After all that, I came here (Johannesburg). I have danced in a lot of places.

NM: How accessible is ballet for a Brazilian young girl? Can anyone take ballet?

MC: It's complicated. But when you want that for your life, you must work for it. It's complicated because you have to pay a lot (for classes); it's not for everyone. You have to be lucky to have a person who likes you a lot, who works with you, who helps you actually become a professional. So, it's not supereasy, even worse when you are Black. When I started in this career, there were no Black girls; it was superhard. There were a few, but you could see that they were afraid to pursue ballet. And they would see that there were others with way more (material things); they had better dresses, better dance shoes, better everything.

NM: Was the challenge race or economic standing?

MC: I think both, because if you are white and you have no money but your physical appearance is for ballet, there is a little more access. The physical appearance of a Black person does not have as much flexibility, it is a common challenge. They don't have these things that a white body is more likely to have. (White women) also have very beautiful feet, and for the Black women, many have to work harder. So, having that mindset of, that's what I want for my life and I will work for that— you have to have that drive.

NM: Can you talk a little more about the mindset?

MC: Yes, there are a lot of people who have a lot of talent, but they do not want to sacrifice their conditions. We give up on a lot of things. If there are parties, I can't go. I have a girl friend who I could move out of my family house to live with, have more independence, but no, I stay at home to study ballet. These are things, values, that have to come from your upbringing; you have to have discipline to dance ballet. It has to be something that you want very much, because it's a very hard job.

NM: Have you ever experienced discrimination because you are Black?

MC: Yes, I did, I went through some problems. Because when you are at a school, you must pay to take a class; people are supposed to treat you like everyone else. But when you are walking towards a professional career, it's not always fair.

For example, one thing that happened to me, I went to audition at a specific place. And some people would discourage me: "No, look at me (with lighter skin), I tried to audition at that place, and I didn't get in; these people are very strict." And I was like, "Okay." Then I went there, auditioned, and passed. Every time people told me it wasn't for me, I would go there, and I would get it. And I passed.

I was a ballerina in Russia! A Russian ballet master went to Brazil and did an audition with everyone and told me "I came to Brazil to find a Black dancer, and I found her."

NM: Can you tell me about a performance experience that was very special to you or a character role you played that was most special to you?

MC: The best role I played? I think when I danced in *Swan Lake*, the complete piece, the white and black swan, with a rebooting made by a Cuban choreographer, Laura Alonso, in São Paulo.

The daughter of Alicia and Fernando Alonso, she is famous all over the world.

NM: Why is it your favorite? What about the role is special?

MC: Because it was a summer festival that happened every year in Brazil, and they did an audition to choose the person who would play the main role, who would be part of the corps, and who would be the soloist. I did that audition, and I was chosen to be the main swan. So, I did the black and the white swan. I did the whole ballet, the four acts.

NM: Can you tell me about the training schools in Brazil and the training that you received? Is it the same as when you take class here in Johannesburg? Or is there a different approach or energy?

MC: I think it's different, starting with the weather. Because for me at least, here in Johannesburg is more humid. So, when I came to dance here, it was very hard. When I am taking classes, I can't feel my feet because there's no oxygen. So, I have to do everything smaller, slower. I can't do everything with full energy. It's different. It's good here, but I think South Africans wouldn't be able to handle the weather in Brazil because of the weather, because of the humidity here. In Brazil our schools are very advanced. In Brazil we have 10-year-old kids who already do everything, and that's normal; that's the way we work.

NM: Do you prefer working in your home country of Brazil?

MC: I like it here too, I like it. I think both places are good, because people have different ways of thinking. Both ways provide results. And we have a company in Brazil too. I think it's because here, these people have all the structure (resources), like a good studio.

NM: What things do they have here that people don't have in your home country?

MC: A good company, like this one, with infrastructure and with everything. Because with the economic crisis (in Brazil), a lot of companies in Brazil had to close, so we have less companies. We have the big companies like São Paulo Companhia de Dança and the Theatro Municipal do Rio de Janeiro. There are also people who are getting paid like in São Paulo or doing a tour in Europe, and they are fine.

But there are other smaller companies that are closing down because they have no money. Dancers are not receiving their payments because of the economic crisis. People try to fight, they protest, they talk to the mayor, the president. They try to do things. They actually want to dance, to be part of a company.

NM: So, what are the biggest challenges for you as a dancer?

MC: Well, my parents are divorced. Since I started with ballet, it was just me, my mom, and my grandfather who always helped us. And when I started to want to do ballet, it was a hard time, because I am from the countryside, not from the big city, a small city, not the capital. Piracicaba is a small town. So, my mom had to work because I was a kid, I couldn't work to help my family to have more money, and ballet is an art that you need a lot of money. So, when I told my mom that I wanted that for my life, she was very happy but worried about costs, but she wouldn't tell me, because I was a kid. I was super happy.

So, my mom said, ok, you will do it; you want to be a ballerina, and you will. My mom told me that when she was pregnant, she used to say "If I have a boy, he will be a great soccer player, and if the baby is a girl, she will be a great ballerina." So, when I told her that I wanted to be a ballerina, without her ever sharing that with me, she got scared! Because it was happening. So, she told me, you will be a ballerina; we will do everything. I used to leave my town on Monday, Tuesday, and Friday. From my house I would go to the capital, São Paulo, to take classes; it's a two-and-a-half-hour trip. I would leave my school in my hometown to go the ballet school in São Paulo. I would do rehearsals, classes, and go to competitions as well. Because there were competitions in São Paulo. I would meet directors of companies. So, think about it, my bus tickets from Piracicaba to São Paulo, and then money for the competitions, money for new costumes, money to pay the dancer that would dance with me, and the tuition of the ballet school. Imagine, a single woman having to pay all this money! It was a very difficult moment in our lives.

My dad was from a different town, and we couldn't count on him, and that's

Monike Cristina with Ruan Galdino in *La Traviata* **(photograph by Lauge Sorensen; courtesy Joburg Ballet).**

why I don't talk to him. Now I don't even know how he is. He is alive but I don't talk to him.

NM: And today? How is your career now?

  MC: Now we are fine. Now my mom has a better job, she is studying again, she is pursuing a career as a psychotherapist, she is with a new husband who is very nice to me and helps me. Now I have new sister; she is three and also studies ballet. My mom's husband is a journalist; they have good jobs, so things now are great.

  And for me, things are much better. Now I have my own money, my work. And I can help my mom if she needs.

NM: Is racism a problem for ballet dancers?

  MC: Here? I think Johannesburg is better than Brazil. I think in Brazil we have

Monike Cristina in *Raymonda*. Men left to right, Thabang Mabaso, Kristof Skhosana, Mahlatse Sachane, and Miles Carrot. Women left to right, Alice le Roux, Erica Vadelka, and Savannah Ireland (photograph by Lauge Sorensen; courtesy Joburg Ballet).

more problems than here. Here it's easier. In Brazil I had problems. But since now I have a name and people know me, when I arrive in Brazil, it's a different thing. People talk to me as if I was from a different planet; it's funny.

NM: Do you think you've ever been color-cast?

MC: I don't think so. I did a gypsy in *La Traviata*. That is a role with a Spanish mother, but I don't think it's because I am Black.

NM: In the States, a lot of Black students are told that you have to be twice as good as white students to get the same part, to get the job. Is that something you have ever experienced?

MC: I think that's something that comes from your house. Some Black people are told it's not enough to be just good, you have to be good and very smart, because you will go through situations, things, that will not please you. But you have to pretend that you didn't go through those situations, because if you argue, you will lose your mind; you won't be right anymore. I think things are better now. I think they speak their minds more, question more things. Before it was different, but now it's better, way better.

NM: How is ballet in Brazil?

MC: The U.S. appreciates the arts, but in Brazil it's different. In Brazil everything is about sports—soccer and carnival. It's very hard for me to answer. It's a lot of struggle, because people don't recognize it. People come to ask me "What do you do for living?" And I answer, I dance. And then they ask, "But what do you actually do, your work?" And I say this is my job. And people say, "Dancing is your job?" And I say, yes, I am a professional dancer; I studied for it, I have a diploma. Because in Brazil you are someone else's employee or you are the boss. That's why I say ballet, or any other type of dance in Brazil, is very hard.

NM: Is ballet perceived as Eurocentric in Brazil?

MC: It's very complicated for you to say (the form is Eurocentric). I studied ballet my whole life. I gave up a lot of things. I missed out on a lot of things in order to be able to say that I am a professional ballet dancer. This is actually my life, my work.

NM: Okay, my last question. What advice was given to you that helped you persevere to where you are that you might share with future students?

MC: Never let people tell you what to do, because what's happening in my life, it can be different from what's happening in yours. So, always have tranquility in your mind and heart, and do your job. Always be nice to yourself—a lot of discipline, a lot of work of course, always.

Monike Cristina Glossary

Brief bio-notes of artists and places mentioned in the chapter. This is not intended to be comprehensive but instead to offer a small amount of information to spark more thorough research if readers are interested.

Alonso, Alicia—Cuban-born prima ballerina. Cofounder of the National Ballet of Cuba and the Cuban National Ballet School in the late 10940s. Danced with Ballet Russe de Monte Carlo, founding member of Ballet Theater (later to be named American Ballet Theatre), and appeared in several Broadway musicals. Suffered from visual impairment for most of her career. Alicia Alonso died in 2019.

Alonso, Fernando—Cuban-born ballet dancer. Cofounder of the National Ballet of Cuba and the Cuban National Ballet School. Performed with Mordkin Ballet, Lincoln Kirsten's Ballet Caravan, and Ballet Theater (later to be named the American Ballet Theater) and danced in several Broadway musicals. Fernando Alonso died in 2013.

Alonso, Laura—Daughter of Fernando and Alicia Alonso. Teacher, coach, and restager for classical ballets. Member of the Cuban National Ballet for 25 years and artistic adviser for the Canton Ballet since 1990.

Bolshi Theater School in Brazil—Affiliate school of Bolshoi Moscow, founded in 2000.

São Paulo Companhia de Dança—Dance company created by the government of São Paulo, Brazil, in 2008.

Youth American Grand Prix—International student ballet competition.

Yinet Fernandez

Past affiliations: Nacional Ballet de Cuba (2008–2014)
Current affiliation: Dance Theatre of Harlem (2017–present)

Country of birth: Cuba
Current residence: New York, New York
Age at time of interview: 30

Excerpts from a June 29, 2019, interview with Yinet Fernandez, in person, at a public library conference room in Queens, New York. I interviewed Yinet in the summer of 2019 when she was on a seasonal break from the company, and we found the library in her area to be a good meeting place. Yinet seemed excited to share with me and a little nervous that her English would not be able to meet the moment. We had a good time together, and I found her ability to communicate excellent.

NM: Tell me about how you began dancing.

Yinet Fernandez (photograph by Steven Vandervelden, Vandy Photography; courtesy Yinet Fernandez).

YF: Well, my mom took me one day. She said, "Hey, let's go to this place. Everybody says you can have fun there." I said, "Okay." I was a little chubby, so she wanted me to, you know [smiling], to get out my energy. She took me to a dance school. I started with Flamenco. I was six years old. So, that's how I started, and I loved it. After that, the teacher came to my mother and said, "She actually has a natural facility. Have a conversation with Yinet and see if she likes it." My mom came to me and asked me "Do you want to take dance classes two days a week?" I was like, "Oh, yeah!" It was just an hour after school. We started like that. And then it got harder and harder [smiling]. Yeah, that was my experience.

NM: And where did you begin?

YF: My first school was ProDanza. It was very close to my home in Cuba, in Havana. It was in Marianao, (a borough of) Havana. The teachers were very good.

NM: How long before you started dancing at the Cuban National Ballet School?

YF: I started with the National School when I was nine years old.

NM: Three years at the first school?

YF: Yeah [nodding].

NM: How long were you at the National School? Can you talk a little bit about your training there?

YF: Well, it was great, but it was very hard. First of all, I lived far away from the school. I had to wake up at 5 a.m. And then I had to take the bus to get to the school.

NM: You said it was very hard. What do you mean when you say it was hard? Do you mean physically, mentally, socially?

YF: It was physically and mentally hard, not socially. We started with ballet class from 7 a.m. to 9 a.m., two hours, and the exercise was like ... it's part of the Cuban training, it's like that. But for a nine-year-old girl, at least for me, it was really hard. At that time, they had different schedules. For example, one group of the girls would go in the morning, like 7 a.m. to 1 p.m., for everything like ballet, conditioning, music, French, everything like that. Then after that they would go to the normal school until 4 or 5 p.m. Like math, Spanish—regular classes. But for me, I started first with the regular classes and then I would go from 4 p.m. to 9:45 p.m. with ballet, repertoire, and the French. So, I would get home at 11 p.m. every night.

NM: At nine years old?

YF: Nine years old. And in Cuba it's very different. It's not like here; it's not like you're done with your classes and you get in your car with AC. It's a developing country; you have to wait for the bus two hours.

NM: I thought the National Ballet School is a boarding school.

YF: You stay there if your home is far away. But if you live in Havana, you have to go home.

NM: So that's another two hours?

YF: Two hours not because it was far, two hours because of the transportation. It was like two hours waiting. My mom was so smart, because she had a schedule for the buses. She would be like, "Okay, you finish at 9:45 p.m., so at 10:15 p.m. the bus is coming, so you have to hurry up."

And the line for the bus was so long, because everybody was waiting. Some of the moms would just wait in the line. My mom would come get me and my friend, and we would catch the bus all together. Then we had to get up at 5 a.m. When you're nine years old you just want to watch cartoons and play. I didn't have time for all that. The classes were hard because we were taking French, music, but it was one of the best times of my life because I had so many friends, and we were together all the time, 7 a.m. 'til 9 p.m. They were my family.

NM: And then the weekends you have for your family?

YF: Yeah.

NM: And how long were you in the school?

YF: For five years elementary school, and then three years like high school/college.

NM: But still at the National Ballet School.

YF: At that time, the elementary school was in one part of Havana and the high school was in another part—different locations. But now they are together, in the same building.

NM: Does it feed into apprenticeship and company, or do you have to leave the school for employment? When you are ready to become professional...

YF: After that, you take a test, like an audition, to select the people they actually want from the school, and they got me like that. I went to the audition, and I was selected to start with them.

NM: So, you auditioned and then you went into the company.

YF: Uh, huh, at that time they took me for like six months, temporary ... to see how I fit in the company.

NM: How did you like it?

YF: It was very hard. It was very hard but also so inspiring, because when you come from school and you see actual professional dancers, you see all the principals that you used go to the theater to see, and now they're right there rehearsing in front of you.

One of my favorite principals was Yolanda Correa. She lives in Europe now, but she was my favorite at the time, and I used to go to every rehearsal and just sit there ... so I could learn how she moved. But it was hard because I didn't know if after that they were going to take me. I would worry. "What am I going to do if they don't?" It was...

NM: Stressful?

YF: Yeah. There is only one national company in Cuba. It's not like I can go to another country.

NM: Then what did you do?

YF: Then they took me. And I stayed there for six and a half years.

NM: And then?

YF: Then I went to Puerto Rico on tour, and I left the company. I stayed with my friends in Puerto Rico.

NM: How was that? What was that day like?

YF: Oh, it was very bad, it was so bad. I was scared. I was sad. I didn't cry or anything. At first, I didn't realize it.

NM: Did you know you were going to leave Cuba and the company when you went to Puerto Rico?

YF: Yes. I talked to my parents first. I said, "I can't do this anymore (dance for the National Ballet of Cuba). I want a change for my life."

NM: Did you have a plan, or did you just say "I'm not going to do this?"

YF: Well, my best friends, they left Cuba before me, like two years before I left. But somehow they found out that the company was going to Puerto Rico, and they called me, and they were like, "Hey you're going to stay with us here." I never had a personal contact there before, a place where I could actually stay in their house. If you don't have papers you can't work, because you have to stay (in Puerto Rico) at least six months. Not everybody will just let you stay there in their house. But (her friends who had left previously) actually called me from Puerto Rico and said, "You're going to stay with us here, right?" I said, "I have no plans of doing that. I don't know." They said, "No, you have to, we're asking you, but we're not asking you, we're telling you what you have to do."

NM: And were they in the company and had left? That's how you knew them; they were dancers.
    YF: Yeah.

NM: And they were dancing in Puerto Rico?
    YF: Yeah. I was like, "Okay."

NM: And were they asking you to leave Cuba or the company?
    YF: It was both. To be honest, at that time in the company I didn't see a lot of fair things happening, at least to me. A lot of things happened that I just didn't understand. When you have a friend, you know you are always going to do stuff with that friend. You (as a director) are going to take that friend on tour instead of the person you should take, you know what I mean? That kind of stuff (favoritism). Or the roles; they (directors) were not going to cast you in the best roles because of the way you look, or they don't like you. If the director or the ballet master didn't like you at the time, there's pretty much nothing you can do about it. At that time a lot of bad things were happening, so I was like, obviously I've been here for six years, and there are no more opportunities for me. And I have to do something, because they're not going to do it for me. I have to make a change for myself; for me that was to leave the country.

NM: So, you go to Puerto Rico, and you don't tell the company you're leaving until you get there, and then what happened?
    YF: My best friends didn't care. They had already left Cuba, so they showed up at the hotel (I was staying with the company in Puerto Rico). I had done all my shows, so I went to the person who has all of our passports.

NM: For the company.
    YF: For the company. She always kept our passports ... we (company members) don't have our stuff (passports).... I went to her room and I asked her for my passport. Because it's illegal for them to withhold your passport when you're outside of Cuba. They have to give your passport to you. You're free, you know; it's not Cuba anymore.
    She was not mad; she was very concerned. Because I had always been very like ... disciplined in my classes, and I would never disrespect anybody. So, she was in shock a little bit. She didn't expect that from me at all. She said, "Are you sure you

want to do this?" I said, "I'm not sure, but I'm gonna do it." Because I didn't know what was coming next, right? So, I asked her for my passport. A lot of my friends were crying. Because it was like seven of us who left the company that day. Yeah, it was not just me. I didn't say goodbye to the ballet master, absolutely not; I just said goodbye to my friends.

NM: How many people were in the company touring, with seven leaving?
YF: Like 45; it was a big company at that time.

NM: Now, these seven people can't all stay with your friends, so everybody had some place?
YF: Different places. One of my friends went to Miami with her family, like four dancers went with her. I think I was the only one that actually stayed in Puerto Rico for six months. Then I went to Miami, and I stayed in Miami for six months, and then I came here (to New York).

NM: Now, when you were in Miami and in Puerto Rico, 'cause now it's a year, were you dancing every day still or taking class?
YF: I was dancing in Puerto Rico for the six months, but then I was not dancing in Miami. It was the worst time of my life, so bad.

NM: Why?
YF: I was working at a bakery. I had to wake up at 4 a.m. I didn't even know how…. I did know how to cook, but not like for a bakery. I had no idea. My whole life I had only known tights, pointe shoes, and tutus. And then I was in this bakery, hat on my head, and sneakers, frying croquettes and *pastelito*—because in Miami everything is like Cuban desserts and… I was like, "What am I doing?" This was not what I wanted for my life, you know, because…

NM: You thought you were leaving Cuba for something better.
YF: Exactly. So I couldn't believe I was in Miami losing all my muscles. I couldn't take class.

NM: Was Miami Ballet not an option?
YF: I was not in shape. I sprained my ankle in Puerto Rico…. I was injured. Miami City Ballet was like Balanchine, my training's Cuban training, classical … ballet … it's not the same. I stayed in Miami for six months; it was the worst experience so far. And then I came here (New York).

NM: What brought you here?
YF: I had a boyfriend, and he got a contract here….

NM: He was dancing?
YF: He got a contract with Ballet Hispánico. And I was like, "Well, yeah, let's go. It's your dream, right?" I didn't have anything (in New York), no job, nothing. But he was gonna work, so maybe I could start, you know. Then we came here, and

then I met Pedro Ruiz and Caridad (Martinez), and I started training with them. They trained me for a year and a half. And I saw the posting for the DTH audition. I went; they didn't take me [giggles] at the audition. After that I started dancing at the Brooklyn Ballet. I was teaching around. I was better, I was much better, because I was doing something, using my skills, using the knowledge I had at least. More than working in a bakery, you know. I was dancing, not full-time but part-time. Then I saw another audition with DTH, and I sent all my stuff. They responded and said, "Come this day." It was a private audition, four hours, by myself.

NM: So, nobody else was auditioning for four hours?

YF: And at that time my English was so bad; I didn't understand a word. I would just say "yes," but I actually didn't understand.

NM: And now how long have you been with the company?

YF: This is going to be my third season (in 2019).

NM: What is it like being a Latina in a Black ballet company? Do you feel your Latinness?

YF: Oh, I always have my Latinness with me; that's 99 to 100 percent. To me, to be honest, in the beginning I was very confused, more because it's a very similar culture to my Cuban culture, but it's not the same. So, sometimes I would get a little bit lost, and I wouldn't understand what was going on. But they took me, they were open to me, to get to know me, and just listen to my story and see me.

NM: Does anyone in the company speak Spanish?

YF: Crystal (Serrano), she speaks Spanish.

NM: It helps.

YF: In the beginning, it was really hard because I didn't understand what they were saying. I didn't talk at all for three months. And people had to come and talk to me. But actually now it's better because they're forcing me to try to speak better English, and I try to speak more English and understand more. They push me to get better; it's a good thing.

NM: DTH has a huge legacy around the African American experience and putting African American dancers forward. Although they're very open, do you think of it as a place open to all dancers?

YF: … If you want to dance with DTH, you have to have … not rhythm … but something more than just classical ballet. You cannot be the ballerina all the time, because I'm the ballerina all the time and I have to push myself to do something else because that's what they are, DTH.

NM: There's a Black aesthetic sometimes called upon.

YF: Yeah, yeah, yeah, there's definitely something more than just pointe shoes and tutus.

NM: When you look back and you say "They (DTH) pushed me," what do you feel like is your biggest achievement in those three years? What do you feel really accomplished about? Is there a role or a dance that now feels comfortable but at first was not?

YF: Oh, have you seen *Change*? It's a modern piece in pointe shoes, and I never took modern before in my life. So, I remember the first week, or more like the second week, we started learning the steps, learning the sequence, and I was like "I'm not gonna be … they're gonna fire me, I'm not going be able to do it." And they put me in the first cast. We were going to Europe, and Ingrid (Silva), one of the dancers, couldn't go, so I was put in for first (cast).… I was like "I'm gonna get fired this week, after just two weeks being here. I can't do this." It was so bad.

NM: Do you feel good in it now?

YF: After like four months of doing it, I felt really good. And now I love it; I ask them to put me in. Yeah.

NM: Dougla?

YF: *Dougla* was okay for me, because I did *Change* first [giggles]. So, *Dougla* was like "I got this." *Dougla*, I remember that we were learning the cell phone turn (informed by current vernacular dance), because Mr. (Robert) Garland (the choreographer) was taking steps from street and social dancing and then fusing with ballet on pointe shoes. I was like "What is this? Not what I learned in school on Cuba, that's for sure." I couldn't even learn the combination. I had to go to my room and practice by myself with the video for like an hour to learn the combination. I was like "Oh my God, this is so hard." Yeah, it was really hard for me. It was harder than doing, I don't know, *Sleeping Beauty* or *Nutcracker*.

NM: What's your favorite role?

YF: My favorite role? I think *Vessels*—have you seen it?—with the red … that one, yeah, for sure.

NM: Why?

YF: I think 80 percent is the music. The music is so beautiful; it's very beautiful. It's like a classic; you can show your lines, and you can just actually dance and live every moment. I really like it.

NM: When I'm reading the bios of a lot of the Latina dancers in a lot of mainstream ballet companies, I notice that these dancers are often not from the U.S. What do you think are some of the barriers to seeing more Latina dancer from the U.S. dancing, because the number of them is few, unlike in Cuba where there is a more concentrated population of Latinx ballet dancers.

YF: I feel like it's the way they cultivate dancers. In Cuba, if you're going to be a dancer, you're going to be a professional dancer. And here it's more like "Ah, let's put her in ballet class because she'll look cute with her tutu, but she's actually going to be

Yinet Fernandez (photograph by Steven Vandervelden, Vandy Photography; courtesy Yinet Fernandez).

a doctor." You know what I mean? I feel like dancing here seems more like a game for little kids, like not actually a professional course.

NM: Something to do on the side.
YF: Yeah, something to do after school.

NM: It's not the substance of children's study?
YF: Yeah.

NM: And that comes from the parents or the community? Do their teachers not look at them and see promise?
YF: I feel like it comes from parents, the teachers. Look at your system.

NM: Everything?
YF: Everything.

NM: Do you see a difference between light-skinned dancers and darker-skinned dancers in casting and opportunities? Do you see it in the Black community or the Latin community?
YF: I actually … don't know.

NM: Okay.
YF: I don't know. I have always heard that if you are very dark skinned you have to be very good. They always said that. And I guess there's something behind that, you know, that phrase. Here I don't have that much experience with the Latino community.

NM: How do you feel about ballet being described as a white dance or Eurocentric? Do you see it as a Eurocentric dance form?
YF: I don't see it that way. In Cuba everybody's Brown. I mean, there's white people, but they are Cubans, you know what I mean, and we all do ballet. I don't feel like the dance is actually white; it's more about the training that you have when you were a little kid, you know.

NM: Yes. What's next for you?
YF: What's next for me.… I want to do more classical ballet.

NM: How do you feel about ballet as an art form?
YF: Well, ballet is my life. I'm a very shy person. I don't talk a lot, so for me it's the way I express myself. That's why I dance, because I have to express myself. Instead of actually having—it's hard for me to have a conversation. The person has to come to me and say like, "Hey, this is my name" I will never go to someone and introduce myself, and that happens in general every day. So, to me (ballet) is the way I express myself; it's my life, pretty much.

NM: Can you go back to Cuba and visit your family?
YF: Yes.

NM: *Can they come and visit you?*
　　YF: No. They have to apply for a visa and ... now, I don't know.

NM: *It's complicated?*
　　YF: It's very complicated.

Yinet Fernandez Glossary

Brief bio-notes of artists and places mentioned in the chapter. This is not intended to be comprehensive but instead to offer a small amount of information to spark more thorough research if readers are interested.

Ballet Hispánico—Latinx/Latine/Hispanic cultural organization founded by Tina Ramirez in 1970.
Brooklyn Ballet—Company based in Brooklyn, New York, with a multidisciplinary and multicultural approach to ballet.
Correa, Yolanda—Cuban-born principal dancer with Berlin State Ballet.
Cuban National Ballet School—Established in the 1940s by Alicia Alonso, it is the largest ballet school in the world, with over 3,000 students.
Dance Theatre of Harlem—A dance company and school founded in 1969 by Arthur Mitchell and Karel Shook. Identified vision to expand opportunities for Black dancers to perform ballet and audiences to see Black dancers perform. Described today as a multiethnic ballet company (Dance Theatre of Harlem website).
Garland, Robert—Former principal dancer for Dance Theatre of Harlem. Choreographer who created works for New York City Ballet, Britain's Royal Ballet, and the Oakland Ballet. Dance Theatre of Harlem School director.
Martinez, Caridad—Former principal dancer with Ballet de Nacional de Cuba. Has served as a dance administrator, educator, or both for organizations such as the Ailey School, Ballet Hispánico, the Brooklyn Ballet Conservatory, and the 92nd Street Y Harkness Dance Center.
Miami City Ballet—Founded in 1985 by Toby Lerner Ansin and founding artistic director Edward Villella. The company was built on the repertory of George Balanchine and continues in this tradition today under the artistic leadership of Lourdes Lopez.
ProDanza—Ballet academy in Havana, Cuba.
Ruiz, Pedro—Principal dancer with Ballet Hispánico for 21 years. Has choreographed Joffrey Ballet, Luna Negra, and New Jersey Ballet.
Serrano, Crystal—Dancer with Boston Ballet. Previous affiliated with Dance Theatre of Harlem, Pacific Northwest Ballet, Sacramento Ballet, Organ Ballet Theatre, and Ballet San Antonio.

Kristie Latham

Past affiliations: BalletMet (2013–2022)
Hometown: Bethlehem, Pennsylvania
Current residence: Columbus, Ohio
Age at time of interview: 30 and 31
Current affiliation: KEZU, digital marketing agency (founding director).

Interview note: Less than a year after this interview, Kristie retired from performing and wanted to share about that experience and decision; thus, there are two

Set II—Dancers Who Are Still Performing or Recently Retired

parts to this interview. Part I was conducted in August 2021, and Part II was conducted in June 2022.

Both interviews took place on Zoom, and I got the sense that Kristie enjoyed sharing about her experiences and valued thinking about intersections of race and her dance experiences. This interview is documented in Latham's account of events as she experienced them. Others may have different accounts of the events described herein.

Part I

NM: Can you tell me a little bit about how you began dancing?

KL: I was a very hyperactive child. I think my parents wanted me to be a bit more constructive in where I put my energy, so I was in a lot of different activities. I did gymnastics, soccer, piano, and ballet—you know, after-school activities. One by one I quit everything because I didn't want to do anything but sit at home or play, because we lived

Kristie Latham (photograph by Jennifer Zmuda; courtesy Kristie Latham).

in a neighborhood with a lot of kids my age. I didn't have any interest in learning anything outside of school. Ballet was the last commitment that I was involved in. I wanted to quit doing ballet so badly and (my parents) said, "No, you have to see it through. You wanted to do it. You're going to see it through the school year." And I would lay on the sidewalk outside of my ballet school crying, trying to fight my mom [laughs], and I was hoping she would just give up on the whole thing, so that is how I started.

NM: How old were you?

KL: Maybe seven or eight years old. And somehow, she (my mom) won that battle, and I continued taking classes. I don't think it was until nine or 10 years old, when the directors of the school recognized me for having talent, that I kind of changed my tune. It was like I felt supported and like "Wow, you're promising," and (they gave me) the attention that I was craving, and once that shift happened, I went on pointe, and I really loved dancing. I definitely went on pointe too young [laughs] or much younger than they recommend.

NM: How old were you when you went on pointe?

KL: I was nine [laughs].

NM: What school was that?

KL: It was the Ballet Guild of the Lehigh Valley. It's the Pennsylvania Youth

Ballet now, but the directors are not there anymore; it was Mireille Briane and Oleg Briansky. I had a French and Russian teacher who were married, and he (Briansky) was a superstar in his day. He was partner to Violette Verdy (and Margot Fonteyn and Maria Tallchief); he had an amazing career. They were wonderful teachers.

NM: Can you talk about a bit about why you dance today?

KL: My journey to dancing professionally was a winding road. I went to the Rock School in Philadelphia on full scholarship, and I really struggled my senior year, I think with my identity in general, and there is a toxic nature, I think, in the ballet world. I think a lot of that comes when you hit puberty—how your body changes, how you can't like how it's changing, and how maybe you go from being a really promising dancer to being a damaged dancer because suddenly you are more womanly (fuller than the traditionally accepted extrathin ballet body).

I am a more womanly dancer, and that's why I love Misty Copeland, because she was the first dancer who, not only being a person of Color but a woman, who I was like, "if she can succeed then so can I." (Body image issues were) a big part of why I quit dancing after high school, and I went to University of South Carolina for broadcasting and journalism. I was there for a year. I was superfortunate and didn't realize how fortunate I was at the time. My dad contacted the director of the dance department when I was down there for orientation. She was like, "Let's have her come in and do a class." They gave me a partial scholarship just to perform with their dance program and not to major/minor in dance. I was really fortunate.

Inside of this opportunity, I was the only nonwhite dancer in the first-year dance major cohort, and half Korean, and everyone called me "Sushi." That was my nickname. I felt like I had made the wrong choice of school to really thrive. I didn't feel accepted there, so I left the University of South Carolina. I was like, maybe I want to dance.

NM: People were calling you Sushi in college?

KL: Yes. Not the teachers obviously, no one on the faculty or staff, but my peers called me Sushi. It didn't feel like the right fit, so I moved back home with my parents. And I decided that I wanted to go try dancing again.

I visited my best friend in Pittsburgh, and I went and saw Pittsburgh Ballet Theater do *In the Upper Room* and *Light/The Holocaust & Humanity Project*. I was so moved by those ballets and how much I missed just being an artist and dancing. It inspired me to rediscover my "why." There are always going to be outside factors that are outside of your control that can take away your motivation, but I needed to recenter myself and do it for me and not for the way others perceive me as an artist. So, I ended up moving back home and working at the mall for like six months, and I didn't dance [laughs], and so then I decided that I actually needed to find a program where I didn't feel so comfortable. I ended up going to Pittsburgh Ballet Theater Graduate Program, and I was there for six months, and I was like "you know what, like I really want to do this." Then I was in it 110 percent and then auditioned for years and years and years and didn't find the right fit until I ended up at BalletMet. I want to say I spent like four years auditioning and not landing in the right place [laughs].

NM: Can you tell me how you describe your ethnicity?

KL: I'm half Korean.... My dad met my mom when he was stationed in Korea. It was really difficult for my mom when she moved to this country. My mom is Korean. Her initial experience in the U.S. was not very accepting of her being Korean [laughs]. So, much of my childhood was trying to be as white as possible, so my mom made the decision not to teach my sisters and me Korean because she felt like if we identified more as Korean that people wouldn't be accepting. I think that was her idea; obviously if I wasn't Korean, people would be more accepting of her and us as her children. So, when I was 11 years old my mom gave me blond highlights. She highlighted all my hair to make me, you know, be more white-presenting and things like that, so we didn't really know much about her culture, her background, until I was in high school. Even now I'm having conversations with her about wanting to go to Korea together.

NM: So, when you're 10 and you get blond highlights, how do you feel about that experience?

KL: I think especially this year, I am seeing a lot of Asian Americans, women especially, talk about that and even the characters that we see in movies growing up....

NM: But were you happy when it happened? Were you like "what's going on?"

KL: Yes, because I wanted that as well. Because I think the beauty standards to me was to be more white.

NM: I get that. My mom is white [laughs].

KL: [laughs] Okay.

NM: Similar. Biracial people have lots in common.

KL: Riiiiight. It's confusing learning how to celebrate all the parts of yourself.

NM: Well, it's hard enough to be in a white-dominated culture; it can be even harder to not want to be included in that.

NM: Especially as a kid, I can see it as an adult, but as a kid you're like "I don't want to be left out" [laughs].

KL: Right.

NM: Did you have a teacher or an advocate in your life who helped you get where you are today? And did that relate to race or ethnicity?

KL: That's a good question. I don't feel like I had a teacher in relation to advocating for me as an Asian American. I did have a lot of teachers who helped me get to where I am in terms of coaching and who really invested in me as a dancer, who I appreciate. I'm realizing sometimes people make comments about your race or look (at you) differently, but I never had that experience with any of my teachers.

I didn't know that (race) would be an issue, because the school I went to after I left my hometown school, the Rock School in Philadelphia, had such a diverse student body. We had students from all over the world living with us, and they always prioritized talent and often they were students from Japan or from Cuba or Mexico. It was always talent forward, so in my mind that was the ballet world. You were seen for what you were capable of doing and not necessarily what you looked like, and so when I started noticing those things in my professional career, I felt a little blindsided [laughs]. It felt strange when I had (these) comments in my professional career.

NM: When did it shift?

KL: It shifted pretty much the first company that I joined. When you do *Swan Lake*, them pulling you aside and saying "You need to lighten your skin more than everyone else" or "You don't have enough makeup on, you're too tan" or, on the summer break, "Don't go in the sun; you're gonna be too tan when you come back into the season" or "You need to make your eyes bigger" or "You need to put more effort into making your eyes bigger" [laughs], random things like that, you know, it's because you're not white. And that's the standard of ballet—whiteness.

NM: Did you ever think about the implicit messages, about who gets what roles in regard to racial representation, and seek out other Asian dancers for support?

KL: Yes. The significance of implicit messages and implicit bias hit me like a ton of bricks at the end of my career. There were two distinct events that allowed me to revisit my experiences and was the catalyst for deep self-reflection. As a young Asian-presenting dancer of mixed race who grew up in the U.S., I never felt especially connected to or affirmed by the achievements of established Asian-identifying dancers. Because many of them grew up and trained overseas, they had different cultural backgrounds and simply didn't look like me. Being a more "womanly" (voluptuous) dancer, I found myself identifying more with Misty Copeland than dancers of Asian descent.

First, during the pandemic the founders of *Final Bow for Yellowface* constructed a series of interviews with Asian-identifying dancers. This took place every day during Asian American and Pacific Island Heritage (AAPI) month to celebrate their achievements and to make space for them to share about their experiences. I was a young dancer freelancing in New York City when I met founders Georgina Pazcoguin and Phil Chan. Meeting Georgina and dancing alongside her, I looked up to her both as a friend and mentor. She was the first professional dancer of mixed Asian American race who I had ever met, and I aspired to be like her … an unapologetic powerhouse. However, it wasn't until after our interview for AAPI month concluded where we were able to go off the record and share our more personal experiences with our racial identities and how it has marked our careers. It was this conversation that allowed me to give myself permission to fully "see" my experiences through a clear and honest lens.

In addition to my conversation with Georgina, *Final Bow for Yellowface* invited the AAPI interviewees to a Zoom meeting where we could connect with each other, as many of us did not dance in the same companies. I was deeply moved and inspired by this experience, and it was the first time I experienced the importance of a broader affinity group.

The second event was a year and a half later, when you held a discussion with my company that made a safe space with the directive for BIPOC dancers to share their experiences, as they were comfortable, with regards to anti-racism and equity in the ballet world. This was the first time I was able to be part of a discussion about how we were connected in our similar unsavory experiences such as blatant racism, microaggressions, typecasting, etc. and how they have affected and continue to affect us. I left this conversation with a deep sense of gratitude and empowerment to have had the space to connect, and to discuss these issues more openly and honestly with peers, young dancers, and others. However, I also left with a sense of helplessness upon the realization that the power to bring forth organizational, structural, and systemic change lies far from BIPOC dancers' hands.

NM: Can you describe the culture at BalletMET?

KL: The culture at BalletMET ... So, I'm going into my ninth nonconsecutive season. With every company it's going to be different. What I love about being in BalletMet [laughing], first and foremost, I am very fortunate to be an Asian American dancer and to work under an Asian American director. There was an incident of racism directed towards me that was so upsetting to the point where I had to talk to (the director) about it, and he couldn't have been more supportive. It was without question "I'm gonna take care of it" (he said). To work under somebody who understands that, where you don't have to explain ... yourself, it is really unique. He's one of just two Asian American directors in the United States. Then, on top of that I just love working in an ensemble company. Seriously, I think I keep dancing, obviously I love to dance, but I also love the sense of community. My closest friends are people in the company, which wasn't my standard of community before I joined BalletMet. I really prioritized having friends outside of work because I wanted work-life balance, but we support each other, and that's just a nice place to be, and I think that's why I stayed so long.

NM: What would you say have been some challenges or achievements that stand out in your mind when you reflect on your dancing career?

KL: I think this is where I feel like I have that internal struggle, because to speak about having an Asian American director and to know that is unique for someone that looks like me, but then to also feel like maybe I'm not cast in certain roles because I look the way that I look and I'm always cast as something exotic....

I understand that that also comes to play, but in being connected to other

(Asian) women in *Final Bow for Yellowface* to discuss the same issues, to always be (cast as) something considered exotic or sensual.... I will be cast to understudy in *Aurora* or to understudy leading ladies. I am never performing as a leading lady; I get a lot of incredible opportunities when it comes to repertoire ballets. On my resumé I'm very proud of some of things I've been able to perform.

(Yet) there are career bucket list items…. I'm coming to peace with the fact that I may never dance the lead of a full-length ballet, and a part of that is hard to rationalize when, in my mind, I'll get first cast for some really difficult repertoire ballets and do them well and be very proud of myself. So, if I'm good enough to do that, then I would argue that I potentially could be good enough to rise to the challenge of a full-length ballet. It could just be that I'm not well suited for it, and I'm okay with that. But then that thought always creeps in: Is it because we prefer to see a blond-haired beauty in *Sleeping Beauty* or in *Cinderella* or… 'cause I find myself doing that as well, looking at other dancers like "Oh, she would be such a beautiful Aurora," and then I'm like, why do you think that [laughs]? It's always (the dancer we) historically see in this industry as an Aurora. So, that's just interesting self-reflection because again, I am in a very unique scenario; I think it would be different and carry more weight if I was not working under an Asian American director [laughing], who I know went through that exact same situation in his career, and it was very real for him.

NM: How do you relate to ballet now versus how you related to it as a young student? How has your relationship to ballet changed over time?
KL: I think what I appreciate now is conversations like this. I wouldn't have imagined this even being on the table when I was a student, so for young students who are maybe having comments said to them and going through those things and feeling very alone and not having the tools to communicate those things … that this discussion is happening and that they can feel seen and supported and the same thing with body types in ballet, which I still think we have a long way to go, but that is also a discussion that is being had openly. Discussing mental health and prioritizing mental health—we're seeing a lot of companies supporting that and also dancers kind of talking about it more publicly, and I think that's something that was never (affirmed before); mental health did not matter. It was like "Why are you crying? … Leave and come back."

I went to one school where it was very bad. Sixteen-years-olds were peeing their pants in class because they were being terrorized by their teachers. Those kinds of things are increasingly becoming unacceptable, and so it restores my faith in this art form; I feel like it's such an archaic model that it's unsustainable for the future. All these conversations just restore my faith in this art, because art should be uplifting and shouldn't contain people in a tiny box. I think that's why a lot of people give up on it, because it feels insurmountable emotionally.

NM: What's your favorite performance role?

KL: Oh my gosh, I loved doing "Fascinating Rhythm" and "Man I Love" in George Balanchine's *Who Cares?* That was like my career highlight; we performed this with the Cincinnati Ballet. It was a collaboration. My performance happened to be with a live orchestra in Cincinnati, which we don't have for repertoire ballet; that was surreal, and I'm really proud. My partner and I worked so hard because we didn't know if we were going to get a show. Then when I finally saw the video like a year later, I cried like a baby because I was just.... I can't believe that was me. I love all the Balanchine ballets. I did "Russian Girl" and *Serenade;* that was also a career highlight. Doing Ulysses Dove's *Red Angels* was a career highlight; that's like a resumé ballet, it's iconic; and then to also perform a ballet by such a prolific Black choreographer ... it was just really special.

NM: Awesome. Can you tell me about a performance experience that was special or memorable for some reason or another?

KL: A specific performance itself? It's funny, because I don't feel like I have that experience in the moment. I put so much pressure on myself that I can't even really enjoy myself until afterwards. I love dancing and I love performing, but I have that moment after the show, like upon reflection (of how special it is), but I think it would be *Who Cares?* for sure.

NM: Okay. Can you tell me your thoughts on Asian representation in ballet?

KL: This one may seem kind of sad, if I'm being completely honest. When I look to audition for ranked companies, I look to see how many Asian women they have in their company. Then, I won't send my materials if I see that they've reached their "quota" for Asian women because there is always only one. You have one Asian soloist, and then maybe you have another Asian woman in the corps, and it's gonna be hard for her to ascend to the next rank, because (there is already one Asian in the soloist rank). You see a lot of Asian women leave companies for that reason and hope to go somewhere where they're looking for that POC [people of Color] quota. I will purposefully send mine. I will purposefully send my audition materials to a company where I see that they at least have one Asian ... but not in the rank that I'm looking to fulfill.

NM: Can you tell me about your time in school as an Asian American dancer and maybe about some of the companies where there were issues around race?

KL: So, in school I didn't really notice that. At my local ballet school, I was the only dancer who left that school who became a professional dancer during my generation. I think there was one other woman who joined Ballet Austin. But I was the only person, so I definitely received special treatment from my teachers—so I felt very valued. I think they valued everyone, but they would give me private lessons, and they were very invested in where I did my summer auditions. I felt very supported.

NM: As a professional dancer in different companies, has race been an issue for you? You talked about it in terms of where you might choose to audition, but I mean company experiences where you actually kind of feel some kind of way in the space.

KL: (Referencing being passed over for roles) I feel that dancing-wise, objectively I could do the role; is (my race) why I'm not doing it? I've actually had people say that to me. Other coworkers come up to me and say, verbatim, "I thought you would be doing that role" and me saying "I was hoping to do it," and then the next phrase out of their mouth: "Oh, it's probably because you're Asian."

We had a dancer who spoke Spanish and who I found to be very disrespectful in general. I had no tolerance for him; (he was) just very disrespectful to our ballet masters, to other dancers. I was in the studio to help teach him his work, which he should have known at this point already, and at the end he kind of like slap-clapped my hand and said "Thanks, China" to me in Spanish and started laughing. I responded, "I know what you said," and he said it in front of another Spanish-speaking dancer and thought he was being hilarious. I went and pulled my director out of rehearsal, and I was like, "I need to talk to you right now," and he was very supportive, and he took care of it.

Then the comments about makeup, I mean, I laughed about it but…. We had a repetiteur here. We were spacing a ballet, and she called my name and another woman's name and said, "I need to talk to you." She told the other woman that she needed to cover her tattoos better, and she turned to me and said, "And you need to shave your armpits." I was so caught off guard, I was like, "I did, this morning, but I am Asian, and I have darker armpit hair, so maybe it looks to you like I haven't." And that wasn't a good enough answer; she asked me to then cover it up with makeup. I was like, "But then I'll sweat onto a white costume and there will be … so I can't do that," and we were already in the theater. She then said, "Can you go buy another razor?" I responded, "I shaved." Then she just looks at me like totally exasperated and said, "I guess I'll just try not to look at it." Incredible! And what's even more incredible is I have worked with her I think at least four times up to this point, so she's seen my armpits before [laughs].

NM: You've probably already engaged this text before, so I am just jogging your memory. It comes from Final Bow for Yellowface, *which you mentioned you read. This reflection is from Danielle I about* Nutcracker. *She wrote:*

> As an Asian American, dancing in the "Chinese Tea" number was incredibly uncomfortable—to be made complicit in the mockery and misrepresentation of your own culture is never a position into which someone should be put. I'm Japanese-Filipino, but since Euro-white-America values simplify "Asian" to mean "Chinese," I still took offense to the way the Chinese number was interpreted, since unfortunately, it influenced the ways that all (East) Asians were seen. I don't just cringe at the end of "Arabian," knowing what is coming next. I'm also offended by the exoticization and often sexualization of the "Arabian" piece. Orientalism applies to both the "Arabian" and the "Chinese" pieces! We should also be standing alongside our MENA (Middle East and North African) allies against the way that the Arabian piece depicts that culture! [2020, 106]

I know that you're familiar with Nutcracker, *and I'm curious what your thoughts are about that reflection. Had you thought of that before? What were your experiences performing in* Nutcracker?

KL: No, I agree with everything that she said, and I think it's very obvious how problematic that depiction is within the industry in watching other people. One, having to depict a caricature of Asian culture as an Asian person.

NM: Have you ever had to perform "Chinese"?

KL: No, although—random anecdote—I do the Spanish doll a lot, but everyone asks me if I'm performing the China doll every year anyway.

But it's like insult to injury watching other dancers wear offensive makeup, which we don't do anymore (speaking to the changes that BalletMet has undergone to affirm dancers' identities and not uphold stereotypes), or make offensive gestures, kind of making a joke of the dance in the culture. I've watched a lot of dancers get corrections about the things that they do while they're bowing, the things that they do while doing something that's not completely choreographed. The things that they choose to do to depict that dance just shows how far-reaching (stereotypes and racism are), normalizing making a caricature of something that's already offensive. It makes them comfortable to continue to do so; that's why I think *Final Bow for Yellowface* is so important.

NM: As you know, BalletMet is one of the two mainstream ballet companies led by an Asian artistic director. You've talked a little bit about it. Can you tell me a little more about how that impacts your experience in the company?

KL: I mean, just referencing that one incident I spoke of earlier, if I felt the need to talk to him about anything else that came up that felt racist and made me upset to the point where I felt like it needed to be escalated.... It's just really amazing knowing that at any point if I needed to talk to him, I know he would support me. And it's because he is a person of Color. We've even had discussions this year about how hard it's obviously been, first and foremost for Black people but also for us, experiencing Asian hate and living in a city where we're not predominant, and even talking to him about, you know, when my husband and I have children, what school district I'd want to live in because I don't know what our children will look like. In all likelihood they will be extremely white-presenting, because my husband is white. But I also want them to be around a diverse population, and (I'm) looking up school districts that have the highest percentage of Asian families. To be able to talk to your boss about things like that is something that I will never take for granted. And I know we both were hurting a lot this year from the state of the world and the hate against Asians; it was really great to be able to have those tough conversations with him. I'm endlessly grateful for him. I'm very lucky.

NM: Yeah, just to know that if ever there was a problem that communications would not be a part of the problem. It means a lot.

In my research, I've noticed a trend I was curious about. Is it something substantive or is it a nonissue? I see a lack of Asian dancers but particularly Asian dancers born in the United States. *I find a lot of the Asian dancers that are working are either from South Korea or China or some other place, and I was curious what you thought about that and if you see that there are challenges for Asian children to train in the United States or if I misread this situation. Is it a thing you've noticed?*

KL: No, I've absolutely noticed that, and it's so interesting because I'm not exactly sure why it is. For example, like me, and another dancer in the company who's full Korean—he was adopted, he's like one of my closest friends, Jim Nowakowski. He was born in Korea but was raised in America, and when they identify you as being Asian, they always assume that you're foreign. A number of times I've been asked at summer programs "Do you speak English?" (I answer) "yes." The dancers that I know who are Asian identifying but were born in the States and who trained here, I could probably list them on one hand. And I don't really know why that is, but it is a trend, and we flock to each other. Like, "Hey! We have similar experience." It is interesting.

NM: How do you think the field of ballet has changed over the last 20 years in terms of opportunities for Asian women?

KL: I definitely think it's changed; I do think we're on the right track. Just the fact that we're seeing Asian American dancers who were born here ascend to the highest ranks of some of the top companies in the United States—when I was younger, that was not the case, from what I saw. The only Asian dancer that I looked up to when I was younger was Yuan Yuan Tan at San Francisco Ballet. I watched ABT almost exclusively, and it wasn't until Hee Seo became a principal that I realized "Oh, nobody dancing here—in the States—looks like me." I think we're seeing more Asian American principals, so I'm hoping that we're on the right path.

NM: Do you feel that you've ever been color-cast or exoticized through a role, and if so can you tell me about that?

KL: Yes, I think I often am [laughs]. I'm trying to think specifically. It's always something I consider when I receive certain roles. I mean, I did Arabian for a long time. No, I don't do it anymore. I've been cast in a few repertoire pieces where the first thing they say about me is "I love your dancing, it's like so sensual" ... I think to myself, "Is it?" A lot of the amazing opportunities I've had.... I've maybe benefited from the fact that I'm viewed that way. But I would like to do other things.

NM: Or not to have to question why you received a role.

KM: I'm never the demure, elegant character. I'm always fierce, sensual, flirty [laughs]—all those things.

NM: Typecast?

KM: Yeah.

NM: How do you feel about ballet being described as a white or Eurocentric dance form?

KL: I would say that it's historically accurate, and I think it takes a lot of conscious effort to work away from that part of its history.

NM: I want to give you time and space to share anything about your experiences in ballet or dance that you want to if I haven't asked you about something that's really special or important to you to share. Do you have any advice to young dancers or anything of that nature?

KL: I think something I recognized in the past couple of years that I try to be aware of is celebrating young Asian dancers. The Asian dancers in our academy, I know that they identify with me, I can tell by the way that they look at me or wave to me in the hallway. I really try to make a conscious effort to talk to them, tell them that they're dancing well, to celebrate them in this space, and to extend support. I feel as though it's my responsibility, because that would have been so meaningful for me as a young dancer. So, I think that's just something that I am trying to do—(to affirm them, let them know) you may be different than what this industry has historically been, and that's what it needs, and that's what we should be celebrating. I've been able to make a career out of it and succeed in this space. It was very hard for me to find a job, and I don't know how much race played into it, but there's space for them here, and not just to be viewed as the Asian dancer, and I do believe that's the direction that we're going in.

NM: Thank you for taking the time out of your day and life to share with me.

KL: Thank you. It's an honor to be a part of it, and honestly I'm so grateful for the work that you're doing.

Part II

Less than a year after I interviewed Kristie Latham, she made the decision to retire. We were also in the midst of editing her chapter for this book and she shared that she wanted to include her retirement. Herein, Latham shares her account of the circumstances around her retirement.

NM: Can you tell me how you came to the decision to retire?

KL: It kind of happened pretty much after you spoke with us on antiracism and equity; that's kind of what made me come to some realizations of historically what has been happening over the past two years. In more recent times, the company has been more open to having conversations like that (about antiracism and equity), throughout the organization. In the meeting, a number of the BIPOC [Black, Indigenous, people of Color] dancers gave anonymous feedback about being typecast or all of our lead roles, especially in in full length (ballets), being white women or white presenting. This caused me to reflect upon my experiences. Because I think I mentioned in our last interview, it's hard to know, because ballet is so subjective: am I being considered for these roles, or not considered for these roles, because of my ability, or is it because of another overarching thing.

NM: Sure, and I think one of the really important parts for people to understand is that not getting the opportunities to practice and build the repertoire is a part of how racism works. Even if you don't have the skill set to do the role, maybe the reason why was race-based.

KL: Absolutely, and I started to really feel that, and it built a lot of frustration, anger, and disappointment. I felt very helpless in that it didn't really matter that I had been working within the company for nine years, and when outside choreographers come in I am cast very well, but when the casting is in-house I kind of stay [in] the same place.

So, after seeing that it wasn't just my own feelings, that other BIPOC dancers in the company were feeling things that I had been feeling, and something that we've never talked about with each other; I was really grateful for just that space to communicate. And then maybe two weeks later, the casting for *Giselle* went out, and the two women cast as Giselles were white women, and the two women cast as Myrtha were BIPOC women. (Giselle and Myrtha are the two lead roles in the ballet.)

I was just floored that we had this organization-wide discussion about just that, about how casting has been historically, and then new dancers getting opportunities, where again, for young white dancers within the company (they get cast, and senior BIPOC dancers are not cast for these prime roles).

And flashback to 2019, I had an artistic evaluation with my artistic director and told him point blank, "I respect you and all the decisions you have to make in casting, you have a very talented company, but I've been here long enough to know that if I if I am to stay here, it is because I want to do principal roles and a full length and there are no hard feelings, if you don't see me ever doing that here. But, please just be honest with me so that I can make certain decisions regarding my career."

From the artistic director's reply, I felt affirmed and that these opportunities for advancement were maybe in the funnel for me, if I continued on the same path.

When that happened, I just finally had this epiphany, "oh wait, there is no space for someone who looks like me to ascend to the roles that I'm hoping to ascend to," that also caused me to reflect upon the experience of other Asian dancers who came through the company.

And, aside from me and another Asian dancer, who also decided to retire this year, other Asian dancers have been let go and had really difficult experiences. There was a dancer who was let go after one season; she was Korean. She was not really cast by the director all season and then left the company, had a pandemic year back at home, and then she joined Atlanta Ballet and is now a principal there. How is it that she wasn't good enough to be here, but she's good enough to be a principal at a company with a larger budget? Same thing happened to another Filipino dancer, same experience. She left, and now she's a soloist with an established ballet company with a higher operating budget. So, that made me conclude that I can't (stay in the company). I love to dance, but for my mental health, I can't continue to subject myself to this kind of environment.

I felt it was important to be honest with the leadership of my company in all the things that I had been feeling. So, I let leadership know why I wanted to retire.

NM: *There's a lot here. Relationships with organizations and the people in them are intense because a dancer becomes a community member, a part of the organization, and often becomes like family with the people, in a very intimate way, as is often the nature of art making with your body and sharing your life. That's why the experience is so deeply felt but also why it's complicated to say anything. On top of these concerns around relationships, this is your livelihood, which quite honestly is why it is not uncommon for many people to not discuss certain things until they've retired.*

KL: My only hesitation is … I just worry about the dancers who are still there and the reputation of the company as a whole. Yet this is important to talk about.

NM: *Yes, it's crucial to understand there's no monolithic Asian dance experience.*

KL: Also, I think a lot of dancers do this race aside thing, where you kind of force yourself to compartmentalize everything, and so you're like "everything's good, everything's fine," and it's really not. So, what's been really amazing for me is the fact that so many people are having conversations about this right now. I feel like finally the veil has been lifted, and I am learning I was not alone; so many other dancers have had similar experiences.

Even with my dad's family, they navigated a race-based society, and there were residual effects that impacted me and my family. They loved me, and yet I have come to understand that stereotypes that are pervasive in our society also impacted my relationships with them, their perceptions of me, and how we related and connected to one another. I did not want to think about race all the time, not with my family and not with my career. But as I look back, I can see connections I chose not to see at the time.

NM: *One thing that I have gotten from you—please correct me if I'm off—is that you were asked in your childhood to assimilate to whiteness and white beauty aesthetics, and so, to have these kinds of circular, reoccurring events in your life, it's kind of culminating to a particular kind of magnitude and trauma.*

KL: One hundred percent, and I feel like I finally started to realize that, and pretty much that is right when I decided to retire. It was like that week. It was like this is too much; I should just unsubscribe.

NM: *You're not the first by far, but I think there's a process of understanding where the line of this beautiful art form is and the social constructs of racism that have, been embedded in the form and when, where, and how they meet your body. And then, how do I fly and soar and be liberated in this beautiful thing without the trappings of our society's "stuff." It's complicated, and sadly, I don't want to say it's normal, but it's typical.*

KL: And it doesn't matter who's kind of steering the ship right. In interviews I've done in the past, I would say, "I'm one of the like very lucky Asian dancers, to dance under an Asian director," but that's, not to say that they don't still kind of prop up the Eurocentric standards of dance.

Kristie Latham (photograph by Jennifer Zmuda; courtesy Kristie Latham).

NM: I think one of the things is that our directors and our leaders don't escape the racism in the water we're all swimming in.

    KL: Right.

NM: Just to plant a seed, you know, maybe in the future, might you be open to an opportunity for you to lead ballet spaces that are very different in who they center?

    KL: Yeah, never know and I'll never say never, but I feel like the break is due.

NM: So many dancers leave and come back in some capacity. I think about Raven

Wilkinson and Delores Browne, who left dance and were called back in some way or another.

KL: We'll just see what happens.

Kristie Latham Glossary

    Brief bio-notes of artists and places mentioned in the chapter. This is not intended to be comprehensive but instead to offer a small amount of information to spark more thorough research if readers are interested.

Ballet Guild of the Lehigh Valley—Founded by Marjorie Berlin Fink in 1958 in Bethlehem, Pennsylvania.

Briane, Mireille—Paris-born dancer and teacher. Taught at Dance Theatre of Harlem, School of American Ballet, and Ballet de Rio De Janeiro, among many other dance companies.

Briansky, Oleg—Belgium-born dancer, choreographer, and teacher. Taught at Dance Theatre of Harlem, School of American Ballet, and Theatro Municipal do Rio De Janeiro, among many other institutions.

Browne, Delores—African American ballet dancer in the 1950s. Danced with New York Negro Ballet. Student of Marian Cuyjet. Longtime teacher at Philadanco and numerous other dance organizations.

Chan, Phil—Arts administrator, cofounder of Final Bow for Yellowface, and author of *Final Bow for Yellowface: Dancing between Intention and Impact*.

Copeland, Misty—First *African American* female promoted to principal dancer with the American Ballet Theatre in 2015.

Nowakowski, Jim—Dancer with BalletMet.

Pazcoguin, Georgina—New York City Ballet's first Asian American ballet dancer, promoted to soloist in 2013.

Seo, Hee—South Korean–born dancer. Principal dancer with American Ballet Theatre.

Tan, Yuan Yuan—Born in China. Principal dancer with San Francisco Ballet.

Verdy, Violette—Choreographer, born in France. Directed Paris Opera Ballet. Formerly a principal dancer with New York City Ballet.

Wilkinson, Raven—First African American woman to join an established mainstream classical ballet company, Ballet Russe de Monte Carlo of New York, in 1955 at age 20. Wilkinson died in 2018.

NOTE

Georgina Pazcoguin, New York City Ballet soloist, and Phil Chan, author of the book *Final Bow for Yellowface: Dancing Between Intention and Impact*, created an organization, Yellowface (https://www.yellowface.org). In 2020 during the COVID-19 pandemic, the organization convened a group of dancers online via Zoom to celebrate the achievements of Asian American dancers and discuss issues in the field that impact them. It was an opportunity for Asian American dancers to be in community with one another and be affirmed around experiences that for some may have felt isolating if they were a minority within their dancing space. In a portion of the interview when Kristie spoke about being exoticized, she noted that in the past she might have questioned whether stereotyping and implicit bias were taking place. However, through this group and hearing the stories of other Asian dancers, Kristie was able to get a better sense of how stereotypes impacted her as well as many Asian American women.

Claudia Monja

Past affiliations: Ballet de Camagüey (2006–2012); Joburg Ballet (2012–2021)
Current affiliation: Nashville Ballet (2021–present)
Country of Birth: Cuba
Current residence: Nashville, Tennessee
Age at time of interview: 30

Excerpts from a March 10, 2017, interview at the Joburg Ballet in Johannesburg, South Africa. The interview took place with an audio recording (as video recording was not permitted) and a translator, Michael Lee. The interview was set up by the company, and I was unsure as to how free Claudia felt to share about her life. The interviews that took place at the Joburg Ballet felt a bit more formal to me. I got the sense that Claudia was not at ease. I intuited that speaking to a stranger in another language in her place of employment was likely not an easy task. I wondered if she had public relations training in her background to keep things positive. I got the sense that was important to her.

NM: *Claudia, tell me how you began dancing.*
CM: Ah, now, I'm 30. But I started at three years old.

NM: *At the Cuban National Ballet School?*
CM: No, that was baby ballet (when I was three). I started at the National Ballet School when I was nine.

NM: *And how long were you at the school?*
CM: In Cuba, the schooling is eight years. Five years for elementary and three years for the more advanced level.

NM: *And did you ever want to be in the Ballet Nacional de Cuba, the company in Cuba?*
CM: It's not that I didn't want to dance in that company (Ballet de Nacional Cuba). But can you soften that question with other choices so I do not sound like "no"? It's not that I didn't want to. At the beginning when I finished the school, I went to the Camaguey Ballet (a reputable and prestigious ballet company in central Cuba). It is very good internationally (referring to Camaguey Ballet). It (Ballet de Nacional Cuba) would have been a good opportunity to dance there, but, no, it is not what I aspire to; it's not my dream.

NM: *What was your dream?*
CM: My dream was to dance ballet. Anywhere. I never had that dream to dance in the national ballet; they are two different things.

Nashville Ballet Company dancers Claudia Monja and Owen Thorne in Paul Vasterling's *Nutcracker* (photograph by Lydia McRae Photography; courtesy Nashville Ballet).

NM: Was it a question of class or color?

CM: You know, many people ask why, in the National Ballet of Cuba, they don't have Black women dancers. Everyone asks me about that.

NM: Why do you think?

CM: I think that…. I have no problem with it. Many people, Black people, have studied ballet in Cuba, and they are very good. More (Black) men dance in the company. But women, not so much anymore. (Speaking of generations past) But a long time ago, there was a principal. But now…

NM: Oh, that was Caridad Martinez?

CM: No, Catarina. Catarina is younger than Caridad. And another lady, she was good but not in the company.

NM: I see. And Caridad is still not dark; she's kind of light.

CM: No, no, no, your color is very different. [She gestures to my skin color, which is caramel-colored, and indicates this is an easier road.]

NM: I see. You mentioned Ana Julia Bermúdez?

CM: Ana Julia Bermúdez from the Cuban school. Yes, she was my teacher.

NM: So, you still have connections there?

CM: Yes, she was my teacher, and when I was dancing there, she came to my classes and rehearsals. She is a very good teacher.

NM: So, you had some good experiences there.

CM: Ana Julia is very good. Very good teacher. She was dancing in the Company Ballet of Camaguey. She was not in the National Ballet, because she was very short. She was a very, very, very good dancer, but they say, "You are short, you can't dance" (in the Cuban National Ballet School).

NM: How did you like dancing with the Ballet of Camaguey, where you danced before coming to the Joburg Ballet?

CM: It was a very good experience there. It is kind of like the second company in Cuba.

NM: How are the two companies different, Ballet of Camaguey and Joburg Ballet?

CM: Oh, everything. Yes, because when I came here, I had too much energy. Here, they're like the same dancing but more calm and soft.

NM: A different style.

CM: Yeah. It's very difficult for me, but it's very good. I think now I'm a completely different dancer.

NM: And you've been here four years?

CM: Yeah.

NM: Can you tell me about a performance experience that was very special or memorable? Your favorite role or your favorite place you performed?

CM: I did before *Don Quixote* and now in March I will perform in *La Traviata*. I love *Don Quixote*—that is me. *La Traviata*, very nice ballet.

NM: In the States, Black women think of race differently from other parts of the world. How do you think of your racial identity? Do you think of yourself as a Black woman? A Latina?

CM: Oh, a Black woman. Of course. Of course.

NM: Before being a dancer.

CM: Of course. I am a Black woman, of course; that is what I am. Now the things I have achieved and how I am. I feel proud of my own color. My family is completely ... we don't have any color complex of being Black, and we never felt humiliated, nothing. My family since I was a child always taught me my own values and that I should not diminish myself in front of anyone because I am Black. Quite the opposite. We have to fight, to move forward.

NM: So, then, as a Black woman, is your experience in ballet, here in South Africa, the same as white women here? Is everybody treated the same? Are there challenges that are different for Black women in ballet?

CM: For me, it's the same. Many people say ballet's not for the Black people. I don't care about that. Here they want to change that; there is a school for kids to study ballet. And most of them are Black, because this company wants this country, South Africa, to have more Black dancers.

NM: Is it the same in Cuba?

CM: In Cuba a lot of Black people study ballet. In Cuba there is not a problem in studying ballet; everyone studies in the same school in Cuba when you take the national exam.

NM: Are they treated differently at the school because they're somehow ... it's communicated to them that they won't be going to the company?

CM: No.

NM: Then why aren't the Black students going into the company?

CM: I don't answer that question.

NM: Okay. But somewhere the children come to understand that that's not going to be possible?

CM: Look, everywhere there is envy and bad thoughts, but I think one should treat everyone the same. That is why I forced myself a lot in my career to achieve the things I have achieved. And now, sometimes people who would not speak to me in the past, will say, "Hi Claudie" and I say "Now you are going to greet me?" No.

These people were not talking to me, never. And after a long time, after they

Claudia Monja, 2022 (photograph by MA2LA).

know everything I'm doing here (with my accomplishments in ballet), they want to say, "Oh, hello, darling." I said, "No, no." Okay.

NM: In the States, they have a lot of things around Black dance and Black arts and having Black pride through the dance. Do you see Black ballerinas taking that kind of agency in Cuba or in South Africa? Where Black ballet dancers come together and are a force? A group? Do you have this…?

CM: No, I don't have that. Because everyone is the same, white and Black. Why do you have to have Black dancers? People are the same.

NM: In ballet, have you ever seen color-casting as a problem? Have you ever noticed it?

CM: No. If you have technique, you can do everything. Here, in this company, I never feel that. Yes. I feel very good in this company.

NM: In other places have you seen it?

CM: I'm not talking about that.

NM: Okay. In Cuba, do you learn at the Escuela Nacional de Cuba, do you learn Cuban national dances or only ballet?

CM: No, we learn everything in the school. French, music, composition, contemporary, Afro, and physical preparation.

Yes. A lot of French. For eight years, it was to support pronouncing the ballet terms in French, because all the steps are in French.

NM: Do you go back to Cuba and visit?

CM: Every year I go, and I see my mom and family.

NM: Yeah. Have they been here?

CM: No.

NM: Maybe someday?

CM: Yeah, of course. Of course.

NM: What's your favorite part about being in the Joburg Ballet company?

CM: What I like is how people are with me. They are very friendly to me, but not only because I'm from another country. No, because every day I work very hard, because I want to do much better. I think that one should gain respect depending on how one is as a person, how she values herself as a woman, and how she values her color.

NM: Muy bien.

CM: Yes.

NM: So, when we look at how Black women become ballerinas, some of them fight racism and some of them say I don't deal with it and go somewhere else that's better. How would you say you navigate racism … would you push against racism, or would you just not deal with it and go somewhere else? I think I know the answer, but…

CM: I am the other type, the ones who don't care. I don't care. I live for myself, I fight for myself, for my mom, and for my family and to be a better person every day, nothing else. I am a very natural, calm person, I live happy with myself. One has to be like that, because if one is like, oh, oh, everything goes bad. One has to be positive. The sun is out, let's go. If I am tired, I have to have the strength to be keep moving forward; no problem.

NM: Muy bien.

CM: *Sí,* Nya, *claro.* It was a pleasure to meet you too.

Claudia Monja Glossary

Brief bio-notes of artists and places mentioned in the chapter. This is not intended to be comprehensive but instead to offer a small amount of information to spark more thorough research if readers are interested.

Bermudez, Ana Julia—Master teacher from the Cuban National Ballet School.
Martinez, Caridad—Born in Cuba. Former principal dancer with Ballet de Nacional de Cuba. Has severed as a dance administrator or master teacher for organizations such as the Ailey School, Ballet Hispánico, the Brooklyn Ballet Conservatory, and the 92nd Street Y Harkness Dance Center.

Margaret Severin-Hansen

Affiliation: Carolina Ballet (1998–present)
Hometown: Long Island, New York
Current residence: Raleigh, North Carolina
Age at time of interview: 41

I interviewed Margaret "Peggy" on Zoom on August 19, 2021, toward the end of her maternity leave. She appeared relaxed in her home, bouncing on a large stability ball.

NM: Tell me how you began dancing.

MS: I was put into ballet when I was a six years old. I'm from Long Island—Huntington. I was in kindergarten—you go to school half days. I had a lot of energy, and my mother didn't want me to come home and kind of sit in front of the TV. She always liked ballet, she had never been a dancer, and she put me into the local ballet school, the Ohman School of Ballet, where I started dance at six. Then I transferred to another school when two of the female teachers there, who had taught me from age six, branched off and opened a school as well. So, I moved with them until I was 12. Then at 12, I went away to the New York State Summer School of the Arts, up in Saratoga Springs. In my class I met a few students from the School of American Ballet. They just talked about it, and honestly, I had never heard of it. I was just a kid taking ballet classes in Long Island, going to Jefferson Elementary School.

Then randomly two of my classmates at the local ballet school said, "We're going to go into the city to audition for the School of American Ballet." I said, "Wait, I just heard about this program." So, I asked my mom if we could go, and for me it was more like a day in the city (New York City). The audition was on the Tuesday after Labor Day for the local New York students for the winter term. We planned to go to the audition, and then go see a Broadway show and go shopping.

This is in 1993, so there were no cell phones, no constant contact of any sort.

We went to the audition. I wound up being asked to stay through different rounds of the auditions. My friends wound up getting cut, so they were not asked to stay as long as I was. They went on to see the show that we all had tickets for. I wound up having to sit there all day long. I wound up getting accepted into B-1, that was the level at SAB. But my dad had no idea that we were going to audition; actually, he just thought we were going into the city with friends from the school. By the time we got home, he (my dad) said, "So, what happened today? I just got a phone call that you're supposed to be in Manhattan tomorrow to start ballet."

I was fortunate that they allowed me to go; then my parents and I commuted together daily for several years. So, I was at the School of American ballet from 1993 to 1998 when I graduated.

Margaret Severin-Hansen (photograph by Yevgency Shlapko; courtesy Margaret Severin-Hansen).

Being from SAB was so fortunate, because all those company auditions come straight through. So, you don't actually have to go anywhere to audition. I wound up doing multiple auditions. I'm kind of short, so I always knew that I wasn't going to get into New York City Ballet.

NM: Can you say your height?

MS: Oh, I'm five-two. But just five-two, you wouldn't mistake me for five-four.

Yeah, I'm petite, I'm five-two, and at the time there really weren't any smaller people, maybe five-four and a half. Basically, because it was still the older generation, and then only recently, years after I had already left the school, they accept Megan Fairchild, who's not super tall, and Ashley Bouder. But before that, there were very, very few shorter dancers.

So, I always knew that, and it never really bothered me or anything; the training was so good that it didn't really make a difference. And then I wound up getting a job with Carolina Ballet, which was a brand-new company in 1998. I did the big cattle call audition in New York, and I was one of the only two people left in the room, and I wound up getting my apprenticeship with them. But I was very skeptical moving all the way down to Raleigh, North Carolina, because it was very South and I had never lived below … coming from Long Island, south to me was D.C.

After that, I had to learn how to drive. In New York, all you do is you raise your hand for that taxi or you take the subway or you walk, so you didn't ever really need to do any of the driver's education stuff, so I had to learn how to drive—very quickly.

So, then I started with Carolina Ballet in August 1998, and I've been here ever since.

NM: How old were you then?

I had just turned 18, so I was 17 when I moved down, and then when the company started, I was 18. This coming season I'll start my 25th season with Carolina Ballet (in 2022).

NM: Why do you dance?

MS: That's a loaded question…. I don't know. I mean, you have to love dance, because it's not an easy profession, you know. It's hard physically, it's hard mentally, it's hard emotionally.

Why do I love to dance?

I don't think I know anything else that I would want to do; there's nothing that drives me the way that ballet has driven me over the years. I enjoy doing other things, but ballet is a driving force. There's something inside that makes you want to dance; it's hard to describe.

NM: Did you have a teacher or an advocate in your life that helped you get where you are today?

MS: Oh, there have been so many. One person that's been with me throughout, from when I was at New York State Summer School of the Arts when I was 12 until even now, has been Olga Kostritzky. Because she was a teacher at Saratoga, and she was a teacher at the School of American Ballet. She had been the ballet mistress for Robert Weiss when he was at Pennsylvania Ballet. So, when Robert Weiss and his wife, Melissa Podcasy, were going around doing a national audition tour to start Carolina Ballet, Olga just happened to be at SAB helping with the audition because there were over two hundred people. There were so many people, so they split the audition up into professionals who had already had a job at one point in their lives and students that hadn't. Olga wound up teaching my barre part. We did the barre separately and then they cut, cut, cut, cut, cut, and then we merged for center.

She had such a close relationship with Ricky Weiss, the director. He would bring her to guest teach and coach ballets; she's literally been in my life since I was 12. I just saw her two days ago on Zoom; she still teaches the company through Zoom, actually. She left the faculty at SAB quite a few years ago, but she guest teaches and she guest coaches and works as a ballet mistress.

She was the woman in *Black Swan*, the movie. She sits in the front with the big glasses with Natalie Portman, and she coached Natalie Portman for all the port de bras and stuff. Yes, she was a major factor in my life.

But throughout my years at SAB it was Suki Schorer, Suzy Pilarre, and Stanley Williams. I was one of Stanley's last generations before he passed away. I had him from when I was in B2 through level D. Then there was Kay Mazzo and Antonina Tumkovsky. All those teachers were so influential and all of their different attributes; they all had something so valuable to say.

As a professional, I honestly would not be where I am without Ricky and his wife Melissa, I mean that's just flat out. Because when I first moved down here, I was an apprentice and I wound up getting to dance huge roles as an apprentice. I mean, I did *The Steadfast Tin Soldier*, which is a pas de deux—a dance for two people.

It just happened to be that (Robert Weiss) hired a really small gentleman, Pablo. He was from Uruguay. Robert hadn't seen him in person; he was hired from a video. So, when we all got together, he was like "Oooh." We were the first couple (Robert) called out for the Balanchine's *Square Dance*, he was like "Okay, Peggy and Pablo," and so we went, and that was the start of my career.

I was fortunate in that sense, that I wound up getting a job and then getting to dance all these roles right away. (Noting that as an apprentice many did not get these roles, but because the company had a smaller male dancer, she was the go-to partner.)

NM: *Can you describe the culture at Carolina Ballet? I'm imagining that you've spent time at different companies and different schools. What are some of the differences? What makes Carolina Ballet special or unique? When you leave and return to Carolina Ballet, you think, "it's home" because...*

MS: Carolina Ballet has always been such a small company but not necessarily in numbers. It started small; it was 21 dancers, and I mean now it's I think 40 or a little over—41 or 42 maybe.

But it's always felt intimate. We all know each other, whereas in other companies that are big of course they commune together, but they have pockets of people, and we have that as well because of whatever, age differences, but as an overall company feel, it has always felt like one.

NM: What challenges or achievements stand out mostly when you think about your career retrospective, looking back?

MS: Challenges—dancing in general is a challenge in itself.

NM: Have you had injuries that you had to navigate?

MS: No, all the seasons I haven't missed a show. The only reason why I'm missing now is because I'm pregnant. And it just happened to be COVID, so I haven't even missed that much.

I've been very fortunate. I have not missed for being injured. Of course, there's always been little aches and pains, but it's never taken me out of a show.

As for achievements, for me, it's always trying to better myself, constantly evolving, nobody puts that pressure on you, but you always should want that for yourself.

Every dance that you do, whether or not you've done it once or three times or seven times, what can you bring out of that role or that part, what more can you give? That's what differs from dancer to dancer, what makes dancers different. What you bring to a role, not just how high your legs are … it's internal artistry, it's not just like, "Oh, I'm Giselle" or "I'm Sleeping Beauty, I'm Aurora." Each part, even nonstory ballets like Balanchine's, they have to have depth. Otherwise, you're just watching a lot of steps.

NM: How do you think you relate to ballet differently now, as a seasoned principal dancer, in contrast to how you related to it when you were just starting out in your career or as a student? How has your relationship with ballet changed?

MS: When I first started it was more just trying to understand, whether it was understanding my body, how did it work, or understand how to project to the audience, how to make myself be all the different roles that you have to be, because when you're younger you don't know, you haven't done those things, so you have to figure it out. Whether or not you watch a hundred videos or read the books if it's a story or try to watch the other seasoned dancers, what do you see when you watch them or other companies? I always enjoyed that. When I was at SAB I got to see City Ballet all the time and ABT all the time, because they were always either at the Met or City Center.

So, that's one thing I still like to do, even as a seasoned dancer. But now I understand more about how to do it. So, now it's more, what can I do differently that I didn't necessarily like last time. But when I was younger, it was more like trying to figure out just how to navigate in the first place.

NM: In previous published interviews, you shared that your favorite roles are Giselle and Aurora from Sleeping Beauty. *Can you talk a little bit about why those roles are special to you? Or maybe you have new favorites today.*

MS: I would say not new favorites, but to pick a favorite ... whenever somebody asks that I never really know how to answer because I put so much effort into each role. I can remember each role so vividly and fondly, like Aurora I've danced it a lot; it's come back four times.

When you've finished Aurora, you feel like you've achieved this momentous thing, because it's one of the hardest technically and longest ballets that you do. Act One, your entrances into the Rose Adagio, into the variation, into the coda, and then into the vision scene, into second act, and then the third act pas de deux, variation, variation, coda. So, when you finish you're like "Wow, I just accomplished something."

But a deep character role, it isn't. It doesn't have as much depth as Giselle. So, that's why the two are so contrasting, because they both take so much technique. But Aurora is much lighter, youthful, and effervescent; that's what I always think about when I think about Aurora. When it comes to Giselle, she's all of those things, but then she has all this trauma because she has a bad heart, and then she falls in love with the worst person that you would ever want to in real life. Then by the second act, you have to be a totally different person but still portray that youthful Giselle in this ghost. It has more emotion to it that you have to then bring out in your technique.

But then all those ballets like *Concerto Barocco* from Balanchine, to dance the first violin, that's technically challenging and has no story behind it at all. Yet again when you finish, you feel "Oh, wow, I did a ballet," and *Allegro Brilliante* when you do those or even *Rubies;* it's so hard to pick one, but I think as I've gotten older, not that I don't love to do those short 20 minutes–30 minutes nonstory ballets, but when you do the full lengths, you feel this different fulfillment when you finish.

NM: Can you tell me your thoughts on Asian representation in ballet? What has been your experience in this art form?

MS: Over the years there's been more Asian presence in the companies within the States for sure. I never really felt or was made to feel, even in SAB or anything, that I was different from anybody. And the one thing that you probably wouldn't know is that I'm also adopted, so I have two white parents. I was always brought up to know where I was from and that I was from South Korea and all that stuff. I've always known I was adopted at 10 months old. When I was at SAB I never was made to feel that I was any different than anybody else, so it was just sort of normal; I never thought about it. But I found out that I was the only Asian one in the advanced levels when I was there. I'm one of the founding members of the School of American Ballet's Diversity Board.

NM: What do you mean "when you found out?" Do you mean that as a student there, race was so not on the radar that you didn't notice at the time?

MS: Yeah, it never occurred to me.

NM: Did it occur to you anywhere in your life, or was it just a nonissue at SAB?

MS: At SAB a long time ago, they used to do this exchange program. The Royal

Danish Ballet—two students would go there, and students would come, and I was one of those two students. My name is very Danish because my dad is actually Danish. So, Margaret Severin-Hansen sounds very Danish, and it was funny because when I went over ... and this was before all of the electronic stuff, back then your pictures were on papers. And I just remember handing over my papers, and the guard at customs started talking to me in Danish. And I'm just standing there, and I don't answer, and then I handed my passport, and he looked at me surprised, like "Oh, I'm so sorry." Because they thought that I would have been tall and blond. That was the only time in my life, actually, that I was not what they thought I was. But it wasn't because of anything negative or bad, it was just because of my name. And then joining Carolina Ballet, that's the one thing Ricky's really big on. He never—whether it was in Pennsylvania or here—he never cast parts because of race, because in his mind it doesn't matter. It's all about can you do the ballet or not; are you talented or not.

NM: Did it ever come up with guest artists or other choreographers outside the company?

MS: No, it's never happened. And I've gone to really, really South places where they probably have not ever seen an Asian person, some of the little towns, and nothing, nobody says anything; they're always super welcoming.

NM: I want to share with you a passage from Final Bow for Yellowface. *I don't know if you're familiar with that text by Phil Chan. Is it okay if I just read it to you, and you let me know what you think of it?*

This is a quote from Danielle I, and she says:

> As an Asian American, dancing in the "Chinese Tea" number was incredibly uncomfortable—to be made complicit in the mockery and misrepresentation of your own culture is never a position into which someone should be put. I'm Japanese-Filipino, but since Euro-white-America values simplify "Asian" to mean "Chinese," I still took offense to the way the Chinese number was interpreted, since unfortunately, it influenced the ways that all (East) Asians were seen. I don't just cringe at the end of "Arabian," knowing what is coming next. I'm also offended by the exoticization and often sexualization of the "Arabian" piece. Orientalism applies to both the "Arabian" and the "Chinese" pieces! We should also be standing alongside our MENA (Middle East and North African) allies against the way that the Arabian piece depicts that culture! [2020, 106]

I'm imagining that you connected with Nutcracker *a lot over the years, and I'm curious in terms of your thoughts about Asian representation within that ballet.*

MS: See, again, I never thought about it. I never thought about it in a derogatory way. It's just like *Madame Butterfly* to me; it's just a representation of a part of the world in that moment, but it doesn't define the person that's dancing it, and it doesn't define the ballet to me. Because all of the diversity and inclusion initiatives that have been coming up in the last 10 years ... seven years, maybe. It's how you internalize it. And I guess other people have experienced such negativity in it that it does affect them in a different way when they see something like that. For example, if something has been brought to light in your life, if somebody has been derogatory towards you when you were younger or throughout your adulthood, you're going to then see things from a particular perspective.

NM: Be triggered.

MS: Yeah. For me, I never experienced it, so then to watch *Nutcracker*, it's like, okay, well, that's what the Chinese and the Russians look like, you know, they have the big babushkas, and that was just that choreographer's interpretation of what that culture was. And every *Nutcracker* is different; it'll have the similarities and the distinctions, whether it's food or culture, but they're all going to have their own—what does that costume look like, what does this look like? Like Spanish, sometimes, is like the flamenco, but does that really represent Spain? For me it's just a ballet; it's not energy towards people meaning to attack their culture.

NM: You talked a little bit about Asian representation in ballet getting better over the years.

MS: Yeah, and same with Black representation.

NM: So, what are your ideas about opportunities for Asians in ballet leadership positions? Has it impacted your career or the way you think about opportunities? What have you seen over the years?

MS: Yeah, again, it's more, what did you do in your life rather than what color is your skin. You know, what did you achieve to be able to apply, for instance, for an artistic directorship? You need specific things that you've done throughout your career. You have to have done administrative stuff, you have to have run a program, you have to have run a successful program. There's all these boxes (to be checked off), and so it's not necessarily a race box. It is what did you achieve, similarly to back in the day, when you didn't see people, if you read this resumé and you read that resumé, you would have no idea what this person looks like. So, I would hope that everybody has an equal opportunity regardless of race. But again, I wouldn't know how the people on the board feel, but you would hope that in these times they really go on merit and not looks.

NM: I agree. Do you feel you were ever color-cast or been placed in a role that was stereotypical?

MS: Mainly height. I don't tend to stand in the back; I was usually in the front [laughs].

NM: How do you feel about ballet being described as a white or Eurocentric dance form?

MS: That's how it started. I mean, that's its history, Again, you can't change history. I think it has evolved quite a bit over the years. It's gotten to be able to give people more opportunities now, in that so many more schools have outreach programs, so that all minorities will have the same opportunities as those more upper-class white people, because that's just, again, a stereotype. We still have the underprivileged white people as well. But I think that outreach of these major schools has been a huge part of it, and the fact that they have more funding as well, so they can offer more scholarships, whether it's to whites or a minority, is a huge thing. I think that one thing that's been very much worked on is having the funds to be able to scholarship people just in general, because ballet is expensive. It's not as expensive when you're little. But then when you get to be advanced, you're buying pointe shoes twice a week; I mean, they are a hundred dollars a pair. It's not for the faint of heart, for sure, and I think with the scholarship programs it's just allowed more people, in general, to be able to accomplish attending these ballet schools, and so then it's been able to, over time, translate into having more opportunities for a person of Color to be able to progress and achieve their goal of becoming a professional dancer.

NM: Does it resonate with you in any different way when you see an Asian ballet dancer onstage versus any other dancer? Do you feel some kind of affinity, connection, or excitement?

MS: No, if they're good, they're good, and if they're not I cringe [laughing].

NM: Do you have any advice for young dancers today?

MS: Pursue what your heart tells you, because it's not an easy profession. There's a mental strength that ballet takes, or dance in general, any form of dance. It takes a strong mind behind it. So, my advice to them is just really follow that because it's not for everybody, and it doesn't have to be for everybody, but if you figure that out while you're going through it and if you really think about it, you can enjoy it once you get there a lot more than if you fight with it throughout your schooling. Because I teach a lot of kids and see their struggles, and you see how they can either overcome them or they succumb to them, and it's not just about that beautiful body or really nice feet or being super flexible or how many turns can you do. Because you can always get better, you know; you can always improve if you work hard and have a drive to get there. It's like anything; it just takes work and dedication. But with dance in general, you have to be strong both physically and mentally.

NM: Well, that's all the questions I have unless there's something else you'd like to share.

MS: I don't think so. I just hope that people have more of an experience, like I had as a child and as an adult, without having to feel that things are race-based, because they shouldn't be made to feel like that. You want people to grow and enjoy their profession and their lives; you don't want that to hinder any part of their life. I've heard people say these things and experience these things, and it's horrible. You know, you never want to be made to feel lesser than, and especially if there's something that you can't change about yourself, you know it's different if you feel lesser because you've been lazy and you haven't been working as a dancer. But there's nothing you can do about the way you look. The only thing that you can do is be the best that you can be.

NM: I'm curious about one thing. I don't want to put words in your mouth, and I'll kind of frame it in the way of African American dancers, and actually I've seen this in ballet as well as in African-based dance forms, when a company or school is looking to hire someone, and they have been criticized for not hiring any Black faculty or you're not hiring any Asian faculty or whatever. The hiring people would say "Well, there's nobody qualified." But if they were to ask me, I would say "Well, there is this person and that person and this person" and on and on. I know these people in the field; they are there. So, I'm thinking there are two Asian artistic directors in the United States at mainstream ballet companies right now—not a lot. Do you think that this is because there are not a lot of Asians qualified, or is it because there might be barriers?

MS: I wonder, because just in general, how ballet has evolved recently, having all of these (people ready): they might actually be too young still. They just might not be ready yet. They might still be dancing or having their careers. Ed (Edwaard Liang) didn't just automatically go to be a director; he was a dancer, then he was on Broadway and then (became an artistic director).

NM: *You have to build a resumé.*

MS: Right, exactly, and so it might just be that too. For instance, in San Francisco Ballet there were quite a few Asian dancers, but I don't know if they would be ready yet to be artistic directors.

NM: *The jury is still out; we still don't know.*

MS: (Speaking to the low number of people of Color artistic directors of ballet companies) I feel the same with Black dancers as well for mainstream ballet. In general, to run a strictly ballet company, because I feel like we've known more African dance or contemporary Black dancers, more so than Black classical ballet dancers. There have been quite a few Black ballet dancers. But that number still reflects a small number group compared to their white counterparts. And, those few that I know, it is not likely that they all even want to be an artistic director. For me, I don't think I would want to be one. Like Debra Austin, who has been a wonderful ballet mistress and teacher throughout our time together at Carolina Ballet, but I do not get the sense that she would want that position. So, the ones that we do know formally that had extensive careers and all these things, I don't think they ever thought about being an artistic director; it also takes a particular mindset. Yeah, that's why in general there's been so many white dancers, and even though they all don't want to be directors there's still seven handfuls of them that do, when there's only a small number of people of Color who have the qualifications to be an artistic director.

NM: *Yes, I can only think of two women off the top of my head, Lourdes Lopez at Miami City Ballet and Virginia Johnson at DTH.*

MS: Right, you're starting to see it now, but because ballet has only started to evolve in the last 30 years. Again, in 30 years not all those people are going to want to become artistic directors; they might just like to run a ballet school or be head of the arts programs; there already aren't that many people, I think, who apply for these jobs in the first place. So, I think over time you will start to see it change. I know Georgina

Margaret Severin-Hansen (photograph by Cindy McEnery; courtesy Margaret Severin-Hansen).

Pazcoguin (could be a good candidate), but she's young, so she wouldn't be ready to apply for an artistic directorship, but maybe in 15 years she would. In time, I think we'll start to see it grow, and you'll start to see more and more of diverse leadership.

Everything takes time, and that's the thing; nothing's going to change overnight even if you wanted it to. You know, all these companies and establishments are all so focused on it that it will change. But it's just not going to change as quickly as people may want to see a change in every genre, whether it's Broadway or ballet or any other art form. Because it has been so exclusive.

NM: Well, thank you so much for your time today. I love to hear everyone's experience. Thank you so much.

MS: And let me know if you need anything else.

NM: I will. Thank you so much.

Margaret Severin-Hansen Glossary

> Brief bio-notes of artists and places mentioned in the chapter. This is not intended to be comprehensive but instead to offer a small amount of information to spark more thorough research if readers are interested.

Austin, Debra—First African American female dancer to join New York City Ballet. Ballet mistress at Carolina Ballet.

Balanchine, George—Arguably one of the most influential choreographers of the 20th century. Cofounder of New York City Ballet, artistic director for the company for over three decades. Balanchine died in 1983.
Bouder, Ashley—Principal dancer with New York City Ballet.
Carolina Ballet—Founded in 1998 and located in Raleigh, North Carolina.
Fairchild, Megan—Principal dancer with New York City Ballet.
Kostritzky, Olga—Ballet master. Taught at various ballet institutions including the School of American Ballet, the Official School of the New York City Ballet, and Carolina Ballet,
Liang, Edwaard— Choreographer. Former dancer with New York City Ballet and Netherlands Dans Theater. Artistic director of BalletMet in Columbus, Ohio.
Lourdes Lopez—Artistic director for Miami City Ballet. Former principal dancer with the New York City Ballet.
Mazzo, Kay—Master ballet teacher. Former principal dancer for New York City Ballet.
Ohman School of Ballet—Founded in 1979 by Frank Ohman in Commack, New York.
Pazcoguin, Georgina—New York City Ballet's first Asian American ballet dancer, promoted to soloist in 2013.
Perez, Pablo Javier—Born in Uruguay. Dancer and founding member of Carolina Ballet.
Pilarre, Susan "Suzi"—Ballet master; former soloist with New York City Ballet.
Podcasy, Melissa—Ballet master; former principal dancer with Carolina Ballet.
Royal Danish Ballet—Founded in 1741 at Kongens Nytorv in Denmark.
Schorer, Suki—Ballet master; danced with San Francisco Ballet and New York City Ballet.
Tumkovsky, Antonina—Longtime teacher at the School of American Ballet. Tumkovsky died in 2007.
Weiss, Robert "Ricky"—Founding artistic director of Carolina Ballet.
Williams, Stanley—Among the first instructors at the School of American Ballet. Williams died in 1997.

Melissa Verdecia

Past affiliations: Ballet Hispánico (2012–2021)
Hometown: Miami, Florida
Current residence: Miami, Florida
Age at time of interview: 28

Excerpts from a December 5, 2017, interview with Melissa Verdecia (Fernandez at the time of the interview). This interview was conducted in a conference room at the Ballet Hispánico (BH) Studios in New York City. Melissa's interview was arranged by Ballet Hispánico. She arrived with a very open energy about herself, willing to share and very at ease.

NM: Tell me how you began dancing.

MF: I began dancing, I was 5 years old. I'm originally from Miami. My parents immigrated from Cuba. They met in New Jersey, and then when my brother and I were born they moved to Miami. So, Miami is my home. When I was 5 years old, the church that my parents and I attended, there was obviously a huge Cuban

Melissa Verdecia and Lyvan Verdecia in *Landscapes*, choreographed by Donna Murray (photograph by Simon Song; courtesy Melissa Verdecia).

population at my church, and one of the ladies in particular, her name was Caridad (Espinosa), she wanted to start her own ballet school. At the time I didn't know this, but she had trained in the National Ballet School of Cuba; ballet was her passion. So, when she came over to the States, she wanted to start a school. She was asking the moms of all the young girls to see if they were interested, trying to recruit. And my mom … my mom's not what you would call a dance mom at all. She's not pushy about anything; everything that my brother and I have done has been because we wanted to. But I guess she saw me dancing around the house and full of energy, so she put me in these classes, and from there on out I fell in love with it. I remember vividly the first time that I wanted to do this professionally. I was six years old, it was my first recital, and we came out onstage, and I don't know, just the feeling of … seeing, like, the pitch-black audience but knowing that everyone's attention and focus was on what I was doing and the elation I felt—at such a young age I could recognize that. And I was like, wow, this is what I want to do.

NM: Tell me about your professional career. How long have you been performing? When did you start performing professionally? And what are your plans for the future?

MF: Well, I guess performing in a professional setting … well, I'll go back. Performing since I was young, like, 6 years old, I've been on a stage. And then, I went to arts middle schools and high schools, and I went to the Juilliard School for college, where I performed a great deal. But professionally, I joined Ballet Hispánico in 2012. So, six years now I've been performing professionally; it's kind of crazy.

NM: And what are you thinking about for the future?

MF: In the future, I honestly, I want to dance as long as I can, obviously, but eventually I want to have a family, and when that transition comes, I still want to be heavily involved in the dance world, whether that means as a teacher in academia. For example, one of my dreams is to teach at the Juilliard School and even a bigger dream, putting it out in the universe, is to perhaps one day be the Director of the Dance Division.

NM: That's awesome. Cool. So, I'm curious about your time dancing in Miami and then going to the Juilliard School. Were those spaces and places where you saw other Women of Color dancing?

MF: Definitely in Miami. Miami, as I mentioned, is predominantly Hispanic—Cuban, and Venezuelan, Colombians, a lot of African Americans. My friends growing up in my art schools, I would like to say we were pretty diverse. If anything, the minority were the Asians. There were very few Asians. But there were a lot of Jewish kids and Cubans and Blacks, and so I never felt segregated. I never felt like I was missing out on a cultural experience.

NM: And the leaders—you talked about the woman who started the school—so, your leaders and the teachers you had were Women of Color?

MF: Well, Caridad, … in the Cuban standards, because there's Black Cubans, white Cubans, she was considered more of a white Cuban. And my teachers in ballet in my art schools were white Hispanics, but it's funny, because my modern teachers were Black. I guess it kind of fit, not the stereotype, but because I grew up in that way, that's what I found to be normal.

NM: Did you find that there was more space for Women of Color in modern than in ballet?

MF: Yes, it was very evident, especially when I transitioned to a performing arts high school, where the level of training was more sophisticated and more advanced. You had to audition to get into the school, and my class, the majority was Hispanic and African American and white. But I did notice that the ones that were considered ballerinas were the white girls and the Hispanics, and then the modern Graham dancers—because we trained in Martha Graham technique mostly and Horton technique—the Graham dancers were mostly Women of Color.

NM: And did that translate also to your experience at Juilliard?

MF: Juilliard was interesting because it's the next step up in terms of training, and they're very exclusive in the sense that they only accept 12 boys and 12 girls every year, and in my class, during my four years there, I was one of the few. There were, I believe, three Hispanics. It was me, an Argentinian girl, and a Puerto Rican boy. So, there were always very few Hispanics and a few Blacks as well, maybe an Asian here and there. So, I wouldn't say we were as diverse, and I guess that's where I noticed it especially.

But the first time I noticed the disparity between races was as a young girl. I used to go to summer intensives, ballet ones especially. And when I was 14 and 16, I came (to New York) to do the ABT summer intensive, and in my class the first year, I was the only Hispanic girl. And then in the second year there was a Brazilian girl, but I noticed that I was clearly different in the sense of my body type; I was more the curvaceous Hispanic compared to the more slender American girls. And I was like "Oh gosh, this is not Miami," where I was used to seeing (a curvier Latina) body. And I guess it opened my eyes and it made me realize that they were going to box me in and say "No, you don't have the perfect feet or the perfect lines and body type to be a ballerina." And for a long time my dream—my goal—was ABT. I wanted to be a classical dancer. But I feel that New World (high school) and then definitely Juilliard opened my eyes and my heart to realizing contemporary dance ... it's not a cop-out, like, oh, I wasn't good enough for ballet, so I go contemporary. No, it really fed my soul in a different way that classical couldn't do alone. So, fusing those two gave me a sense of empowerment as an artist. And then when I came to Ballet Hispánico, it gave me a sense of empowerment as a Latina, which was, like, on a whole different level.

NM: *Do you think that you saw a space for yourself in contemporary where you didn't in ballet?*

MF: Yeah, in the sense that contemporary, when you just look at the art form, it's a fusion of all these other forms, classical modern and classical ballet. So, it doesn't have so many restrictions. There's so many different body types that can achieve the same kinds of movement. No, not the same, different styles, whether it's more grounded, or staccato ... a Jiri Kylian piece, which has classical lines, is different than a Gustavo Ramirez Sansano piece, which is very grounded. So, the fact that there are so many possibilities—it's not just the classical training of the Cubans or Cecchetti or Vaganova. I can hone these skills and excel beyond them too.

NM: *When you think about your time with Ballet Hispánico and your experiences either guesting or interacting with other companies, how would you describe the culture of Ballet Hispánico, and what makes it different as a company member?*

MF: It's funny, we get asked that question a lot, and—not because I'm biased, but because I've witnessed it and experienced it—I think Ballet Hispánico is unique because we are founded in our cultural principles. Like, we're Hispanic, and Hispanic people tend to be very warm and family-oriented, and I think our mission statement—we stay true to that.

You can sense it if you come to one of our rehearsals, and you just sit down and watch how we interact day to day, there's a really nice ease. Ninety percent of the time. Of course, there's always moments where there's tension ... it's life, like any relationship, but we truly are a family. I love these guys like my sisters and brothers. Especially me, because I've been here for so long, so I've had the honor to see the ebb and flow and the changes. And so, it's something that I really try to cultivate.

NM: Do you have a teacher or an advocate in your life who's helped you navigate the space as a woman of Color in dance?

MF: My very first teacher, Caridad (Espinosa), instilled in me the pride of being a Cuban dancer and the technique and how important the technique was and how rich it is. So, I guess without knowing it at a young age, she empowered me to stay true to that, to being a Latina. And then, as I got older, it didn't necessarily have to do with my race, but I give a lot of credit to my teacher, Charla Glenn, who was my instructor at Juilliard. She was a great mentor as well. I love that she was one of the teachers ... it was really evident in her teaching style that it didn't matter what color or what body type you had or what conditions you had. She was willing to bring out ... to find the piece of you to expand on, and she was willing to bring out your strong suits even when you didn't believe that they were there. And she helped me a lot during those four years, because it's a difficult school, and mentally, psychologically, it can mess with you. I'm really grateful for her support. And even now as a professional, she still comes and sees all my shows.

NM: That truly is wonderful. What challenges and achievements stand out for you in your experience in ballet and in dance?

MF: I would say my biggest challenge was myself. Like, mentally, psychologically, I think a lot of dancers struggle with this, especially when they're in that adolescence age where you have to decide whether this is going to be your career or not because it requires so much sacrifice in terms of time—your life and discipline.

And I think my biggest challenge during my training was during my years at the Juilliard School. I really had to reorganize my thoughts and make them become more positive, because when I got into Juilliard, I went from being the best in my school, and then all of a sudden I was the little fish in a bigger pond. And I was like, wow, everyone's amazing! And for me, instead of allowing that to push me further and excite me, it brought me down because I became negative. I said, "Wow, I'm the worst one. What am I doing here?" It's funny how throughout the four years, I was learning how to cope with these negative thoughts; I had to reorient them and shift them. And then, by the end of my four years there, I realized that the mind plays the biggest part in your success. And then when I got into a company, I was really grateful and superlucky.

The goal of everyone graduating from Juilliard is to have a job by May 15, your graduation date, and if you don't, you start freaking out. But I was fortunate that I had this contact with Ballet Hispánico, and by the time I graduated I was in the process of auditioning, and by August they gave me the contract, so it was a huge blessing, and I was so grateful. The fact that I had gotten a contract with a company that I admired was a huge relief, and it made me realize that all that mental strife and physical strife too that I had put myself through in college was paying off.

Once I became a professional, the first year is always the hardest. You have to transition from thinking in an academic mindset, like a student, to a professional.

And that, for me, was liberating because I realized I didn't have to hyperfocus on all my flaws. At the end of the day, my job was to perform well, with integrity and my technique, but more so it was to perform in a way that my director would be pleased, that he would notice I'm offering something to the audience. Because I know that one thing Mr. Vilaro loves is a dancer who can offer themselves genuinely—like, who they are as a person—to the audience. And that's where I found my voice. Like, who Melissa was, not who the student at Juilliard was or who the student in Miami was.

NM: That's beautiful. I'm under the impression that Juilliard has a certain amount of turnover among the students. So, when you talk about 12 males and females coming in, how many students were in your class when you graduated?
MF: Eighteen. We were at 18, yeah.

NM: That's not...
MF: It's not that bad, but I know that after us, they started accepting 26, because they were like, oh my god, if so many kids leave.... It happens; it's a difficult, strenuous program. I have a really good friend, and she only stuck it out for six weeks because it just wasn't for her. And, you know, everyone has their own path.

NM: Do you remember any significant works that you performed that for you related to the social climate of the time in a significant way?
MF: Recently, at the Apollo—and last year, at the Joyce, in April (circa 2016)—we presented an all–Latina program. All the choreographers were Hispanic women, and that was fun because of today's focus on feminism and women's rights. It was cool to present a whole evening where everything was driven by the female voice. And each piece was very different, so it was nice for us, the dancers, to experiment with that and also to see how the public would react.

But even more relevant, I think, is the Apollo season, which we just had on Friday and Saturday; our theme was immigration. So, the three pieces touched upon different cultures. For example, the first piece, which is called *Bury Me Standing* by Ramón Oller, it's about the Roma people, the Gypsies, and how they were constantly immigrating and their desire to belong, but they know that they always have to keep moving. Moving on, moving forward. And that was very relevant at the time we set it, because there were a lot of immigrants, for example, the Syrians going to Spain to find refuge. And for me, that connected the ideas, and it helped me portray the character at a deeper level than just dancing it.

Aside from that, we did Ronald K. Brown's *Espiritu Vivo*, originally choreographed seven years ago. It was about the tragedy and the loss of those that had died on 9/11. The singer, Susana Baca, wrote these songs inspired by that event. And so, the beginning of the piece is very somber and could evoke those feelings of loss, but as you go on to the middle and the end, it's very joyous. In song she's talking about *fin de la esclavitud*, so it's the end of slavery, and I didn't take that in a literal way; I took it in a metaphorical way. It's like the end of fear. We're getting over this fear of terrorism and fear of being suppressed in our own city, New York City. And it was a challenge, but it was beautiful in the end—Ballet Hispánico had tackled Afro-Cuban work. And, honestly, it was so hard, because the majority, 99 percent of us (struggled), because the only one who achieved it was my boyfriend, who is Afro-Cuban. He had that in his bones, in his blood, because he was born dancing that style in Cuba. But for the rest of us, we had to get in touch with it and learn about the history of the Orishas, the Santos—Shangó, Elegua. Because that's what Ronald was inspired by. And also, he fuses other African cultures, so it was cool to see what step came from what culture or what tradition.

Then, finally, the last piece was *Con Brazos Abiertos* by Michelle Manzanales, who used to be our rehearsal director; now she's the director of the school of dance at BH. And her piece was, for me, it's the one that I'm the most attached to, because she started the process two years ago and she finally realized it this past spring. We premiered it at the Joyce in April, and it talks about her evolution as a person and a choreographer while being Mexican American. It's that struggle of finding her identity, because when she's in the U.S. living her life—she's from Texas—people saw her as, oh, you're the ethnic girl. But when she would go to Mexico, her relatives were like, no, you're *la gringa* (a white girl). So, it's that constant battle: where do I belong and how do I embrace this culture that I knew when I was young—how she lived her daily life. I related to that. I lived in Miami, so to me, Cubans are normal, but when you go elsewhere, you notice that perhaps mariachis at your birthday aren't normal. Things like that, and it was funny, because the whole process was beautiful to hear her anecdotes, her stories. She created the piece based on these vignettes in her life and the evolution of it; it's very colorful and eye-pleasing. The crowd loved it, so it was fun.

NM: Awesome. Great. Have you spent time in Cuba?
MF: Yes, many times.

NM: What part?
MF: My family is from Oriente, the eastern part. They're from a town called Bayamo. The first time I went was four or five years ago. I went with my mother, who hadn't been back since she left, like 25 years. My mom's one of three; she has two brothers. She and her older brother live in Miami. Her eldest brother stayed in Cuba, and when my grandfather, her father, passed away, his wish was that the brothers be reunited. So, she made a decision to go to Cuba and took me with her. That was the first time I went. It was so emotional and eye-opening. To meet, like, cousins and uncles in the flesh that I had known about my whole life and seen pictures of but never talked to, never interacted with. And on a more obvious note, seeing the conditions they live in. It was so humbling—it gives you so much perspective. I miss them. Then in 2014, Ballet Hispánico had the honor to go to the International Festival in Havana. That was the first time we (BH) had gone, and that was my first time in Havana, the capital, actually.

NM: I bet that was really special.

MF: Yeah. I had always wanted to go and, obviously Havana is totally different than the eastern part of the island. The eastern part is more, what we would call, like, *campestre.*

NM: Less touristy?

MF: Yes, less touristy and more, like, farms and people and little towns, where Havana's a big city, very populated. And that was beautiful. We saw old Havana, and we went to the ballet school and the company, I got to see a lot of things.

NM: Did you take class there?

MF: Yeah, we took class at the National Ballet Company.

NM: What was that like?

MF: It was amazing, because I thought of all my Cuban teachers and I thought of all the stories they had told me, and I was like, that happened in this room, the blue studio; I'm right here. It was interesting to see how such phenomenal dancers come out of such a humble space. Like, for example, something so simple as their floors are wood. They don't have Marley, so the floor is super slippery. I don't know how these girls do it on pointe, and because it's wood, it wears out your pointe shoes so quickly. And, there's no AC, which is normal; I was used to that in Miami (in the home). But here in the U.S., heaven forbid you don't have AC in the dance studio. Just simple little things you notice. Despite those adversities, these dancers are phenomenal, and they give just as much time and dedication and effort.

NM: Maybe more.

MF: Yes, and maybe more. More sacrifice than a kid in the States would, you know?

NM: I just took one trip to Santiago this summer, and I noticed that the Afro-Cubans were in the contemporary works and the white Cubans were in ballet, not exclusively but generally.

MF: There is a lot of racism in Cuba in dance, unfortunately. It's sad to say that, but I'm going to be really honest because I think it's a topic that they still haven't tackled head-on. Like, for example, my boyfriend, Lyvan Verdecia, he was in the school, and he danced for the company for two years, and he's Black and white. He's what we would call mulatto, and he was not given many opportunities in the ballet company because he was Black. And it's very noticeable. They like to cast white dancers, and it's sad; that still goes on. Whether they acknowledge it or not, that's a different story, but it happens.

NM: And it certainly happens in the United States. Do you see it as same story, different country, or do you see that it's in some way different?

MF: No. I honestly believe now, in this day and age, yes, racism exists, but I think in the dance world, because we've had so much success in terms of a Misty Copeland figure, who's brought light to Brown girls that can dance ballet, I think people are more aware of it. And especially in the art world, where it's like a utopian society. We're not looking at color or all these barriers that exist in our day-to-day life. I think as an artist, outside the commercial world, if that makes sense. Art for the sake of art, because that's what we love; we're color-blind. Or maybe that's me being naive, but living in New York City, a more liberal city, more art educated, and cultured, I don't think that we're as close-minded. For example, ABT is not only going to cast white girls to do their production. I think we're taking the steps to erase that.

NM: How do you relate to ballet as a young student and now?

MF: I'm a perfectionist, and I think ballet fed into that need and desire to achieve the step and constantly work towards achieving the aesthetic. Perfect technique is something that's so elusive, and very few people have it. You know, nobody has it. As a child, ballet was grounding, to know that instead of letting my perfectionist tendencies drive me crazy, I could use dance as an outlet.

As I got older and transitioned into contemporary—I (still) train in ballet every day. Ballet is always a big part of me. It's not like I said, okay, goodbye, ballet. To be a contemporary dancer, you have to be very close to ballet. For example, I take ballet class every morning. I've started to notice how my approach to the class and the technique changed. It wasn't about, oh my god, I have to achieve that triple pirouette and land perfectly in fourth. It was about this class is to prepare me for the long, six-hour day of rehearsal I have ahead, and in that rehearsal I'm not just going to be dancing one classical piece. I'm going to be going from really grounded to more upright. So, this class has to benefit me in a whole body-mind experience, and I think these are things that every dancer learns as they go through the trajectory from being a student to a professional. You have to approach your daily technique as something that's going to prepare you. It's going to mold you and warm you up. It's not about being the best one in the class. I still aspire to that perfection, but it's not the goal. The goal is the journey. The journey is more important.

NM: Cool. Okay. How do company officials, PR, marketing, talk about art for the Latino community?

MF: That's a good question. I've never had that asked. I can only speak for Ballet Hispánico; our mission is to expose our communities, especially in New York and at large, to what it means to be Latino. So, I think they approach it in a very visual way. These posters right here, these are for the Apollo, and in the back that's Dandara Amorim, one of our newest dancers. She's Brazilian, beautiful Black girl, Latina, Brown girl. And in front is Eila Valls, she's Spanish, from Spain. If you look at our posters throughout the years—we've been around since 1970, so 47 years—you see how there's never just one prototype. There's Hispanics of all colors and shapes and races, and for us, I think that's how we best approach it. We showcase an image that is obviously beautiful. Our dancers are physically beautiful, but we're not selling one body type or one face or one hair color.

NM: *The diversity of the culture.*

MF: Yeah.

NM: *Okay. What was your favorite performance and role?*

MF: I have a couple. One of the most recent has been dancing in Annabelle Lopez Ochoa's *Línea Recta*. She set it on us, choreographed it on us, last year, and we presented it ... actually, I got to premiere it in Cuba, which was so special, at the 2016 festival alongside my boyfriend and one of my really good colleagues and friends. That was really special, because it was the first time that a leading lady role was set on me. And I had the opportunity to work really closely with Annabelle, who is a choreographer I've always admired, because she's a woman and her assertiveness.... I was always drawn to that, how she was able to create movement that looks good on contemporary companies and classical companies. She's just a really smart woman. So, that was one of my favorite roles. But before that, Gustavo Ramirez Sansano, a Spaniard, set his version of *Carmen* on Ballet Hispánico, like three years ago, and the role I was given, I was one of the *cigarreras* (cigar factory workers), one of the factory worker girls, friend of Carmen's. And that role, well, first of all, if you know anything about Gustavo, his movement is very challenging and very musical. It's like a contemporary dancer's dream to dance his work. Being given the responsibility of that role and that movement was very liberating for me because I could get in touch with my sensual, sassy side, and for the first time I didn't feel like a young girl in the company. I was a woman, just like the rest of my colleagues. These are things that I remember. Now we're going to revisit that work. We're going to tour it in Europe. It's going to be fun.

NM: *There's a lot of diversity and diversity of Latinos, and that's amazing, but there are times when the company has more non–Hispanic people than others. I'm under the impression that it fluctuates. Can you tell me about that?*

MF: It fluctuates. For the past six years that I've been here, there's been years where 80 percent of us are bilingual. We speak English and Spanish or have come from Spanish-speaking countries. And now, over the past few years, sometimes it's half and half, but lately there's more English-only speakers or Americans than Hispanics, Latins. Amongst the dancers, we've never felt that's a problem. On the contrary, if there's a lot of Hispanics, you'll see, the way we communicate where we speak more in Spanish, we'll always get the non–Spanish speakers to learn. Or, vice versa, if there's more English speakers, then we'll joke in English. So, among the dancers, it's never been a problem.

But I think, obviously ... because of the nature of our company ... like at Ailey, they will always have more African Americans ... they're never going to have 17 white people and 10 Black people; that's just not going to happen. So, for us, I think we have to stay true to the idea of being Hispanic and Latinidad. And in a way, that's even a broader genre, because a Hispanic comes in so many shapes and colors. You can see it. A Brazilian is not going to look like a Colombian, a Cuban American is not going to look like … you know, a Haitian. And we've had Italians and Taiwanese people in the company. So, I think at the end of the day, Eduardo's looking for that diversity, and I don't think he's ever going to hire seven blond blue-eyed people.

However, we do have them. We have three blond-haired people with light eyes and light skin, and I feel that they're just as in tune with their Hispanic side as we are and true to the message. But I think along the road, yeah, we want to establish our brand, and that means having a larger portion of the company that does represent what we would consider Latino. But not making stereotypes, if that makes sense. It's hard. It's a very fine line, because if everyone's looking the same, then we are stereotyping. But it's a balance. I know that Eduardo doesn't sit there and say "Okay, we already have three blonds, so we can't have another one next year." No, if that dancer appears in the audition and they're incredible and they embody the qualities we're looking for, he will hire them. But naturally, there will always be more Hispanics, because that's what this company attracts.

NM: That makes sense. So, you talked a little bit about race, and you talked a little bit about competition in dance regardless of race. But have you ever had an experience where you felt your race was part of that competitiveness? Where you had to be twice as good as the white dancers or anything in that kind of realm?

MF: I only felt that way, honestly, when I was in a very classical ballet setting. Like, auditioning for summer programs and things like that. But honestly, in college and now in the professional environment, no, I've never felt that. Perhaps because my professional career has been associated with Ballet Hispánico, and I'm always in a zone where I feel safe. I've always felt proud of my culture. But I always feel that of course they're not going to be racist against me because I'm representing this.

NM: I wonder how many young Women of Color don't pursue ballet because they lack that feeling of acceptance. Like, when I look at the roster at ABT or New York City Ballet and I don't see a lot of Latinas, maybe it's because the ballet didn't extend that feeling of acceptance, but it's not something that can be measured.

MF: Maybe. But there's a lot, when you really dig deep into that, I think, it's also a socioeconomic thing. At the end of the day, it draws back to that. For example, in Miami growing up, a lot of the girls at my studio were middle class, lower middle class. Ballet is expensive—it's so expensive, between the dancewear and the pointe shoes and the classes themselves. A lot of these girls required scholarships. I required scholarships. That time that I went to ABT, I didn't get a scholarship, but fortunately, one of my aunts was able to help my mom pay for it, and that was a huge blessing. She did it because she knew how much it meant to me, and I'm very grateful, because now I'm a professional. But, I think at the end of the day, especially in companies like that, I think it's a socioeconomic thing. Most of these girls—it's funny, because I would meet these girls in summer programs, the American white girls that lived in Connecticut, New York, or New Jersey—came from more affluent families. So, it's easier for their moms to pay $10,000 in tuition.

NM: And to stay in New York while they're taking these summer intensives....

MF: Yeah. I had to stay with that aunt that helped me pay for the program. I would stay with her in Jersey, and every day I would take the train to ABT. If we were to dig deeper and maybe get out statistics, girls like me, regardless, it's not to say that they don't make it because of any one thing. There are many factors; aside from socioeconomic, it's the talent and the body type and the perseverance.

NM: But economics is an obstacle they're climbing.

MF: I think that's a really big, evident obstacle. If you don't have the money, even if you're the most talented, if you can't go to the summer program, and maybe they gave away all their scholarships already.

There weren't a lot of us, and ballet is such an elitist art form ... by nature. It was created by the bourgeois, you know, the French elite. So, that's the ideology it's always going to be based on. And not that we do it on purpose to exclude Blacks or Hispanics or Asians, it's just that these (white) girls have the money, so they can go to these programs.

NM: You talked a little bit about body issues in ballet. Is there a specific incident related to body or body image that you can remember? Can you share?

MF: Hispanics or Latinas are known for being more curvaceous. When I was young, I always had a big butt for ballet. A more, like, round butt. And I'll never forget, I was in high school, and I had a teacher, and she was like, "Your butt is so big. Why can't you tuck it in?" And I was like, "I can't," in my mind, obviously. You don't respond to these things; you just try to make it happen. But I was like, it's not going anywhere. I got this butt from my mom and my Cuban ancestors, you know? Honestly, I was, like, obsessed with being flat-chested and flat and being anorexic skinny, which is not healthy, in retrospect. I had seen all these girls at ABT, and ... my body will never achieve that unless I go to some unhealthy extreme. But that idea that some body parts or some curves or shapes are not acceptable in a body that should do ballet was frustrating for me. It's funny, because I even struggled with that at Juilliard, and that was a more contemporary school. Well, we train in everything, but we perform contemporary. But this idea of being skinny and the perfect body, it's something very prevalent in dance culture, and that's something I think we need to work on just as much as race. Because these issues are psychologically impacting a lot of young girls. That was one instance, in particular that, as a young kid, informed me. Whereas in that moment I saw it as a bad thing and I was like ugh, why can't I have that skinny body? And what could I do to get rid of my butt?

On a brighter note, an instance that happened in this company, I think it was my first year, we performed at the Kennedy Center, and one of my friends, he saw a clip of us dancing, and he commented on Facebook, "It's so nice to see girls with curves dancing beautifully onstage." And I was like, whoa, he just praised my curves! And all this time, I was like hating on them, but there are people out there who appreciate them just as much as they appreciate an emaciated girl. Like, okay, there's people for both camps. Yeah, every dancer has a story in which their body was shamed.

NM: For sure. I think a lot about this when I talk to my students. I say, "Many of us have problems here, including myself. We've danced in studios for 10 and 20 plus 20 years, with mirrors and thin women everywhere, and many of us feel like there is always something not right with our body." And then, the goal of so many classes is to examine what you're doing wrong (so you can improve).

MF: Yeah, right there, that's…. Yeah, I'm psychologically a little damaged, but…

NM: Who's not? Can we talk a little more about community?

MF: It's funny, because when you become a professional, your goal is to dance the lead, be in every piece, be onstage, and the longer you spend in this profession—and especially in this company, because outreach is such a pivotal part of what we do—you're not just going to dance onstage, you have to interact with the community. You start realizing that the most profound experiences are not necessarily the ones you have onstage; they're the ones you have with the people.

One of my most impactful moments was when we were in California, I don't know how many years back, but we were in Bakersfield in this community, like a farming community, Mexicans, and they have this community house. So, the Wonderful Foods company, if I'm not mistaken, gave money to this community to help rebuild. Because it was a very impoverished community, lots of problems with drugs and crime, and they were able to infiltrate money and bring it up. So, they built this beautiful community center and started programs in the schools to empower kids.

Ballet Hispánico went to teach workshops, and one day we spent a whole afternoon in this community center teaching what we like to call "Latin social." It's pretty much like a salsa, merengue class, but we engage people at all levels and all ages. There were grandmas and little kids, and I remember my boyfriend was teaching, he was leading the salsa lesson, and then—because we had two that day, so one had just passed, and the second one was starting—and the little girl that I had been dancing with us in the first lesson, she came up to me and she tapped my knee, because she was so little, and I turned around. She was like, "This flower's for you." She had gone outside to pick me a flower, and I was like, oh my god. And she was so young and, when I work with children, that's the most impactful.

Especially now, the older I get, and I want children. You mold these kids, especially when you see you're molding kids that feel like they had no future. Like, they lived in a really impoverished town in Bakersfield, and their parents are migrant workers, and you feel like, well, what is their future? What do they have to look forward to? And so, when you give them a glimpse into what you do…. When we do questions and answers after our performances for kids and they ask questions like … one day, a really cute African American boy goes, "Do you guys get paid to dance?" And we were like, "Yeah, we do." And he was like, "Yes! Yes!" And I was like, whoa, we got him enthused! I think that's a really important message, for kids to know that if your soul yearns for dance and art, then do it, and you can make a living out of it. We showed these kids that you can make something of yourself, you know? For me that was beautiful.

Another one was when we went to Israel, and Shelby and I were partnered up and had to teach a roomful of Palestinian and Israeli girls, and none of them spoke English. So, this was a challenge, but it was amazing to see how dance is truly a universal language. Because we were teaching salsa, we paired them up, and by the end of the class they were catching on. Knowing the political climate in Israel, to see Palestinian girls and Israeli girls get together and, you know, unify for a moment through something like dance, it was really groundbreaking, and it gave me hope in society.

NM: That's beautiful. And I know that you've had extensive dance training: Juilliard, Complexions, Netherlands Dance Theatre. But what does it mean to be part of a company that's connected to Latino culture as opposed to a more mainstream space?

MF: Well, it's funny because at Juilliard, when I was there, my dream was to be in a European company. That was like the goal, and then I got into this company, and I realized, when I speak to my friends who are Hispanic but are in … not normal companies but European companies that aren't associated with a culture, like Hispanic culture … how do I put this? Not that they don't have the same pride for their culture, but when you're immersed in it all day long, we are here, and that is our mission statement. You become more aware of how your culture really does inform everything you do. And especially in this day and age, being proud of that and embracing that and advocating for that, is … important, because without your roots, who are you? Especially now in America with all the issues with immigration. This country was built on immigrants. So, recognizing that, especially now that I've been to Cuba and know my family's history, it's an integral part of my life.

I'm an artist, but I'm a Hispanic artist, and aside from that, I'm Melissa. I'm not just the Cuban American girl. So, there's so many different facets to it, but I think knowing and embracing that I am a Latina is something very empowering, something I want to share everywhere I go as an artist. Whereas, perhaps, being in a company like NDT (Nederlands Dans Theater), for example: I have a friend who danced there, and she's Argentinian, like, that wasn't her focus. Her focus wasn't educating others on her Argentinian roots, and that's cool, but for people who aren't immersed in what Ballet Hispánico is about (cultural heritage and connection to dance), perhaps they don't get to tap into that culture (in an embodied way). So, maybe she didn't tap into her Argentinian roots when she was dancing a piece by Yuri or Lightfoot, you know?

NM: Sure.

MF: And that's something that I'm grateful that I can do here, because it gives my work a different richness. Yeah.

Melissa Verdecia and Lyvan Verdecia in *Landscapes*, choreographed by Donna Murray (photograph by Luis Corona; courtesy Melissa Verdecia).

NM: That's lovely. You talked about the racism in Cuba in ballet. I've spent a very little time in Cuba, and I've also spent a little time in South Africa, and I've noticed that South Africa, like some other countries, but particularly the Joburg Ballet, wants to have an image of being diverse, and if you look at the PR on the ballet company, they are more diverse than our most financially endowed and established companies. But one of the things they do is bring dancers from Cuba or Brazil, so what I'm seeing, as a hypothesis, is that in Cuba, as an Afro-Cuban, you can train in ballet, but opportunities to get into the national company are scarce. But if you're trained at the national ballet school, you can often get employment in a company in some other country.

MF: Yeah. It just goes to show you the hypocrisy, in a sense. It's not that the Afro-Cubans can't be in the company; there are some who have been and are super successful. Carlos Acosta, he was trained and brought up—well, he had issues too; if you go read his story, you'll see how he had some opposition in the Cuban ballet. But he became the star of the Royal Ballet, and he became successful in London. And Ociele … his last name escapes me, also an Afro-Cuban, incredible star, and now he dances in Europe as well. So, it's what you're saying, these people are brought up in this tradition, and they're honed in this incredible technique, but in their home countries they don't always get the same opportunities or it's very short-lived or the roles aren't the principal roles. It's never solos, never principals. So, it's interesting how … these other countries are like, okay, so they are the best, and we need them.

NM: We need color, we need diversity!

MF: Yeah. So, I think it's sad (from) the standpoint of the Cuban Ballet; why not elevate your own dancers? They're phenomenal, regardless of their color. But at least in other realms they're getting more opportunities, and to be honest, a lot of these dancers would prefer leaving Cuba. Because if we want to really get into it, the political climate of living in Cuba is rough, and the standard of living is rough. A dancer doesn't make much. To be honest, they'd probably prefer to leave.

NM: Melissa Fernandez, thank you so much for giving me your time and information and your story, I really appreciate it.

MF: Thank you.

Melissa Verdecia Glossary

> Brief bio-notes of artists and places mentioned in the chapter. This is not intended to be comprehensive but instead to offer a small amount of information to spark more thorough research if readers are interested.

Acosta, Carlos—Cuba-born choreographer and dancer. Artistic director of the Birmingham Royal Ballet.

Ailey, Alvin—Founder of Alvin Ailey American Dance Theater in 1958. Choreographer and activist.

American Ballet Theatre (ABT)—Founded in 1939. Known for presenting classical ballet repertory in contrast to New York "City Ballet," known for presenting and preserving Balanchine repertory.

Set II—Dancers Who Are Still Performing or Recently Retired

Amorim-Veiga, Dandara—Dancer with Ballet Hispánico.

The Apollo—A famous theater, nonprofit multidisciplinary arts commissioner, and presenter located in New York.

Ballet Hispánico—Latinx/Latine/Hispanic cultural organization founded by Tina Ramirez in 1970 in New York.

Brown, Ronald K.—Choreographer. Founding artistic director of Evidence, A Dance Company, in Brooklyn, New York, in 1985.

Cecchetti, Enrico—Dancer and creator of the Cecchetti Method, a ballet training method.

Copeland, Misty—First African American female principal dancer with the American Ballet Theatre.

Espinosa, Caridad—Cuban born. Melissa's first dance teacher.

Genn, Chara—South African born. Ballet teacher on faculty at Julliard and numerous other dance organizations.

Graham, Martha—Founder of the Martha Graham School of Contemporary Dance in New York.

The Joyce Theater—Dance theater in Chelsea, New York, built in 1982.

Juilliard School—Private performing arts conservatory founded in 1905.

Kylian, Jiri—Choreographer. Former artistic director of the Nederlands Dans Theater, 1975–1999.

Lopez Ochoa, Annabelle—Belgian-born choreographer. Director of the Contemporary Classical Summer Program of the School at Jacob's Pillow.

Manzanales, Michelle—Choreographer, dance educator. Cofounder of the Latinx Dance Educators Alliance.

New York City Ballet—Founded in 1948 by George Balanchine and Lincoln Kirstein. Known for presenting Balanchine repertory, in contrast to American Ballet Theatre, which is known for presenting classical ballets.

Oller-Martinez, Ramon—Dancer, choreographer, and founder of the Metros Company.

Orishas—Deities that are part of a spiritual system related to and deriving from the Yoruba religion of West Africa.

Ramirez Sansano, Gustavo—Choreographer. Former artistic director of the Chicago-based Latino-focused contemporary dance company Luna Negra Dance Theater.

Vaganova, Agrippina—Russia ballet dancer, choreographer, and creator of the Vaganova Method, a ballet technique and training method.

Valls, Eila—Dancer affiliated with the Peridance Contemporary Dance Company and a member of the DeMa Dance Company.

Vilaro, Eduardo—Artistic director and CEO of Ballet Hispánico.

Reflections

Themes and Variations: In the Experiences of the Women Interviewed

Resilience lives in all of these dancers, as seen in their lived experiences and the paths they have the paved for young artists still to come. The next section is a synthesis of themes I discerned from the interviews with theoretic underpinnings exploring race and Black and Brown dancing bodies, followed by a chapter on progressive antiracist approaches to ballet.

The experiences of the women featured in these interviews illustrate the significance of how race identity markers operate and impact life experiences and livelihoods within a country. These identity markers had great significance, creating the obstacles as well as the opportunities for Women of Color (WOC) who wish to pursue a career in ballet. There can be no question that these women have had a presence in American ballet for over a century even though many people do not know about any of them. Why was Misty Copeland framed by so many, rewriting history, as "the first"? Why was there such a lack of information that this falsehood could emerge and be widely accepted?

The absence of Black and Brown people in ballet is not accidental but rather institutional, commonplace erasure. It is also informed by location and people, which also means that such circumstances are malleable. As we see in the lives of many of the women featured in this book, national cultural identities are expressed through the arts. Art forms positioned to gatekeep around social constructs of power enact the cultural norms and social construct of the locale. Similarly, countries that want to see themselves in ballet find ways to express their national identity through the form. South Korea and Cuba are models of this, with South Africa also working to create a South African ballet identity. As dance scholar Thomas DeFrantz wrote, "Ballet technique, in and of itself, is not racist, but the people who teach it, as well as its company managers, artistic directors, patrons, critics, and choreographers, live in a racist society and succumb to its vicissitudes" (2004, 146).

To Include or Not to Include: Representation Matters, Geography Matters

As distinct as each of the 13 interviewees are, what can be said of them collectively? Each interviewee chose to focus a significant portion of their life in ballet. Their ideas about who gets to perform ballet are often laced with implicit notions that none of these women belong. But for some, these notions were not part of their socially constructed identity; in fact, for some it was quite the opposite. For example, the whole reason why ballet has thrived in Cuba harkens back to subverting a white supremacy model. The art form was embraced by Fidel Castro's government when Alicia Alonso advocated for national development as a signature of culture and refinement for the country (Tomé 2011). Cuba wanted to be looked upon as a global center; its dancers excelling in this Eurocentric dance that signified high art would certainly support such a goal. How better to subvert white supremacy, exemplifying capitalism and European aesthetics, than for those suppressed by the model to take the dance treasured by dominant world powers and master it, to insist on inclusion, on their own terms? This could also be said of the work of Arthur Mitchell through Dance Theatre of Harlem (DTH).

Ballet brought the dancers featured herein from a wide variety of places. Lauren Anderson and Caridad Martinez brought forth the experiences of two women from previous eras. Their stories explore ballet from very different places: Houston, Texas, and Havana, Cuba. The support Ben Stevenson extended to Anderson at the Houston Ballet shaped her experiences in monumental ways that transcended race. In contrast, race was a social and institutional obstacle for Martinez to navigate from the beginning and throughout her career. Both women surpassed the challenges of racial constructs yet remained acutely aware of discriminatory practices that can impact the lives and livelihoods of talented ballet artists. Further, this awareness and lived experience hangs in the balance for these women every day as an added hurdle that white dancers, in the past and today, do not have to understand, engage, or climb over. Dancers today have very different stories. Yet, to be sure, race is still a part of their stories.

Another observation of great significance is geographic location. Where a person lives and is raised has an immeasurable impact on who they will be in the future. As we look at WOC in ballet historically, one can see that only in certain parts of the country could WOC train to become ballet dancers in the 1940s or 1960s or 1990s; typically during the earlier years most opportunities would be on the East Coast. Access, opportunity, and representation includes where ballet teachers are accessible across the United States at any given time. Then, one would need to consider whether the accessible spaces were welcoming for people of Color (POC). Many POC today express some level of discomfort or cultural alienation in predominantly white spaces. How might this have looked 30 years ago in terms of demographics and racial tensions. It is important to think about how location had an impact on each woman's experience.

Lauren Anderson achieved the position of principal dancer in part because she was born and raised in Houston at a time when Stevenson was at the helm of the Houston Ballet and saw a vision for the organization that surpassed skin color. Anderson might have fared differently in, say, Marion, Indiana, where less opportunities in ballet and for children of Color were available when Anderson trained in the 1980s. One might also consider some of the blatant racism Endalyn Taylor experienced in a different part of the country training at relatively the same time. Also consider the training experiences of Margaret Severin-Hansen just a few years later on the East Coast, who reported no experiences of discrimination in her training and career.

In 2014, I presented a talk about the scarcity of Black ballerinas at Swarthmore College in Pennsylvania, and a white student in the front row was absolutely bewildered by my presentation. When I completed my talk, during the question-and-answer period she said, "I do not know what you mean that experiences are limited for African American women. I have been going to the ballet all my life, and there was always an African American principal dancer." My answer was "You're from Houston, aren't you?" And she said, "Yes." This exchange gave me hope that we really can shift our society and culture so that no children see limitations in front of them if we reimagine our politics of who gets to dance and who gets to dance what roles.

National Identity and Ballet

The common denominator in identity markers for the 13 women interviewed is that they are not members of the global dominant culture. I want to focus on what that means in ballet. First and foremost, it is most significant to understand that race and "being outside the dominant culture" do not mean the same thing from country to country or even from ballet company to ballet company. As a social construct, the national identity in which one lives contributes immensely to the way that nation-state organizes race relations: the racial contract (Mills 1997), social understandings, and customs. I found that this was one of the variations in how ballet was experienced as a dance form during each interviewee's training and career. Depending upon their country, she may not see ballet as Eurocentric or even as a gatekeeping tool to keep POC out. This was most evident with those interviewed from Central and South America, and it also aligns with what I have gathered through personal relationships with South Korean dancers.

The notion that ballet can be an expression of nation-state identity might be no more pronounced than the case of the United States. Ballet in the United States embodies, expresses, and displays the image of the stratified caste system of the nation. In many ways, the U.S. image of the mainstream ballet company belies the true nature of this country. The white dominant culture is centered, and POC are included on the periphery as token gestures and platitudes of diversity and inclusion.

Ballet can be employed as an expression of nation-state identity, both explicitly and implicitly. The United States is known for diversity. But the nation also harbors racism, and there is a public understanding that national institutions (such as the educational system, the health care system, the criminal justice system, and financial banking structures) were constructed to support the white middle class, marginalizing and deterring people outside the dominant culture (Bonilla-Silva 2006). These structural arrangements, also known as whiteness (Castagno 2014), are reflected in all the arts, including ballet. In this way, ballet mirrors, embodies, and personifies the racial tension and, yes, racism that permeates and plagues the United States.

There are dance companies beyond the United States in places such as Cuba, Brazil, and China that have successfully utilized ballet to bolster national pride. This has been written about at length by many dance scholars as in the case of *The Red Detachment of Women*, a Chinese film from 1961 that was transformed into a ballet. The ballet carried forth the goals of Chairman Mao Zedong and the cultural revolution at the time (Colville 2021). Originally performed in 1964 (Zhang 2016), this historic ballet exemplifies the slogan coined by Mao in 1956: "Use the past to serve the present and make the foreign serve China" (Brady 2003, 1). The second part of the quote, "make the foreign serve China," speaks to the way in which this European art form was appropriated and utilized as political propaganda art to support the cultural revolution and the Communist Party. But what is significant is that in contrast to the way that ballet is commonly used in the United States, *The Red Detachment of Women* serves as one model of how ballet can express a non–Eurocentric culture. In this ballet, a body type not typically featured in Western-based ballet is centered, and communist sociopolitical values are promoted, presenting affirming artistry (Clark 2010, 178).

Similarly, Cuba also developed a cultural arts identity, in part, through ballet. The country established an internationally acclaimed national ballet company in 1948 and school in 1950 that have been in operation for decades (Ballet Nacional de Cuba 2021). As mentioned by Caridad Martinez, the ballet school developed a Cuban ballet technique to provide a particular Cuban-informed approach to the form. Martinez notes that this technique is more suited to the physical attributes of the Cuban people than those purported by the Russian Vaganova technique that was a common option at the time the school was establishing its ethos.

In-group Messaging

The dancers featured in this book possess intersections with many individual identity themes such as nationality, race, and ethnicity. Where one can see affinity around nationality, this at times intersects with other identity markers. Many of the dancers interviewed describe experiences that aligned their identity with others in their group relating to country and race, especially in the case of the Cuban dancers. This intersection also points to moments when in-group messaging was active. The Cuban model of ballet exemplifies in-group messaging as subconscious messages that people receive from others in their in-group. As introduced in Part I, an in-group message is a message sent from a person with a salient identity marker to other members in that same identity group. These messages are implicit and communicated through actions, positions/roles, representation (print, digital, text, video), and examples in history as well as real-life experiences.

Historically, WOC receive few affirming in-group messages from other WOC pursuing ballet as a career. More specifically, within a U.S. context, African American women may receive the in-group message that few African American women can actualize their dreams in ballet. The anomaly to this could be young women with the financial resources to have seen DTH perform. Due to the size and large presence of DTH, including its legacy of African American dancers, it is possible for many African American women from this particular part of the United States or with financial means and access to see and believe that African American women can achieve in ballet. Consider the experience of Lauren Anderson as she talks about her first trip to the DTH school long after her retirement:

> Yeah [emotional shift in her voice], wow ... so, I never danced with them, by the way.... Virginia Johnson, who is the ballerina I looked up to as a young dancer ... called me and asked me to come teach. And I said "sure," and I got there. Just walking in and seeing that giant picture of Mr. Mitchell.... It was ... tears came to my eyes. Walking around and seeing that many little Brown ballerinas in one place, I'd never seen it before; I never ever witnessed that before. So that was, it choked me up, and when I think about it, I still get a little choked up [Anderson interview].

It is hard to deny the power of these in-group messages when you hear from a dancer who missed on out on such affirmation in a consistent manner as a child. The loss of not being affirmed by like images in one's training is immeasurable, which comes across in Anderson's recounting.

Similarly, young Cuban dancers training at the Cuban Nacional Ballet School would see a plethora of dancers they could identify with, which would enable them to experience ballet in a culturally and identity-affirming space. This experience is unlike the experience of many dancers of Color who navigate U.S. mainstream ballet schools that historically embrace and uplift the white dancing body. Many U.S. mainstream ballet institutions have often, both explicitly and implicitly, asked students without white–presenting bodies to approximate whiteness.* Further, in-group messaging is powerful and can send messages that are encouraging or discouraging, depending on the context.

---

*I use the term "white-presenting" instead of "white–passing" because presenting as white is not synonymous with passing for white.

Throughout Part II, affirming in-group messaging came up as a point of inspiration from African American, Asian, as well as Latina dancers. The U.S.-based Latina dancers interviewed knew Caridad Martinez. In my interview with Fernandez, she spoke with affection about Martinez and noted that she was one of the first people she studied with when she came to New York. When talking about her role as a teacher, Martinez articulated the importance of representation in this way:

> You know, it's important for Black people, for African Americans, and Latinos, to see people like them teaching them, performing. They came every single weekend (referring to her students). And I realized that the problem was that they were surrounded by white people. That's why they came. (They would say to me) "We want to stay with you. We want to take classes with you" [Fernandez interview].

This first had account demonstrates how these dynamics can play out for students seeking affirming in-group messages to support them through their training and employment.

Similarly, Verdecia mentioned that Caridad Espinosa, her dance teacher from Cuba, was a formative role model for her. These Latina dancers shared a particular affinity and interest in being connected to other dancers with similar backgrounds. This is a common occurrence, and as such I intuit that this is often a subconscious choice. However, when one considers their friendship circles, often there are shared interests, which further connects them to cultural and identity markers to those they are closest. To that point, it is not surprising, then, that Martinez pointed me in the direction of Lopez. Of course, Martinez and Verdecia also worked together at Ballet Hispánico.

In-group messages do work to affirm, disaffirm, or redirect. Verdecia noted the implicit (in-group) messages she received in her training that directed WOC toward modern and contemporary techniques and white dancers toward ballet. In contrast, the in-group messages that students at the Cuban National Ballet School received from company members carved space for them to imagine futures in the company. Moreover, individuals from marginalized groups have a heightened need for those intracultural connections, so their networks tend to be substantive.

Kristie Latham shared generously in her interview about the impact of connecting with other Asian dancers through the work of Georgina Pazcoguin and Phil Chan's organization, Final Bow for Yellowface. "Meeting Georgina and dancing alongside her, I looked up to her, both as a friend and mentor. She was the first professional dancer of mixed Asian American race who I had ever met, and I aspired to be like her ... an unapologetic powerhouse" (Lathan interview). Kristie also spoke about how the opportunity to be in a space to share stories about ways race intersected with her career gave her the ability to see the larger landscape with a new perspective. It was not just her experiencing discrimination and microaggressions. She said that

> it wasn't until after our interview for AAPI month concluded where we were able to go off-the-record and share our more personal experiences with our racial identities and how it

has marked our careers. It was this conversation that allowed me to give myself permission to fully "see" my experiences through a clear and honest lens [Lathan interview].

It is important to understand that in the absence of such affinity groups or mechanisms that allow us to see others whom we look like, one can be subject to gaslighting and feeling alienated. These experiences can also intersect with a bootstrapping mentality, suggesting that if we are good enough we will be selected, and if we make too much noise or cause too many problems we will not be selected or promoted, making for dangerous mental stress and anxiety.

The interviewees revealed many connections among the African American dancers as well, with Stephanie Powell noting that Endalyn Taylor adopted her into Dance Theatre of Harlem (DTH) when she joined the company and Lauren Anderson sharing about all the African America ballerinas she admired and looked up to from afar while growing up. These were tacit in-group messages. They were also positive, affirming messages within an art form with limited mirrors for these women. Members of DTH sent Lauren Anderson in-group messages as they grand jetéd across the stage. These messages, sent by people with whom one can identify through their most salient identity markers—often race and gender (Earick 2009)—are powerful. Anderson explains that she did not think of being a ballerina until she saw DTH perform.

It was in-group messages that Powell sought when she left the Oakland Ballet to dance with DTH; she wanted the experience of holding space onstage with dancers who looked like her:

> Judy (Tyrus) came back, to do a performance as a guest, so she did Plum and I was doing Flowers. ... And I remember walking out, and there's like a little pas de quatre, right before Plum goes out. ... Well, I walked out and (Judy Tyrus) walked out, and I looked across the stage and I was like, "oh my God, I've never been on stage with another Black ballerina, hmmmmm"—that did it, that was kind of my impetus to get to DTH. I thought, "There's another one like meeee right now" [speaking with emotion in her throat] It had never happened, ever, in my whole life [Powell interview].

In-group messaging is a powerful socializing tool. It's a signal of belonging, the notion that you do not have to be "the only one." For marginalized and oppressed groups, it is also an opportunity of healing and resilience. This was evident in 2015 at Misty Copeland's historic American Ballet Theatre premiere as principal ballerina in the role of Odette in *Swan Lake*. To be sure, Lauren Anderson and Raven Wilkinson were there to affirm the soaring young dancer with bouquets onstage. Consider how these messages operated in the lives of the interviewees.

A Black feminist theoretical lens is another vantage point that calls for consideration to better understand the experiences of Stephanie Powell and other interviewees. The words of Black feminist scholar Brittney Cooper resonate: "Black girls of every age need other Black girls who can hold their truths" (2018, 18). There is great significance in being seen and understood in one's lived experience, particularly for marginalized people outside the dominant culture. For many, only those who are also marginalized in similar ways can truly provide the soothing affirmation that the experiences of racial marginalization were real and not to be placated. For these individuals, being seen often requires leaving the building in which we work or dance. Cooper draws further significance to the need for Black women's affinity connection, writing that "Blacks girls find each other as a means to survive" (2018, 117). In the 21st century when our society has accepted racism as a public health issue and has identified the numerous physical and mental health problems related to racial trauma, the urgent need to connect to someone experiencing the same marginalization is deeply seated within many WOC. This reality calls for a greater understanding of in-group messaging; it also highlights the need for mainstream ballet companies to go beyond hiring one or two POC for a greater drive toward inclusive representation. In recognition of this reality in a post–George Floyd world, many mainstream ballet companies are working hard to form groups around antiracist practices and affinity groups. To these efforts, I say, "great, continue and do more." Just as I believe these companies would say to their dancers after a great show or to their boards after a great fundraising year "Great! And let's do it even better next time."

Approximating Whiteness

Dr. Brenda Dixon Gottschild, renowned dance historian, writes extensively on the demands to approximate whiteness in financially endowed and established U.S.-based ballet companies in her book *The Black Dancing Body*. Of skin color, she writes,

> More than any other contested sites in the black dancing body, skin is the alpha and omega of racial difference. The darker the skin, the more likely will its inhabitants be excluded from white power and privilege, or even the chance to approximate it. Skin so personal, so all encompassing ... skin protects us; skin reveals us [Gottschild 2003, 190].

To be sure, skin is the most salient identity marker of race for many WOC. In Endalyn Taylor's interview, she talks about experiences of racism at her dance school in Chicago—a school she also credits for her foundational training. As an example, she shared that she was told she did not look like "snow" but instead looked like "slush." She acknowledged her acceptance of discrimination motivated by the desire to access training, something not abundant in her community. In my interview with Stephanie Powell in 2009, she shared a similar experience while dancing with the Oakland Ballet (McCarthy-Brown 2011). She spoke of the Oakland Ballet being like a family while also relaying that she had fewer racial experiences there than at DTH. Yet, she was asked to powder down for *Les Sylphides* while performing for the Oakland Ballet. She complied and stayed with the company for several years thereafter. It is worth noting that ballet training often included teaching dancers to be obedient and agreeable about their appearance as representatives of their employing dance company; language related to appearance is typically included in dancer employment contracts.

Taylor described requirements to powder down and being color-cast into the Arabian role, and of these things she remarked,

> [T]hat early lesson was hard, although I couldn't put my finger on why it felt so uncomfortable. Because nothing was ever spoken. You know how that is, it's all the things that are not said [Taylor interview].

Caridad Martinez in her interview discusses the gatekeeping around skin color that she experienced in her training and career in Cuba. Melissa Verdecia also notes these things in her understanding of ballet in Cuba. Claudia Monja was guarded on the topic but acknowledged that Black men had more access to the company and only mentioned the opportunities of Black women in the national ballet school. The stories go on, from Wilkinson being hired temporarily to see if she could make it as a performer without anyone noticing she was Black (*I'll Make Me a World* 1999) to Aesha Ash being told by the ballet mistress that she did "not want to see one tan body on the stage," in reference to the row of swan dancers (Craig 2018). Gatekeeping exists in the stories of those unable to approximate whiteness, such as Anderson being excluded from choreography when a choreographer outside the Houston Ballet organization came into the space. The decision served to alienate a competent African American dancer.

These experiences do not simply teach those discriminated against; these moments of discrimination also communicate cultural codes to other company members, students in the academy, staff, leadership, audience, and beyond. They are a part of the organizing structure within a race-based society. Eduardo Bonilla-Silva explains in his 2003 book *Racism without Racists: Colorblind Racism and the Persistence of Racial Inequality in America* that racist people are not needed to hold the line on racism when institutional structures have been coded to reflect the racist psyche of the institution and the nation.

One of the ways in which whiteness as a structural arrangement operates in the United States is that people are indoctrinated into a culture where it is inappropriate, impolite, and improper to discuss race in professional settings. In not talking about the structures of inequity, we uphold and protect them and allow institutions and cultural practices to go unchecked. In this way, racism functions as a caste system, one that is described by Isabel Wilkerson in her book *Caste* as an invisible program: "The unseen master program fed by the survival instincts of an automated collective" (2020, 34). People accept the program, system, and structure because it is unseen. Some people are genuinely unaware of the structure; there are examples of this throughout these oral history interviews. For instance, Endalyn Taylor recalled that performing in *Nutcracker* as a child, she was cast as Arabian with three white dancers. Stephanie Powell shared similar observations.

> [E]ven at DTH … there were skin tone preferences. And you see this with roles like Medea, which was Charmaine (Hunter), always, you always had a Brown-skin figure that was

doing those ... there's just certain roles. Like Virginia was never going to do Medea, Virginia (a lighter-skinned woman) was going to do *Creole Giselle*. There's just certain things, so (Mitchell) even fell into that trap of what is expected of a Black swan. Almost maintaining the stereotype of this music, which is very robust and strong, so that was Karen Brown (a darker-skinned woman who fit the description of that strong music) versus the sylph and all these ethereal creatures, the lighter-skinned girls; it happened at DTH. ... [I]f you look at the videos and the casting, it's clearly there [Powell interview].

Endalyn Taylor notes:

It happened here sometimes, whether intentional or not. Certain roles appeared to go to dancers because of their coloring. I mean, I always played strong roles. Myrtha, who's ice cold, Medea, who killed her children and convinced them to kill someone else. It wasn't until the birth of my child, that roles switched for me. I got to portray romantic roles and the femme fatale; I was the flirtatious one.... I reflect on it in hindsight, actually. Other people pointed out the color-casting. We were questioned as to why there were so many light dancers and so few dark dancers. These questions were directed towards Mr. Mitchell at times. We would hear it in conversation from people who came backstage for autographs. They were like "Wow, you are brown. There aren't that many." It was noticed, and sometimes you attributed that to some people are always going to look for the negative side of things. Other people, not so much. Was it there? Yes, it was there [Taylor interview].

Claudia Monja spoke matter-of-factly about it at the Ballet Nacional de Cuba. "You know, many people ask why, in the National Ballet of Cuba, they don't have Black women dancers" (Monja interview). The codes, structure, and "caste" are taught to all members, not just the marginalized or less powerful ones. Often these messages are encoded in actions such as directing people where to go. That is to say, encoded messages are not explicit statements.

The above examples from Powell, Taylor, and Monja note color-casting within the Black community. This phenomenon is common knowledge to members of the Black community. As indicated by the examples, even many with power within these structures of whiteness are compelled to uphold the structure. As caste structures operate, I would argue that often these actions are programed and not intentional. As Stephanie Powell notes, Arthur Mitchell of DTH fell into a (commonly understood) trap.

Whiteness maintains a veneer of niceness and neutrality. As a result, social constructs are nuanced and often conflicting in message. Shelby Colona experienced messages of "niceness" along with a clear understanding of not belonging: "So, I think it was difficult growing up there. No one ever treated me mean or awkward, but I always felt a little out of place" (Colona interview). Looking back to Lauren Anderson, who did not experience racism in ballet until an outside choreographer came to set a work, told me, however, that when initially cast as Alice, she thought there was a mistake because "Alice is white." This speaks to an unawareness of whiteness, of the socially ordered structure of power aligned with race. This structural arrangement is actually where racism and whiteness hold the most power to grow and dominate. By contrast, the examples shared above of Endalyn Taylor and Stephanie Powell being asked to powder down reveal how both were aware of the structure that required them to appropriate whiteness. But they lived in a society that normalized these types of experiences; they accepted their "place." For women in ballet there is an underpinning feeling of being dispensable; this is magnified for WOC. When training and dancing, one is often groomed to be grateful for the opportunity and privilege and would not dare challenge a teacher or ballet mistress. Thus, even when aware of the structure, many outside the dominant culture are not in a position to challenge or change it. Examinations of whiteness in relation to Blackness find "the construction and reproduction of racial prejudice at levels that are simultaneously social, interpersonal, and intrapsychic" (Hamer 2007, 132). Through these oral history interviews, numerous incidents of understanding a person's placement and belonging is seen through where dancers are directed and positioned.

There are examples throughout this book of moments where racism is so deeply entrenched within the fabric of a person's reality that they are unaware of its existence. At times, I imagine that even the perpetrator of the comments is unaware, as the most fertile proliferations of racism are the forms and maneuvers that go unnoticed and unchecked. Also note that the women interviewed were poignantly aware of these moments. But they did not protest, refuse to perform, or quit the school or company. In many cases they understood that outside the studio doors was a very similar race-based world. Just as racism is implicitly taught to white people, distrust is taught to POC (Kendall 2020), along with an understanding that POC will be held to a higher standard for entry and a higher level of scrutiny in general. For many, this is an accepted fact of life that goes along with all the unfairness related to racism. Often this understanding is not verbally articulated or even understood on a conscious level, but it shows up in other ways and operates subconsciously.

These women do not speak of racial incidents as being surprising; they framed them as, "just the way things were." I think of this when Lauren Anderson describes her dance history and notes that she did not experience racism or limitations of race. She did not think she could be Alice in *Alice in Wonderland* and yet did not see this as a racist paradigm. I imagine that she met no people pointing limits to her in relation to her race, but I would argue that there were other likely indicators that would usher her into an understanding of where she belonged and where she did not, as caste systems and racism operate. A similar mindset is described by South African dancer Monike Cristina, originally from Brazil, when sharing: "So, it's not supereasy (pursuing ballet), even worse when you are Black" (Cristina interview). Caridad Martinez also explained her understanding of these codes as they were explained to her as a small child by her mother (Martinez interview).

Today, approximating whiteness in ballet persists today in uniform, costume, and dress code policies. There is a whole chapter dedicated to this issue in Gottschild's *Black Dancing Body* (2003). One example is the requirement of a hair bun. Crystal Perkins, a ballet-trained contemporary dancer, explained how she thought about the hair component of her ballet uniform when she was an adolescent training: "I just thought, 'Oh, if I straighten my hair like this, I can dance? OK, as long as I get to dance,' and I sat for pressings that enabled my hair to be worn in the proper bun" (Perkins interview).

African American women in the United States have faced hair discrimination since they entered the workforce (Thompson 2009; Craig 2020). This expression of anti–Blackness requires approximating white hair texture that (most often) can easily be brushed into a bun. While some African American women can attain this aesthetic look, many cannot without chemical processing using hair lye or pressing a 400-degree hot comb to their head and hair. These processes are counteraffirming of one's identity. All of these processes require women to reach for and attain a beauty standard designed for white women. Approximating white skin color, the use of pink tights is also a long-held ballet tradition. Working against this understood racist tradition, many inclusive and progressive mainstream companies support students and company members by supporting the practice of wearing flesh-matching tights.

Considerations of Stereotypes

The Latina stereotype of "hot Latina" or "vamp" did not surface much as a direct or explicit barrier to dancers I interviewed, as I had hypothesized upon entry into this research. Most dancers did not identify being typecast into roles at great length. While such practices were mentioned here and there, I did not find the theme to be a throughline. Still, it is possible that this stereotype, operating as implicit bias in hiring and casting, might have prevented these women from being cast in more central and lead roles. However, this was impossible to assess within the parameters of this research project, and to the extent that it could have been the case, it is likely we will never be able to quantify and know for certain.

African American Stereotypes

African American women are historically stereotyped in a number of ways that are unfitting to classical ballet. The jezebel, the strong/angry Black women, the tragic mulatto, the mammy: none of these stereotypes easily fit into balletic embodiments of the pure, innocent, delicate fairy princess or swan (Deans 2001). In addition to the challenge of overcoming typecasting and stereotypes, African American women also deal with colorism that plays a divisive part in these archetypes. Often although not always, lighter-skinned African Americans are given more opportunities to approximate whiteness and perform some of the classical leads than are darker African Americans. Additionally, darker-skinned African Americans are more likely to be typecast into "powerhouse" roles, capitalizing on the perceived strength of the Black woman (McCarthy-Brown 2011). Stephanie Powell mentions tensions among dancers while in DTH; Endalyn Taylor also notes this occurrence. Endalyn Taylor's candor is powerful in that she describes how race operates. Even people outside the dominant culture can and do operate within the oppressive structure. It is my belief that most Americans operate within this structure by default at least some of the time—even members of oppressed groups, even people who consciously work against it. There are reasons why one might tap into the structure to survive, and there are also times that the caste system is so deeply ingrained that one may operate within the structure without even realizing it. This is why it is so insidious.

In 2021 Lin-Manuel Miranda, internationally acclaimed writer and producer renowned for his color-conscious casting in *Hamilton*, released his film *In the Heights*. The film is based on the 2009 musical about a Latinx community in New York set in Manhattan's Washington Heights. With Miranda's full knowledge of the spectrum of colors in the Latino community, few darker-skinned cast members appeared in this film, and there were no named roles for darker females. The film was released to acclaim for many attributes but also criticism in terms of colorism. Many in the Latinx community were disappointed and hurt. When questioned about this at the time, Miranda acknowledged the privileging of Latinos who could come closer to approximating whiteness and stated, "I am truly sorry.... I promise to do better in my future projects" (Romano 2021). I bring this example forward to demonstrate how race politics are insidious, calcified, and hard to transcend even by those who have accomplished the tasks at other points in time.

Arthur Mitchell's legacy and the work of Lin-Manuel Miranda have made great contributions to our society in term of breaking racial barriers. Both men's accomplishments and errors were informed by the race-based society of the United States. It is important to examine these issues of racism and colorism wherever they exist in order to remove oppressive barriers. However, diminishing the accomplishments of Mitchell and Miranda does not have an impact on the structural racism that permeates our society. It is important to remember that our society, not any particular person, made space for these moments of inequity to appear in the first place. But recognizing the shortcomings of Mitchell and Miranda should not overshadow the monumental accomplishments that have been culture-shifting and legendary in ballet and musical theater respectively. Too often, groundbreaking accomplishments are diminished through critical examinations—our leaders and their legacies are tarnished, and the white supremacy culture and structures remain unscathed. Further, we cannot allow individual leaders to bear the brunt of society's ills of racism. We must examine and acknowledge inequity everywhere, but let's not tear down the leaders who are working to advance the overall cause and are, to be sure, also working against active operations of oppressions themselves.

Asian Stereotypes

Not surprisingly, the three Asian women I interviewed had varying experiences with Asian stereotypes. As previously discussed, racism and bias do not elicit monolithic responses. As the interviewer, I assessed the personal pain of racist encounters and experiences that made the issue of race in dance more salient for some of the interviewees. Dancers who experienced typecasting, such as Kristie Latham and Shelby Colona, feel differently about stereotypes in ballet than Margaret Severin-Hansen, who did not experience typecasting. Severin-Hansen, by her own account, did not experience racism in ballet. Similarly, she was unbothered by the depiction of Asians in *Nutcracker*, which others found quite hurtful. I argue that both of those truths are intertwined. The dancers injured by racial stereotypes have a heightened awareness and are cautious of racism in a very different way than an individual never experiencing racism. Not surprisingly, these individuals also have different triggers as well.

Margaret Severin-Hansen is a principal dancer who has not experienced a ceiling above her. Kristie Latham was a soloist, aspiring to principal, who experienced that ceiling on many occasions. Even more troubling in the case of Latham is that even those around her acknowledge that the ceiling is there, and they express no outrage and show no interest in calling out inequity where it exists. "I've actually had people say that to me. Other coworkers come up to me and say, verbatim, 'I thought you would be doing that role' and me saying 'I was hoping to do it' and then the next phrase out of their mouth: 'Oh, it's probably because you're Asian'" (Lathan interview). To be sure, it is better that people who witness the injustice of racism acknowledge the injustice, because ignoring that this is happening results in another form of racial violence. However, it is wrong when others witness the act and do not call out the injustice. We see people willing to put energy into saving nature reserves, animals, and historical sites, but for WOC, too bad for you. For these women, there is a full embrace of the structure, and those within the structure are complicit with the status quo if not full endorsers.

In the "Chinese" section of *Nutcracker*, Kristie sees a cultural reference that symbolizes marginalization and othering. What she doesn't see is a character that can transcend into the Sugar Plum Fairy. Further, Kristie problematically acknowledges that she sees young white women as fitting lead roles (Lathan interview) even though she desires to undo these stereotypical type-castings.

When asked about racial stereotype casting, Shelby Colona knows that she has experienced it. She notes that as an athletic dancer, being cast in the exotic sexy role was an odd directorial choice, but knowing about the cultural stereotypes in the United States, such artistic choices registered with her as stereotypical:

> I've definitely been [stereotyped]—people view Asian women, I think they sexualize them in a way. ... [T]his is what I've perceived over the years. ... And I think that I've been cast in certain things because of that, absolutely [Colona interview].

This was interesting, because I presumed that Shelby and others of her generation had experienced less stereotyping than the dancers from previous and less politically correct generations. However, when I asked Shelby about stereotypes, her response was swift and affirming, clearly noting her knowledge of the issue. In contrast, many of my university students (who are primarily white women) are often unaware of stereotypes in relation to Asian women.

Kristie Latham's interview was one of the hardest for me emotionally. I was moved and deeply saddened to hear the experiences of racial discrimination she endured, particularly as a young person still dancing; her personal accounts were not from 50 years ago. It cut a little deeper each time Kristie laughed it off or couched the behavior in the understanding that POC hold: "It is what it is," and we must move forward in spite of these obstacles if we are to succeed or have a productive life. She had a clear understanding of the racial contract and her choices within the paradigm: work around the racism, accept your position, or leave. But for many, questions quickly arise: "Where would I go if I left?," an inquiry for another discussion.

Kristie's encounters with racism in performing extended to experiences with makeup, casting, and costuming, affirming what is already known about the work of dismantling racist structures, it takes the labor of everyone in the building. It cannot just be the teacher or administrator who attends implicit bias and inclusion trainings; it must be everyone in the building. To be sure, dismantling systemic racism goes beyond training and professional development; it is an invested and lifelong quest for equity for all.

Throughout this text I have discussed the value of in-group messaging at length. However, it is important to note that the way Kristie Latham experienced ballet worked in a very different way. She was not led by in-group messaging in relation to race. She spoke to me about her affirming experience in an affinity group of Asian ballet dancers, organized by the writers of *Final Bow for Yellowface*, Phil Chan and Georgina Pazcoguin. However, she also noted that she did not pursue work with ballet companies that already had more than one Asian dancer employed. I deduce that this placed Kristie in a position to have a minimal number of in-group messages, and to be sure, they were few and far between. Shelby also noted the small number of women with whom she shares an ethnic and racial affinity who are working in ballet. The magnitude of how this paradigm of in-group messaging translates is great and reflects in the small number of women interested in or willing to pursue this same path.

Additional Codes

In this discussion of race, I want to hold space for those uninterested in the discourse of race. For some, surviving the caste system, the racial contract, and daily oppression means not always having to push against it, not always fighting, not always calling it out. There is exhaustive labor in all those acts. In the shared oral histories of this book, sometimes racism was ignored, dismissed, and at times even allowed. I know that even in my own professional experiences I have found the burden of undoing racism too ginormous at times; I have been resentful of those who faulted me for not saying, doing, or fighting more.

A number of the interviewees noted not pushing back in certain moments or even being disinterested in doing so. To be sure, at times people outside the dominant culture align with those in power for survival, education, and opportunities, and at times this includes the opportunity to dance. We see examples of this in Raven Wilkinson's life in her willingness to "pass" in certain venues for the opportunity to perform. In the words of Monike Cristina: at times "you have to pretend that you didn't go through those situations [of discrimination], because if you argue, you will lose your mind" (Cristina interview). Monike's strategy of pretending she did not experience discrimination in order to not lose her mind is a common coping mechanism for marginalized people. Stephanie Powell and Endalyn Taylor talk about being asked to powder down, complying, and not pursuing an immediate exit. Shelby Colona shares her response to racist comments around her: "I started to brush things off" (Colona interview). I understand these actions to be at a minimum coping mechanisms and in more severe cases survival maneuvers to allow the individual to cope, survive, or be employed within a racist structure. Where racism is not addressed, you are subjecting your dancers to similar psychological abuse and racial violence.

Throughout all the interviews I noted how race was talked around. If the topic could have been avoided and I had not asked about it, I think it would not have been discussed in many of the interviews. For some, not focusing on race can be a survival skill. The "r" word—"racist"—was only used once, in Martinez's interview, and only after I asked her to explain what she was implying. Latham had a particular focus on race in part due to painful race-based experiences. Other's shared stories or examples but only when asked. This relates to my work as a consultant for inclusive dance spaces. In many instances, assumptions are made by leadership in a particular organization or dance program that people outside the dominant culture are having positive experiences and feeling included. However, it becomes important to consider how these assessments of inclusion are being made. Are these observations of inclusion, and are they substantive or performative? Are individuals offered private or anonymous space to share about their experiences? When seeking to understand the experiences of others, nothing can be taken for granted or assumed particularly in an industry where people work so hard to get a small number of positions. Many dancers would rather not be perceived as disruptive and often keep workplace grievances to a minimum. Providing space for all members to show up fully is essential.

Entrepreneurship and Agency

When people speak of women empowerment, agency, and entrepreneurship, the first image to come to mind is usually not a ballet dancer. Ballet dancers have an image of a choreographer's muse or a delicate entity that is molded and shaped to take on different roles; few images revolve around ballet dancers wielding great power and acquiring financial independence. Yet, financial barriers are the first barriers many met when pursuing a career in ballet—it is not an inexpensive or easily funded endeavor. Thus, the stakes are high when dancers think about securing their future through ballet as a livelihood. While this component of a ballet dancer's career is not explored at length in this text, I have highlighted a few poignant moments.

How women in dance navigate business is an aspect of the profession often overlooked by young artists, yet it is quite significant to the journey of all dancers. Stephanie Powell shared several career choices in her interview. When discussing the circumstances that caused her to leave one company, she shared about feeling exploited, performing roles above her company rank, and not being compensated at that rank of pay. In the quote below, she shares part of her reasoning to depart from the company:

> I also was doing principal work and not getting paid for principal work. I submitted a letter and I got no response, and I submitted another letter and I got no response. And I resigned. You know, I just finished my contract and I said, "It's OK." Like, "You can't just keep putting me out there and not give me the contract that honors the work that I'm doing" [Powell interview].

In this instance Stephanie Powell acknowledges the choices before her and chose to leave the company over not being paid to do the roles she was performing. In our interview she also notes being instilled with financial values from her parents and coming from a home dance studio that taught her she could be anything she wanted. Both of those foundational values likely factored into her ability to leave the company when she did.

Kristie Latham shared her strategic considerations when thinking about where she would apply for company positions. She noted race as being a component of her thought process in where she would pursue her profession. "I will purposefully send my audition materials to a company where I see that they at least have one Asian ... but not in the rank that I'm looking to fulfill" (Lathan interview). I find Kristie Latham's thought process illuminating and honest. For those who feel that our society has transcended race, I wonder if they count the number of people who share their racial identity and are already employed before making the decision to apply for a position.

Last, I point to the words of Lourdes Lopez when deciding to take a two-year hiatus break and begin a family and go to school:

> The greatest thing about being away from a ballet company is that when you come back, you realize you've changed; it hasn't. The company is exactly the same, meaning your class is at 10 a.m., your rehearsal's at 12:00 p.m., performance is at 8:00 p.m., you have a weekend. It's this machine that just keeps on going even if the dancers are different; it's a machine that keeps on going, whereas you've changed [Lopez interview].

For so many dancers who believe that dance will leave them behind if they take the time to attend to their health, I lift up these words of Lourdes Lopez.

Examining What Is Not Seen: What About the Others?

I recognize the contrary nature of many of the questions explored in this book. It is hard to ask people who have persevered and were able to access a number of opportunities if there were enough opportunities; indeed there were, in most cases, enough for these women. But what of the hundreds of thousands of women who were not offered those opportunities? I believe there are countless dancers we will never know of. To be sure, the future of ballet in terms of WOC will be up to our society. I have no doubt that there are and will continue to be talented and prepared dancers ready to dance, but will our nation rise to the occasion and extend the opportunity that has been historically privileged to white dancers? Indeed, it is our history to live and write.

The (S)heros

As I sit with the interviews and the experience of writing this book, I think of the parents, most often hopeful mothers, who placed these women in ballet classes as young girls. Then I think of the teachers. The one thing I would say is true of all these women is that they all had a great teacher, and many of them had several. The interviewees' whole countenance, demeanor, and tone changed when they spoke of their teachers. Often, interviewees recounted descriptions of intense and personal relationships with emotional significance. As I write, I think of Lauren Anderson and Ben Stevenson; Caridad Martinez and Fernando and Alicia Alonso; Stephanie Powell and Cindy Trueblood; Endalyn Taylor and Larry Long; Melissa Verdecia, Caridad Espinosa, and Charla Glenn; and Crystal Perkins, who choked up when she thought of her teacher, Shelley Berg and spoke of Debbie Blunden-Diggs with affectionate esteem. To be sure, dance teachers are the change agents and way makers in these stories.

A Liberatory Approach to Teaching Ballet

Note about this chapter: Since the publication of my book, *Dance Pedagogy for a Diverse World: Culturally Relevant Teaching in Theory, Research, and Practice* (2017), many people have asked me for resources on teaching ballet. While I have taught ballet on more than one occasion over the years, I must be transparent in stating that it is not my area of expertise. However, I have developed teaching tools and approaches for the dance studio classroom that I believe would be an asset to all dance teachers, including ballet instructors. This section is designed to be a resource for ballet teachers and soon-to-be-teachers of ballet.

I began researching diversity in dance in higher education in 2008. In my dissertation research I examined how dance departments went about diversifying their offerings. When it came to ballet, it seemed that programs and instructors got a pass. I examined sequential BFA/BA curricula and asked instructors about methods to diversify content; they would share their resources and describe their teaching methods. But most of the ballet instructors I spoke to at the time would say something along the lines of "Yes, diversity is very important. I teach ballet technique, so we do not really address it in my class, but it's so important." They would point to the fact that there were few text resources for them to share, and they were already teaching so much in a small amount of time, so unfortunately the bulk of the diversity work fell outside the ballet class.

This was over a decade ago. I am convinced that today very few teachers believe they are exempt from the work of diversifying curriculum and addressing issues of inclusion. There are few to no administrations in higher education who do not ask each department and instructor how they are addressing these issues in their classroom. However, ballet continues to be a content area where instructors are often at a loss as to how to make this genre of dance more inclusive. In this section I refer to liberatory practices for teaching dance. This is analogous to antiracist practices for teaching, but instead of pushing away from oppressive structures, one focuses attention on modes of accessing liberation. Liberation is inherently antiracist but provides a positive versus oppositional frame.

Because historically ballet in the United States was taught through a lens of whiteness, many instructors have deep-seated bias, trauma, or both related to the form. Teachers need to check their feelings about ballet and ask themselves questions: Do you believe ballet is the foundation of all dance? Do you believe every student needs ballet? If so, ask yourself why. How did you get to this understanding? What does this idea mean for students and dancers outside the dominant culture? How can you communicate to students and parents that ballet is not a part of a white supremacy model if you believe that all students need it in order to dance? Reflect honestly about your ideas around whose body is pliable for ballet, who has the "look" for particular roles in regard to casting, and who is an overall "fit" for the culture.

I use the word "culture" because every dance community has its own culture. Beyond genres (ballet, contact improvisation, hip hop, classical Indian), particular dance genres have subcultures (such as Cecchetti, Vagonova, Royal Academy of Dance in ballet and, in hip hop, popping, locking, krumping, jukin', breaking, and so on). These dance subcultures hold various customs and practices. Cultural differences show up in the space, such as the need for barres and mirrors for ballet. We're aware of the need for a floor that dancers can wear shoes on for hip hop; and, that breakdancers require a particular type of floor to safely perform head spins. Other differences can be seen in dance forms that desire wooden floors, such as tap and flamenco. How these dance forms are talked about—the lexicon, the attire worn in these spaces, and the accepted and expected audience etiquette—are all aspects of each of these dance subcultures. How do you as an instructor treat the particulars of ballet? Are the needs for your genre above those practicing other forms?

Given ballet's widely understood history of exclusion, implicit bias has seeped into the cultural knowledge and understanding of this form. At times, I have even seen students discouraged from pursuing ballet to prevent disappointment and experiences of racism. To be sure, ballet is not an easy art form for anyone to pursue; it requires an absolute commitment that eludes many competent dancers. However, the challenge of excelling in ballet is compounded for those seeking to break through structures of racism evident in the ballet world. As such, it is imperative for ballet teachers to be reflective of their experiences in ballet as they relate to race, including their training and employment experiences. I encourage all teachers to ask themselves and reflect on the following questions:

1. What was the racial makeup in the places where you studied ballet as a child and teenager?
2. Who were the dancers affirmed in this space? What was their racial background? What was their body structure?
3. Did the school or your teachers make strides to explicitly include people of Color?
4. Do you recall whether students of Color received affirming messages? Were these the same or different from those offered to other students?

5. Did the school or your teachers make strides to explicitly include people who did not possess the typical ballet body?

6. What was the racial background of the dancers who got leading or sought-after roles in productions?

7. When you were directed to watch other ballet performers, what was the racial background of those dancers?

8. What was the racial background of the ballet dancers you saw in books, print magazines, on websites, or in poster photographs on the walls of your studio/school when you were growing up?

9. If you lived in a white and homogeneous community, such that white people were all you saw or were surrounded by, consider why that was. Consider the possibility that there are no segregated spaces in the United States that are segregated by accident.

10. Were you ever excluded from ballet for reasons of race?

11. Did you ever witness others excluded from ballet for reasons of race?

12. When you are in ballet spaces where everyone is white, does this feel normal?

13. Have you been taught to believe that the centering of white people in the space is normal? If so, does it feel as though a person of Color holding center stage would be abnormal?

14. Have you been connected to a ballet program, school, or company led by a person of Color? If the answer is never, consider how that might have subconsciously impacted your ideas about where people of Color belong and where they do not belong.

15. If these questions point to a history of whiteness in ballet for you, how might you be a different teacher if you had a more inclusive training experience?

As a teacher, it is important to examine the racial history you bring into the classroom. What have you seen? What are your knowledge gaps? If you have never had to consider the implications of race in ballet, consider what in your life made that possible. If you see that any of the above questions left you feeling uneasy or insecure about the vantage point you come to your classroom with, spend some time reflecting on class experiences and dynamics. Talk to other teachers and adult students about their experiences. If you can influence hiring, hire a specialist or consultant to come into your school or program and speak to inclusive practices around body image, representation, hairstyles, makeup, and costumes or advocate that such a person be hired. For starters, many dancers, costume designers, and makeup artists who have worked with Dance Theatre of Harlem or other ballet companies outside the dominant majority have a wealth of knowledge in these areas.

In my work as an educator working to dismantle racism, I defined several anchors for antiracist and liberatory teaching practices.

1. Teachers must reevaluate their curriculum and mine for spaces of implicit racial bias as well as opportunities to inject diversity.

2. Students need to be engaged in conversations about privilege and power. They need to be encouraged to think critically about how privilege and power operate in learning and dancing spaces. It is operating in all spaces, and to not acknowledge that supports the dominant culture and those who hold an imbalanced share.

3. Interrupt whiteness (Singh 2019). Where conversations, print images, and class demographics foreground white people in positions of superiority or as the only race being valued in an image or space, point out the absence of people of Color. Failure to do so normalizes this absence. Debunk white as the unstated universal norm. Further, if you are in a space where only or mostly white bodies are being positioned for representation, ask why. What would be lost by changing these images to dancers of a different hue or body type? If indeed it would not matter, then change it as an intentional act to affirm and lift up those who are often underrepresented.

4. Look for opportunities to affirm and build up the often underaffirmed. As a practice, I like consider in addition to race gender-inclusive representation beyond the binary as well as nonnormative bodies. Ask who in the room likely gets the least affirmation around their body image. Is every person in this room given the support and encouragement to feel good about their body and what it can do?

5. Learn about racial trauma and how it lives in the body. Offer opportunities for healing in the body. This means empowering students with choice and moments to reflect on how their body feels, how their being feels, and how their feelings sit/rest in their body. Show students how feelings (expressed through the body via varied cultural norms) change and modulate (Duggan 2020). Rejoice in collective healing, provide space for this, and create space for students to witness resilience (Menakem 2017). This often works with movement phrases that use lots of space, jumping, and whole-body movement exertion; and can be done in a circle as well.

Embrace Inclusion

There are many ways to think about inclusion in your ballet class, and they are all significant and important in creating a welcoming space for all students. Also remember that as a teacher you are modeling the tools and strategies your students will need in the future to create and be members of welcoming dance communities. Create customs that give structure to how students will interact with one another. This might include how students come into the learning space and how they see, affirm, and greet each other each day.

When students and dancers experience exclusion in dance spaces, this is often coming from their peers and not their teachers. Students often do not report these instances of peer alienation for fear of retaliation and suffering even more exclusion. I think of how Delores Browne described her dance training as lonely. She noted that the teachers were wonderful, but the students did not speak to her and often acted as if she was not there. As previously shared in Kristie Latham's interview, she suffered name-calling in college, with her classmates calling her "Sushi." I would venture to say that these verbal derogatory slurs were likely not spoken in the presence of teachers. Be sensitive to what students from diverse backgrounds might be experiencing in as well as outside the studio, in the locker room and the lobby, and cyberspace. When I say "diverse backgrounds," I am speaking of differences from the majority of enrolled students. In different settings, the difference varies; it could be body size, language, religion, race, age, or transgender and gender nonconforming students. If a student reports an incident of othering, accept this as feedback that your dance community needs more development in the area of inclusion, and be proactive in addressing the situation with the whole community. Ideally, focus on the teaching moment and the opportunity to embrace the different identity marker that is being alienated in your community.

Think about how you can teach students to look out for each other and express true community, citizenship, and allyship. I think back to Crystal Perkins's interview when she talked about how much it meant to her when she did not have to explain her culture to others. When other students in her community came to learn about her culture and then when her culture was questioned or alienated, these brave allies stepped forward in the gap of knowledge to explain the cultural difference. In this action, members of Crystal's community took on the labor of educating others about the celebratory affirmation in performance that is a cornerstone of the African American community. This is one expression of allyship and support, and its impact can reduce the racial battle fatigue and exhaustion that people from diverse backgrounds often experience in spaces that privileges the dominant culture.

Consider approaching dance students as diverse language learners, with ballet being one language of movement. How can all students be welcomed into the space? Position students as experts (or soon-to-be experts) of their body and the dances they enjoy. Affirm their movement history and prior knowledge of dance no matter what package it comes in. Seek to add ballet to that movement history in a manner that does not presume superiority over students' primary (dance) language, which is also an extension of their culture and identity. Understand and lift up the hip hop, flamenco, and bharatanatyam dancers. These are culturally informed physical practices. These dancers are trained dancers. Their dancing will be informed by ballet, just as any ballet dancer's movement would be informed by West African dance training. No one form is the foundation of all dance, and to suggest such is to impose a colonizing, imperialist ideology that supports white supremacy culture in the United States.

Messages

Utilize in-group messaging. Lift up dancers who look like your students. Lift up differently abled dancers, nonnormative bodies, and people of Color. I have explained in detail why in-group messaging is important, but it is also important to lift up those who are different or marginalized in other ways. Your students will grow up to be dancers, teachers, parents, friends, spectators, and community members. When they see differently abled and disabled dancers in their classroom or onstage, do you want them to see the limits facing the dancers or the opportunities? Shifting culture takes the intentional actions and practice of everyone. As teachers, we must prime, prepare, and maintain the space for our class and school communities and cultures if we want to achieve sincere inclusion. Model these practices of inclusion.

Are you showing a video of a ballet adagio? Who is dancing? Are you showing dance magazines in the academy or studio lobby or dressing rooms? Whose bodies are centered? Whose images are hanging on the halls and in the studios? I am not suggesting erasure of the white dancing body, but what does the American dancing body look like? Do your students have the opportunity to create a pluralist idea of who gets to dance? As teachers, if we do not want people to presume exclusivity around ballet, then we must instill inclusive practices into ballet pedagogy.

Controlling Codes, Customs, and Traditions

Who is the dress code designed for? Do students have to mute their identity to participate? Whose identity do you not want to see and why? Ask critical questions. Can people of different faiths feel free and included through this dress policy? Is the policy gender-inclusive, or does it rely on socializing binary gender constructs? Can students with various hair textures participate with ease or with an experience comparable to those of the dominant culture? Can students with darker shades of skin color participate without being made to feel as though the dress code was designed for people with lighter skin color (i.e., extending the line of the dancer with similar color tone in pink and white tights)? What is the cost to the dance school or class of including flesh-matching tights in the dress code? For all of these questions I apply the "impact over intent" rule. Understanding the impact of harm or affirmation must be weighed and valued more than the intentions behind traditional policy. If a negative impact is plausible, then this outweighs one's good intentions, and the policy should be nullified.

It is possible to cloak racism in "tradition," in the "rules," in "the way we've always done things." Another phrase name this is institutional racism. Take a moment to google some of your favorite ballet schools. Look at how the schools choose to represent (and market) their desired image. Who is there? Who is dancing? Who is centered? How is hair worn? What color are dancers' tights? Who is best positioned to fit into these pictures, these stories of who gets to take ballet class? Who will need to cloak their identity to approximate whiteness in order to be included? Who will suffer through this process?

If you or your organization is unsure about how to approach this type of inclusion, seek guidance from a consultant. There are many individuals steeped in this work who can support you and your dance community.

Families

In teaching ballet, one must relate to students, connect to their families, and let people know that you—the teacher—and the art form must welcome each child. This also means welcoming families. Talk to students, learn about them and what they care about—including their families. This is counterintuitive for some. But to be sure, parents will not support their child's study of an art form that keeps them at arm's length and feels racist. What does it mean to "feel racist"? As I discussed earlier and as established by Wilkerson (2020), race relations in the United States operate like a caste system, an unspoken program and structure that is implicitly communicated and is palpably felt as to where one belongs. If white bodies are historically and currently centered, with no clear and measurable plan to address exclusionary culture and structures, the racial contract is in place, and parents will be inclined to direct their children to more supportive institutions. Inclusion cannot be accomplished by one teacher. It must be a systematic organizational shift and a way of working that includes everyone from the administration and leadership to the custodial staff.

What do you and your team think of difference? Are you more comfortable with people who come from a similar place? Is there acknowledgment that pursuing inclusion is not easy? It requires working against the common desire to be exclusionary. But let's consider this further. If you are seeking a more diverse student population, what are your strategies to get there? Does everyone in the building know that your institution values inclusion? Do you hold auditions for entry or scholarships? Are families treated with care or disinterest or, worse yet, disaffection? Are families greeted and welcomed into the space? Who is welcoming your soon-to-be students and families? If families look different than your typical family, what then? Many families of Color include extended family in ways that many white American institutions are not familiar with. This means you may have more people accompanying an auditionee; have you set up the space for that? Inclusion practices and policies are an ongoing process and look different within every dance education setting. What is most important is that they be well thought out and designed to meet the needs of each particular community and location.

In closing, I leave you with two thoughts. First, acknowledging racist practices within U.S.-based ballet would go a long way toward moving race relations forward. It is very hard to convince someone you are aware of a problem if you are unwilling to acknowledge that there even is a problem. Second, I bring forth the words Caridad

Martinez shared with me as we were setting up for her interview. She asked me if I was a ballet dancer, and I explained that I wasn't very good. Caridad corrected me and asked, "who told you that?" Then stated, "when you are very young, the opinion about how you are as a dancers is your teacher's opinion. That opinion stands, influences, and informs your idea of yourself as a dancer. That's why the responsibility of the teacher is huge. We have a huge responsibility with the kids."

Further reading on this topic is available in chapter 4 of *Dance Pedagogy for A Diverse World: Culturally Relevant Teaching in Theory, Research, and Practice* (McCarthy-Brown 2017). The chapter includes many teaching strategies to diversify the ballet class. I recommend that text for more specific teaching tools.

Afterword

BY MELANYE WHITE DIXON

Note about the afterword: I asked Dr. Melanye White Dixon to write the afterword because she was one of my most significant in-group messengers, as one African American woman, doctoral student at Temple University to another. Her dissertation sparked my interest in women of ballet outside the dominant culture. I asked her to approach the afterword through an autoethnographic lens and to include some of her experiences that carried her forward as a dance scholar focusing on African American ballerinas. To be sure, her story gives voice to many dancers denied opportunities in ballet yet also sheds light on alternatives modes of dance discovery nurtured by dance educators and leading to significant contributions to the field.—NM

Finally, a publication that celebrates African American, Latina, and Asian ballerinas. Dr. Nyama McCarthy-Brown's *Skin Colored Pointes* directs our attention to the narratives of women who have survived, thrived, and persevered through seemingly insurmountable challenges in the ballet world. She is filling a void and placing the stories of African American, Latina, and Asian women center stage. This groundbreaking scholarly work brings forth restorative herstory and creates a powerful space for redefining the place of women of Color in the dance history ballet canon. The interviews presented dig deep and unearth thought-provoking, revealing, and fascinating journeys from the voices of the ballerinas profiled.

This book is revelatory because it makes visible the stories of dancers of Color in ballet. My newfound knowledge of their testimonies has augmented my personal understanding and appreciation for the significance of women ballet dancers of African, Latina, and Asian descent. *Skin Colored Pointes* answers the call of cultural relevance in dance history and interrogates the necessity of antiracist dance pedagogy. The book also called me to reflect on the barriers and opportunities I encounter in dance that were impacted by race.

I have always been drawn to the stories of nonwhite dancers, choreographers, and teachers. Their paths have not always been clear of the debris of prejudice, bigotry, and economic uncertainty. In 2011, I wrote *Marion Cuyjet and Her Judimar School of Dance: Training Ballerinas in Black Philadelphia, 1948–1971*. This book was my contribution to documenting the impact and legacy of African American dance educators in 20th-century Philadelphia, Pennsylvania. Learning about the tenacious Marion Cuyjet revealed that Black dance educators devoted to teaching ballet to African American children existed in select regions of the United States.

I grew up during the 1950s in racially segregated Chattanooga, Tennessee, a key location for direct-action sit-in protests of the civil rights movement. I still remember the morning phone call my father, a high school teacher at the time, received from his seniors with a request to bail them out of jail after being arrested the day before at a sit-in protest at a whites-only lunch counter in downtown Chattanooga. In my hometown, dance studios that offered formal dance studies were closed to Black children.

Unlike the women interviewed for this book, I did not receive the opportunity to take dance classes in Chattanooga until the age of 12. A family friend arranged for Mrs. Severance, a wealthy white dance instructor, to teach ballet and tap dance to Black children in our community at the Black YMCA for 50 cents on Saturdays. We used metal folding chairs for our ballet barre work, there were no mirrors, and the floors were linoleum. Mrs. Severance was kind and very encouraging, and we performed throughout the community. I relished this experience, and thus my love affair with dance began.

During the 1960s my parents did their best to expose me to cultural arts through visits to the Hunter Museum of Art and attendance at the downtown Tivoli Theatre's national opera and ballet company series. This afforded me my first opportunity to witness a Black ballerina, Llanchie Stevenson, performing with the National Ballet of Washington, D.C. (Stevenson was a founding member of Dance Theatre of Harlem.) I also remember attending a wonderful performance by the American Ballet Theatre at 12 years of age during the era when Ivan Nagy was emerging as one of its star principal dancers.

In 1969 I entered Spelman College and loved my four-year participation as a member of the Atlanta University Center Dance Theatre, established by Mozelle Spriggs and Shirley Rushing, a member of the Rod Rodgers Dance Company. My dance life at Spelman included intense study in ballet with supportive teachers Hildegarde Tornow of the Atlanta Ballet and Duane Dishon. We engaged with artists such as Pearl Primus, Arthur Mitchell and the Dance Theatre of Harlem, Geoffrey Holder, Bill Mackey, Mary Hinkson, Eleo Pomare, Thelma Hill, Rod Rodgers, Carol Johnson, George Faison, Debbie Allen, Chuck Davis, Clover Mathis, Rex Nettleford and the National Dance Theatre of Jamaica, and Capitol Ballet of Washington, D.C., with Sylvester Campbell and Sandra Fortune. As a first-year student, one of my fondest memories was traveling to Statesboro, Georgia, in 1970 to attend a performance of the Alvin Ailey American Dance Theater at Georgia Southern University. Our teacher and artistic director of the Atlanta University Center Dance Theatre, Mrs. Shirley Rushing, was a friend to many of the Ailey company members.

Although I majored in sociology and elementary education, Spelman College laid the groundwork for my pursuit of a career in dance. Some of my dance professors who served as significant role models were accomplished dance professionals from New York City (Shirley Rushing and Diana Ramos). They steadfastly supported my aspirations as an artist/educator, and I often reminisce about them with immense gratitude. I am also grateful to Mrs. Christine King Farris—sister of Martin Luther King, Jr., and one of my professors at Spelman—who vigorously supported my intention to focus my first collegiate research paper on the impact of Black women in dance. The ability to navigate the dance world with confidence was a result of the African American and white dance teachers who recognized my talent, always making me feel validated. This may not have happened if my training had occurred in predominantly white dance studios.

In 1973, the summer after graduating from Spelman College, I attended ballet classes at a newly established white ballet school in Chattanooga as the only African American student. I enjoyed the classes but at times was "called out" for my body type, thin with a prominent derriere. On one occasion we traveled out of town for a nearby regional dance convention. The owner of the school only allowed me to take the modern dance workshop. I was mystified because my technical ability in ballet was solid. While observing the ballet workshop, an older dancer from our school noticed that I was perturbed, sad, and confused. She stated, "I cannot understand why you were not chosen for this ballet class." Rationalizing that the owner of the school wanted her favorite male student to be showcased, I did not realize that it was probably a case of racial discrimination.

I arrived in New York City in 1973 to pursue my master of arts in dance at Teacher's College, Columbia University. My goal was to be an artist/educator with hopes of teaching dance in a college or university, and my graduate school professors rendered an abundance of support. My movement technique studies were supplemented with professional contemporary dance classes at Clark Center, Dianne McIntyre's Sounds in Motion Studio, and ballet classes at Dance Theatre of Harlem. In 1974 I received an Alvin Ailey American Dance Center merit scholarship, the result of auditioning for the newly formed Alvin Ailey Repertory Ensemble, now known as Ailey II. I was fortunate to be in New York City during the dance boom of the 1970s and the Black Arts Movement.

When I reflect on some of the barriers experienced by some of the women in this book, such as Crystal Perkins getting so close and then cut at the last minute at the Fort Worth Dallas audition and Kristie Latham being called "Sushi" by classmates and "China" by another dancer, I question how might things have been for me and the women featured in this book if race were not a factor in their training or employment. I am grateful for Dr. McCarthy-Brown's extensive research and opportunity to consider these realities. While we are called to work collectively for future generations, *Skin Colored Pointes* reminds us to also hold close our personal histories that got us here and provides the inspiration to continue the work of seeking representation, equity, and inclusion for all.

Dr. Melanye White Dixon is an associate professor emerita, Ohio State University Department of Dance.

References

Alvin Ailey American Dance Theater. 2023. "Mission & Core Values." https://www.alvinailey.org.
American Ballet Theatre. 2020. "Lupe Serrano." https://www.abt.org/people/lupe-serrano/.
Ballet Nacional de Cuba. 2021. Ballet Nacional de Cuba Official Website. Retrieved June 17, 2021. http://www.balletcuba.cult.cu/es/paginas/la-compania/hitos-historicos.
Banes, Sally. 1994. *Writing Dancing in the Age of Postmodernism.* Hanover, NH: University Press of New England.
Bergner, Gwen. 2009. "Black Children, White Preference: Brown v. Board, the Doll Tests, and Politics of Self-Esteem." *American Quarterly* 61, no. 2: 299–332.
Bonilla-Silva, Eduardo. 2006. *Racism Without Racists: Color-Blind Racism and the Persistence of Racial Inequality in America.* Lanham, MD: Rowman and Littlefield.
Bourne, Sandra. 2018. "Tracing the Evolution of Black Representation in Ballet and the Impact on Black British Dancers Today." In *Narratives of Black British Dance,* ed. Adelsola Akinleye, 51–64. London: Palgrave Macmillan.
Brady, Anne-Marie. 2003. *Making the Foreign Serve China: Managing Foreigners in the People's Republic.* Lanham, MD: Rowman & Littlefield.
Burch, Traci. 2015. "Skin Color and the Criminal Justice System: Beyond Black-White Disparities in Sentencing." *Journal of Empirical Legal Studies* 12, no. 3: 395–420.
Case, Kim. 2013. "Beyond Diversity and Whiteness." In *Deconstructing Privilege: Teaching and Learning as Allies in the Classroom,* ed. Kim Case, 21–34. New York: Routledge.
Castagno, Angela. 2014. *Educated in Whiteness: Good Intentions and Diversity in Schools.* Minneapolis: University of Minnesota Press.
Clark, Paul. 2010. "Model Theatrical Works and the Remodeling of the Cultural Revolution." In *Art in Turmoil: The Chinese Cultural Revolution, 1966–76,* ed. Richard King, 167–87. Vancouver: University of British Columbus Press.
Classically Cuban: Alicia Alonso and the Cuban National Ballet. 1982. A BBC TV production, directed by Michael Dibb. Arena Production.
Classic Black Panel. 1996. Videotaped by Penny Ward at the Bruno Walter Auditorium, February 12, cassette 2. New York: New York Public Library for the Performing Arts.
Coleman, Nancy. 2020. "Why We're Capitalizing Black." *New York Times,* July 5. https://www.nytimes.com/2020/07/05/insider/capitalized-black.html.
Collins, Patricia Hill. 2000. *Black Feminist Thought: Knowledge, Consciousness, and the Politics of Empowerment.* New York: Routledge.
Colville, Alex. 2021. "When Ballet Became Revolutionary: Xue Jinghua and the Red Detachment of Women." SupCina (online platform). Retrieved June 17, 2021. https://supchina.com/2021/02/22/xue-jinghua-and-the-red-detachment-of-women/.
Cooper, Brittney. 2018. *Eloquent Rage.* New York: St. Martin's Press.
Copeland, Misty. 2010. Personal Interview by Phone in July of 2010.
Craig, Greg. 2018. "Aesha Ash Danced Her Way from Modest Life in Rochester to New York City Ballet." *Rochester Democrat and Chronicle,* December 6. https://www.democratandchronicle.com/story/rochester-magazine/2018/12/06/aesha-ash-new-york-city-ballet-swan-dreams-project-rochester/1440436002/.
Craig, Veronica. 2020. "Does My Sassiness Upset You? An Analysis Challenging Workplace and School Regulation of Hair and Its Connection to Racial Discrimination." *Howard Law Journal* 64, no. 1: 239–66.
Dahl, Izabela, and Melin Thor. 2009. "Oral History, Constructions and Deconstructions of Narratives: Intersections of Class, Gender, Locality, Nation and Religion in Narratives from a Jewish Woman in Sweden." *Enquire,* no. 2: 1–20.
Daly, Ann. 1997. "Classical Ballet: Discourse of Difference." In *Meaning in Motion,* ed. Jane C. Desmond, 111–19. Durham, NC: Duke University Press.

Deans, Joselli. 2001. "Black Ballerinas Dancing on the Edge: An Analysis of the Cultural Politics in Delores Browne's and Raven Wilkinson's Career, 1954–1985." EdD dissertation, Temple University.
De Baca, Miguel, and Makeda Best. 2015. *Conflict, Identity, and Protest in American Art*. Cambridge, UK: Cambridge Scholars Publishing.
DeFrantz, Thomas. 2004. *Dancing Revelations: Alvin Ailey's Embodiment of African American Culture*. New York: Oxford University Press.
Desmond, Jane. C. 1997. "Embodying Difference: Issues in Dance and Cultural Studies." In *Meaning in Motion*, ed. Jane C. Desmond, 29–54. Durham, NC: Duke University Press.
Dixon, Melanye White. 1987. "Marion Cuyjet: Visionary of Dance Education in Black Philadelphia." EdD dissertation, Temple University.
Duggan, Diane. 2020. *Healing Our Students and Ourselves*. Webinar presented via Zoom, NYU Dance Education MA Program, June 22, 2020, New York.
Dunning, Jennifer. 1974. "A Dancer Who Had a Dream." *New York Times*, 91.
Dunning, Jennifer. 1997. "An Uphill Path to Swan Lake." *New York Times,* February 24, 1997, C11.
Dunning, Jennifer. 2003. "Janet Collins, 86; Ballerina Was First Black Artist at Met Opera." *New York Times,* B7.
Earick, Mary. 2009. *Racially Equitable Teaching: Beyond the Whiteness of Professional Development for Early Childhood Educators*. New York: Peter Lang.
Fisher, Jennifer. 2016. "Ballet and Whiteness: Will Ballet Forever Be the Kingdom of the Pale?" in *The Oxford Handbook of Dance and Ethnicity,* ed. Anthony Shay and Barbara Sellers-Young. New York: Oxford University Press.
Frankenberg, Ruth. 2001. "Mirage of an Unmarked Whiteness." In *The Making and Unmaking of Whiteness,* ed. Birgit Brander Rasmussen, Eric Klingenberg, Irene J. Nexica, and Matt Wray, 72–96. Durham, NC: Duke University Press.
Glass, Barbara S. 2007. *African American Dance: An Illustrated History*. Jefferson, NC: McFarland.
Gottschild, Brenda Dixon. 1996. *Digging the Africanist Presence in American Performance*. Westport, CT: Praeger.
Gottschild, Brenda Dixon. 2003. *The Black Dancing Body*. New York: Palgrave Macmillan.
Gottschild, Brenda Dixon. 2012. *Joan Myers Brown and the Audacious Hope of the Black Ballerina: A Biohistory of American Performance*. New York: Palgrave Macmillan.
Grant, Stan. 2015. "Black Writers Courageously Staring Down the White Gaze—This Is Why We All Must Read Them." *The Guardian*, December 31. https://www.theguardian.com/commentisfree/2015/dec/31/black-writers-courageously-staring-down-the-white-gaze-this-is-why-we-all-must-read-them.
Hamer, Forrest. 2007. "Anti-Black Racism and the Conception of Whiteness." In *The Future of Prejudice*, ed. Alaf Mahfouz, Stuart W. Twemlow, David E. Scharff, and Henri Parens, 131–39. Lanham, MD: Rowman & Littlefield.
Hausman, Carl R. 1989. *Metaphor and Art: Interactionalism and Reference in the Verbal and Nonverbal Arts*. Melbourne, Australia: Cambridge University Press.
Haynes, Kathryn. 2010. "Other Lives in Accounting: Critical Reflections on Oral History Methodology in Action." *Critical Perspectives on Accounting,* no. 21: 221–31.
Homans, Jennifer. 2010. *Apollo's Angels: A History of Ballet*. New York: Random House.
Horwitz, Dawn Lille. 2002. "The New York Negro Ballet in Great Britain." In *Dancing Many Drums: Excavations in African American Dance*, ed. Thomas DeFrantz, 317–19. Madison: University of Wisconsin Press.
Houston Ballet. 2020. "Lauren Anderson." Houston Ballet, retrieved June 23, 2020. https://www.houstonballet.org/about/ece/teaching-artists/lauren-anderson/.
I'll Make Me a World. 1999. Series, Blackside, Alexandria, VA. PBS video.
Johnson, E. Patrick. 2003. *Appropriating Blackness*. Durham, NC: Duke University Press.
Kealiinohomoku, Joann. 1983. "An Anthropologist Looks at Ballet as a Form of Ethnic Dance." In *What Is Dance? Readings in Theory and Criticisms,* ed. Roger Copeland and Marshall Cohen, 533–49. Oxford: Oxford University Press.
Kendall, Mikki. 2020. *Hood Feminism: Notes from the Women That a Movement Forgot*. New York: Viking.
Kerr-Berry, Julie. 2018. "Counterstorytelling in Concert Dance History Pedagogy: Challenging the White Dancing Body." In *The Palgrave Handbook of Race and the Arts in Education*, ed. A.M. Kraehe, Rubén Gaztambide-Fernandez, and Stephen B. Carpenter II, 137–55. Cham: Switzerland.
Klapper, Melissa. 2020. *Ballet Class: An American History*. New York: Oxford University Press.
Kourlas, Gia. 2007. "Where Are All the Black Swans?" *New York Times*.
Kyunghee, Kim, and Kim Hyunjung. 2008. "Representing the Historical Memory of War in Lim Sung-Nam's 'Prince Hodong.'" *Dance Chronicle* 31, no. 3: 412–35.
Leary, Mark. 2012. *Handbook of Self and Identity, Second Edition*. New York: Guilford.
Lewin, Yael T. 2011. *Night's Dancer: The Life of Janet Collins*. Middletown, CT: Wesleyan University Press.
Maher, Erin. 2014. "Ballet, Race, and Agnes de Mille's Black Ritual." *Musical Quarterly* 97, no. 3: 390–428.

McCarthy-Brown, Nyama. 2017. *Dance Pedagogy for a Diverse World: Culturally Relevant Teaching in Theory, Research, and Practice*. Jefferson, NC: McFarland.
McCarthy-Brown, Nyama. 2011. "Dancing in the Margins: Experiences of African American Ballerinas." *Journal of African American Studies* 15, no. 3: 385–408.
McCarthy-Brown, Nyama. 2014. "Decolonizing Dance Education: One Credit at a Time." *Journal of Dance Education* 14, no. 4: 125–29.
Meadows-Fernandez, Rochaun. 2018. *Investigating Institutional Racism*. New York: Enslow Publishing.
Menakem, Resmaa. 2017. *My Grandmother's Hands: Racialized Trauma and the Pathway to Mending Our Hearts and Bodies*. Las Vegas: Central Recovery.
Merskin, Debra. 2011. *Media, Minorities, and Meaning: A Critical Introduction*. New York: Peter Lang.
Mills, Charles, 1997. *The Racial Contract*. Ithaca, NY: Cornell University Press.
MoBBallet. 1948. https://mobballet.org/index.php/2017/10/04/1948-therrell-c-smith-school-of-dance-is-founded-in-washington-d-c/.
Osato, Sono. 1980. *Distant Dances*. New York: Alfred Knopf.
Romano, Aja. 2021. "The Backlash Against *in the Heights,* Explained," Vox Media, retrieved June 15, 2021. https://www.vox.com/culture/22535040/in-the-heights-casting-backlash-colorism-representation.
Singh, Annalise. 2019. *The Racial Healing Handbook: Practical Activities to Help Challenge Privilege, Confront Systemic Racism, & Engage in Collective Healing*. Oakland, CA: New Harbinger Publication.
Solórzano, Daniel G., and Tara J. Yosso. 2002. "Critical Race Methodology: Counter-Storytelling as an Analytical Framework for Education Research." *Qualitative Inquiry* 8, no. 1: 23–44.
Tatum, Beverly D. 1997. *Why Are All the Black Kids Sitting Together in the Cafeteria?* New York: Basic Books.
Telgen, Diane, and Jim Kamp, eds. 1996. *Latinas! Women of Achievement*. Detroit: Visible Ink.
Thompson, Cherly. 2009. "Black Women, Beauty, and Hair as a Matter of *Being*." *Women's Studies* 38, no. 8: 831–56.
Tomé, Lester. 2011. "The Cuban Ballet: Its Rationale, Aesthetics and Artistic Identity as Formulated by Alicia Alonso." PhD diss., Temple University.
Tomé, Lester. 2017. "Swans in Sugarcane Fields: Proletarian Ballet Dancers and the Cuban Revolution's Industrious New Man." *Dance Research Journal* 49, no. 2: 4–25.
Tonkin, Elizabeth. 1992. *Narrating Our Pasts: The Social Construction of Oral History*. New York: Cambridge.
West, Cornel. 2001. *Race Matters*. New York: Vintage Books.
Wilkerson, Isabel. 2020. *Caste: The Origins of Our Discontents*. New York: Penguin Random House.
Wilson, Julee. 2015. "Ballerina Misty Copeland Talks About Being Unapologetically Black and More." Huffington Post, August 10, 2015. https://www.huffpost.com/entry/ballerina-misty-copeland-talks-being-unapologetically-black-for-essence_n_55c80ac6e4b0923c12bd4714.
Yow, V. 2005. *Recording Oral History: A Guide for the Humanities and Social Sciences*. Walnut Creek, CA: AltaMira.
Zhang, Enhua. 2016. *Space, Politics, and Cultural Representation in Modern China: Cartographies of Revolution*. New York: Routledge.

Index

Abarca-Mitchell, Lydia 22, 131
Acosta, Carlos 218
Addison, Katlyn 46
Aïda 36
Ailey, Alvin 73; *see also* Ailey II
The Ailey School 10, 21, 77, 141, 150
Ailey II 250
Akinleye, Adeshola 26
Alice in Wonderland 44, 232
Alicia Alonso Ballet Company 78
Allegro Brilliante 197
Allen, Debbie 49, 249
Allen, Pamela 132
Allen, Zita 1
Allison, Guy 31
Alonso, Alberto 86
Alonso, Alicia 2, 29–30, 78, 85–87, 156, 223, 239
Alonso, Fernando 78–79, 80–82, 86, 156, 239
Alonso, Laura 156
Alvin Ailey American Dance Center 250
Alvin Ailey American Dance Theater 21, 110, 112–117, 122, 152, 212, 249,
Alvin Ailey Repertory Ensemble 250
American Ballet Theater (ABT) 19, 26, 32, 38, 56, 77, 81, 88, 180, 196, 206, 211, 213–214, 228, 249
American Ballet Theatre Jacqueline Kennedy Onassis School (JKO) 90
American Indian Ballerinas 30
Anderson, Lauren 2, 10, 21, 23, 35, 42–52, 121, 143, 148, 223–224, 226, 228, 231–232, 239
Apollo Theater 149, 208
Araújo, Loipa 80, 85
Arja, Alice 70
Arja, Nathalia 70
Ash, Aesha 6, 35, 230
Ashley, Merill 71
Atlanta Ballet 182, 249
Atlanta Ballet Center of Dance Education 13
Atlanta University Center Dance Theatre 249
Augusta, Georgia 93–94, 97
Augusta Ballet 93–96, 100–102
Augusta Mini Theater 94–96
Austin, Debra 201

Baca, Susana 209
Bakersfield, California 110
Balanchine Method 39
Balanchine, George 18, 27–28, 57, 59, 112–113, 120, 134, 165, 177, 195, 197
Balanchine Trust 115
Ballet Austin 177
Ballet Bus 67–68, 70, 72
Ballet Caravan 81
Ballet de Camagüey 186; *see also* Camagüey Ballet; Company Ballet of Camagüey
Ballet Guild of the Lehigh Valley 171
Ballet Hispánico 10, 20–23, 29, 32–33, 77, 87–88, 90, 141–143, 145, 149, 165, 203–204, 206–207, 209, 211–213, 215–216, 227; *see also BH Dos*
Ballet Nacional de Cuba 58, 71, 186, 231; *see also* Nacional Ballet de Cuba
Ballet Nacional de Mexico 32
Ballet Russes 18, 27, 29, 31–32; *see also* Ballet Russes de Monte Carlo
Ballet Russes de Monte Carlo 28, 30–32, 35
Ballet Theatre 27; Negro Unit 27
Ballet West 46
Ballethnic Dance Company 13, 129
BalletMet 22, 170, 173, 175, 179, 181
Ballo della Regina 71
Banegas, Joaquin 78–79, 80
Barnes, Fabian 129
Barnhart, Beverly Jane 96
Bartenieff Fundamentals 124
La Bayadère 87
Baylis, Meredith 1
Beatty, Talley 106
Bell, Karen 22
Berg, Shelley 103, 239
Berlin, Germany 155
Bermúdez, Ana Julia 188
Bethlehem, Pennsylvania 170
BH Dos 142
Black, Maggie 1
Black Arts Movement 250
The Black Dancing Body: A Geography from Coon to Cool 2, 39, 229, 232

Black feminist thought 15
Black Ritual 27
Black Swan 195
Blunden-Diggs, Debbie 239
Boal, Peter 66
Boléro 113, 118
Bolshoi Theatre 155
Bonilla-Silva, Eduardo 230
Boston 134
Boston Ballet 26, 38, 115
Bouder, Ashley 194
Bournonville Method 39
Braine, Mireille 172
Brandenburg 66
Brazil 28, 29, 39, 153, 225, 232
Brenau Women's College 97
Briansky, Oleg 172
Bristle 119
Broadway 21, 31, 76, 92, 106, 109–110, 125, 127, 135, 140, 193, 202
Brooklyn Ballet 77, 90, 166
Brown, James 131
Brown, Joan Myers 11; *see also* Joan Myers Brown & the Audacious Hope of the Black Ballerina
Brown, Karen 10, 121, 231
Brown, Madison 49
Brown, Ronald K. 105, 208
Brown vs. Board of Education 27
Browne, Delores 11, 14, 31, 185, 244
Bryant, Willa Walker 11
Burke, Elena 78
Burmann, Willy 115
Bury Me Standing 152, 208

California 20
Camagüey Ballet 186
Campbell, Sylvester 31, 249
Capitol Ballet of Washington, D.C. 249
Carmen 145, 212
Carolina Ballet 22, 192, 194, 195, 198, 201
Carousel 135
Carpentier, Alejo 86
Carrot, Miles 159
Caste: The Origins of Our Discontents 6, 230
Castogna, Angela 34
Castro, Fidel 223
Cecchetti 206

Index

Cecchetti Method 39, 241
Cedar Lake Contemporary Ballet 150
Chan, Phil 174, 198, 227, 236
Change 167
Charlotte Ballet 38
Chateau, Yvonne 18, 25, 29
Chattanooga, Tennessee 249
Chen, Nai-Ni 143
Chicago, Illinois 128, 133, 229
Chicago Opera Ballet 29
Children of the Passage 105
Chile 32
China 28, 29, 31, 225
Chu, Peter 143
Cia Estável de Dança 153
Cincinnati Ballet 177
Cincinnati Conservatory of Music 104
Cinderella 176
Cirque de Soleil 122
City Ballet 119
City Center 116
Clark Center 1, 250
Cleopatra 46
Cleveland Ballet 32
Collins, Janet 32, 36, 37
Collins, Patricia Hill 17
Colona, Shelby 21, 23, 141–153, 231, 235, 236, 237
colorism 11, 12, 229–231, 233–234, 245
Columbus, Ohio 170
Communist Party 225
Company Ballet of Camagüey 188
Complexions Contemporary Ballet 129, 150, 216
Con Brazo Abiertos 146, 209
Concerto Barocco 119, 197
controlling codes 245
Cooper, Brittney 6, 228
Cooper, Duncan 22
Copeland, Misty 6, 10, 14–16, 19, 22, 49, 121, 148, 172, 174, 210, 222, 228,
Copélia 83
Cornejo, Erica 26
Correa, Yolanda 163
Creole Giselle 82, 231
Criação Ballet (Ballet Creation) 155
Cristina, Monike 22, 24, 25, 153–160, 232, 237
critical race theory 14
Cuba 9, 28–30, 34, 39, 22, 31, 41, 53, 77, 81, 83, 86, 89, 161, 186, 189, 191, 203, 218, 222–223, 225, 230
Cuban Artists Fund 71
Cuban Ballet Technique 225
Cuban Method 39, 40
Cuban National Ballet 85, 87
Cuban National Ballet School 39, 161, 186, 226, 227
Cuban Revolution 29, 30
Cunningham Technique 122
Cunxin, Li 47
Cuyjet, Marion 11, 249

d'Addario, Edith 56
Dahl, Izabela 15
Dallas, Texas 42
Daly, Ann 16
Dance Magazine 45, 145
Dance Spirit Magazine 103
dance studies 18
Dance Theatre of Harlem (DTH) 10, 13, 20, 21–23, 25, 29, 32, 35, 37, 41, 43, 45, 100, 110–111, 113–118, 120, 121, 125, 128–131, 133, 135–136, 148, 160, 166, 223, 226, 229–231, 242, 249–250
Dance Theatre of Harlem School 128
Dance/USA 38
Dances at a Gathering 65
Dancing Many Drums: Excavations in African American Dance 26
Dandara Amorim 211
Danielle I 178, 198
Danskin 102
Davis, Chuck 249
Davis, Thaddeus 113
Dayton, Ohio 93
Dayton Contemporary Dance Company (DCDC) 93, 99, 103–105, 109
Deans, Joselli 11, 13, 22
DeFrantz, Thomas 26, 222
de Mille, Agnes 27
DePrince, Michaela 50
de Saá, Margarita 80
de Saá, Ramona 80
Desmond, Jane 31
Diaghilev, Sergei 18
Dialogues 137
Digging the Africanist Aesthetic in American Performance 28, 120
Dishon, Duane 249
Distant Dances 32
Dixon, Melanye White 11, 248
Don Quixote 46, 189
Donald Byrd/The Group 110, 112–113
Dorsey, Essie Marie 11
Dougla 119, 131, 167
Dove, Ulysses 177
dragon lady 17
Dulzaides, Felipe 55
Duncan, Theodore 31
Dunham Technique 122
Dunning, Jennifer 37

Earick, Mary 15
Eda 155
Ellis-DuBoulay 135
English National Ballet 85
"The Equity Project" 37
Escuela Nacional de Arte de Ballet 2, 77–78; see also Escuela Nacional de Cuba; National Ballet School of Cuba
Escuela Nacional de Cuba 191
Espinosa, Caridad 203, 207, 227, 239
Espiritu Vivo 208

Essler, Fanny 27, 81
Études 47
Europe 27–28

Fagan, Garth 100, 116
Fairchild, Megan 194
Faison, George 249
Fancy Free 65
Farrell, Suzanne 115
Farris, Christine King 250
Feijóo, Lorena 26
Fernandez, Yinet 22–23, 35, 160–170, 227
Final Bow for Yellowface 174–176, 178–179, 198, 236
Firebird 44, 65–66, 119
Fisher, Jennifer 33
Fleming, Ward 31
Floyd, George 229
Fonteyn, Margot 172
Ford Foundation 57, 71
Fort Worth Dallas Ballet 102, 250
Fortune, Sandra 249
Four Temperaments 134
Franklin, Aretha 13
Franklin, Frederick (Freddie) 74, 117
Funakoshi, Aoi 104

Gaddis, Bernard 119
Galdino, Ruan 158
Garland, Robert 131, 167
geisha girl 17
gender-inclusive 243–245
Georgia Southern University 249
Gilreath, Nena 13
Giselle 36, 83, 87, 138, 130, 138, 182
Glenn, Charla 207, 239
Gomes, Bethania 131
Gottschild, Brenda Dixon 1, 2, 11–12, 28, 33, 39, 120, 229, 232
Goudie, Sylvia M. 55
Graham, Martha 73, 100, 102, 205
Graves, Lorraine 112, 114
The Green Table 118
Guidi, Ronn 117–118
Guillén, Nicolás 79

Harlem, New York 29, 115
Harlem Nutcracker 118
Havana 144
Havana, Cuba 223
Havana Ballet Theater 77, 86
Haynes, Kathryn 21
Herrera, Paloma 26
High School for the Performing Arts (HSPA) 42
Hightower, Rosella 18, 25, 29
Hill, Thelma 1, 31, 249
Hinkson, Mary 249
Historically Black College and University (HBCU) 97
Holder, Geoffrey 120, 249
Holland, Edith 11
Horton Technique 114, 122, 205
Hot Latina 17
Houston, Texas 141, 143, 223–224
Houston Academy 44

Houston Ballet 2, 21, 23, 25, 41–42, 44–45, 223–224, 230
Howard, Theresa Ruth 13, 37
Hubbe, Nikolaj 66
Hueso, Cayo 78
Hunter, Charmaine 112, 115, 121, 130, 230
Hunter Museum of Art 249

I'll Make Me a World 31
in-group messaging 15, 225–229, 245
In the Upper Room 172
inclusion 12, 23, 37, 63, 198, 223, 225, 236, 243–246, 250
Indiana University's College of Arts and Humanities Institute 20
International Association of Blacks in Dance 38, 42
International Festival 209
Ireland, Savannah 159

Jackson, Michaelyn 31
James, Adrian Vincent 45
Jamison, Judith 11, 49, 53, 113, 115, 122,
Jazz Train 119
Jezebel 17, 233
Jimenez, Frances 31
Joan Myers Brown & the Audacious Hope of the Black Ballerina 2, 12
Joburg Ballet 19, 20, 22–23, 29, 38, 56, 153, 155, 159, 186, 218
Joffrey Ballet School 1, 100, 102
Johannesburg, South Africa 22, 41, 153
John S. Davidson Fine Arts School 95
Johnson, Carol 249
Johnson, Christina 115, 130
Johnson, Graham 31
Johnson, Louis 31
Johnson, Virginia 14, 23, 35, 45, 74, 121, 131, 226, 231
Jones, Bill T. 105
Jordan, Kimberleigh 13
Joyce Theater 208
Judimar School of Dance 11
Juilliard School 32, 50, 143, 204–208, 216

Kammermusik No. 2 65
Kennedy Center 84, 214
Kent, Allegra 66, 115
KEZU 170
King, Alonzo 112
King, Alonzo LINES Ballet 150
King, Martin Luther, Jr. 250
King, Sydney 11
Klekovic, Patti 135
Kosmovska, Irina 56
Kostritzky, Oleg 195
Kourlas, Gia 37
Ku Klux Klan 32
Kylian, Jiri 206

Lane, John 112
Laracey, Ashley 119
Larkin, Moscelyn 18, 25, 29
Larsen, Mike 30
Las Vegas Contemporary Theater 110
Latham, Kristie 22, 24–25, 170–185, 227, 235–238, 244, 250
Latin diasporic studies 18
Latina 5–6, 12, 17, 21–22, 25, 68, 72, 143, 166–167, 189, 206, 207–208, 211, 213–214, 216, 227, 233, 248
Latinx 10, 12, 16
Latinx critical race theory 15
Lauer, Meryl 19
le Roux, Alice 159
Letras de Amor 119
Lewis, Yael T. 32
Liang, Edwaard 24, 201
Lichine, David 57
Light/The Holocaust & Humanity Project 172
Limon Technique 122
Linea Recta 152, 212
The Lion King 21, 109, 110, 127, 135
Livingston, Lili Cockerille 30
Long, Andrea 121
Long, Larry 137, 239
Long Beach, California 110
Long Beach City College 110
Long Beach Community College 21
Long Island, New York 192
Lopez, Lourdes 21, 23, 38, 53 76, 201, 227, 238
Lucas, Waverly 13

Mabaso, Thabang 159
MacDonald, Brian 84
Mack-Graff, Alicia 50
Mackey, Bill 249
Madame Butterfly 198
Mahr, Martha 58
mammy 233
Mantsoe, Vincent 116
Manzanales, Michelle 142, 146, 209
Mao's Last Dancer 47
Marion, Indiana 224
Marion Cuyjet and Her Judimar School of Dance: Training Ballerinas in Black Philadelphia, 1948-1971 248
Marsalis, Wynton 100
Martinez, Caridad 2, 6, 10, 21, 23, 77–92, 166, 188, 223, 225, 227, 230, 237, 239, 246
Martins, Peters 59
Marymount 150
Mathis, Clover 249
Mayfair Academy 133–134
Mazzo, Kay 195
McDowell, Yvonne 31
McIntyre, Diane 105, 250
McKayle, Donald 105, 112
McMillan, Ayisha 46
Méndez, Josefina 78, 80

Metropolitan Opera Ballet 32, 36
Mexico 89
Mexico City 32
Mexico City Ballet
Miami, Florida 53, 203
Miami City Ballet 21, 26, 38, 32, 53, 63, 165, 201
Miami City Ballet School (MCBS) 38, 67
Miller, Bebe 105
Mills, Charles 35
Mills, Shirley 136
Minnesota Dance Theater 32
Miranda, Lin-Manuel 234
Mitchell, Arthur 18, 27, 29, 31, 66, 82, 103, 114, 116, 121, 129, 130–131, 134, 136–138, 223, 226, 231, 234, 249
MOBBallet 37
Molnar, Marika 60
Monja, Claudia 22, 24–25, 186–192, 230
Myers, Milton 114

Nacional Ballet de Cuba 77, 84, 86, 160, 210
Nagata, Corrine 23
Narratives of Black British Dance 26
Nashville, Tennessee 186
Nashville Ballet 22, 186
Nasser, Esther 24, 39
National Ballet de Cuba 21–22, 77
National Ballet of Canada 38
National Ballet of China 31
National Ballet of Cuba 2, 10, 21, 30, 188
National Ballet of Washington, D.C. 249
National Ballet School of Cuba 204
National Dance Theatre of Jamaica 249
National Endowment for the Arts and Humanities 71
National identity and ballet 9, 224–225
National School for the Arts 39
nationality 9, 12, 15, 20, 225–226
Neal, Charles 31
Negro Ballet Company 27, 120; *see also* Ballet Theatre's Negro Unit
Nemchinov, Vera 1
Netherlands Dance Theatre (NDT) 143, 216
Nettleford, Rex 249
New Dance Group 1
New Orleans 74, 100
New World High School 206
New York, New York 77, 128, 141, 161, 250
New York City Ballet (NYCB) 19, 21, 27, 29, 38, 53, 59, 88, 121, 155, 194, 196
New York City Opera 59
New York Negro Ballet Company 31

New York Public Library 19, 22
New York State Summer School of the Arts 192, 194
New York State Theater 59
New York Times 5, 37, 84, 119
New York University (NYU) 59, 150
Night's Dancer: The Life of Janet Collins 32, 37
Nigodoff, Alexander 55
Nijinska, Bronislava 118
Nonnormative bodies 243, 245
North Carolina School of the Arts 128
Nowakowski, Jim 180
Nutcracker 14, 46, 84, 98, 111, 118, 133–134, 147, 179, 198–199, 230, 235

Oakland, California 133
Oakland Ballet 10, 21–22, 110, 113, 115, 118, 121, 123, 228–229
Ochoa, Annabelle Lopez 145, 212
Ochoa, Arantxa 70
Odette 10
Ohio State University (OSU) 93, 109
Ohio State University Department of Dance 250
Ohio State University Global Arts and Humanities Discovery Themes 20
Ohman School of Ballet 192
O'Keefe, Timothy 43
Oklahoma 29, 111
Oklahoma Five Moons 26, 29, 30
Oller, Ramón 208
Olympia, Washington 141
Organ, Sandra 45
Orientalism 17
Osato, Sono 18, 29, 32
Othello 85

Page, Ruth 6, 134–135, 137
Paris Opera Ballet 29
Pas de Quatre 82
passing 31–32, 237
Patterson, Arnoldo 86
Pavlova, Anna 81
Pazcoguin, Georgia 174–175, 201, 227, 236
Pennsylvania Ballet 195; *see also* Pennsylvania Youth Ballet
Pennsylvania Youth Ballet 171
People of the Global Majority 5
performance studies 18
Peridance 77
Perkins, Crystal Michelle 24, 41, 93–110, 232, 239, 244, 250
Perry Mansfield Performing Arts Camp 142
Phelta, Kitty 39
Philadanco 12, 104
Philadelphia, Pennsylvania 11, 249
Phillips, Edna 31
Pilarre, Susan (Suzy) 195
Pilates 142

Piracicaba, São Paulo, Brazil 155
Pite, Crystal 143
Pittsburgh Ballet Theater 172
Pivot, Kidd 143
Podcasy, Melissa 195
Pointe Magazine 121
pointe shoes 49, 55, 57, 66, 85, 98, 102, 113–114, 122, 124, 128, 165–167, 200, 210, 213
Pomare, Eleo 249
Portman, Natalie 195
Portuondo, Omara 78
Powell, Stephanie Marie 21–23, 110–128, 228–231, 233, 237–239
Primus, Pearl 249
ProDanza 161
Prodigal Son 113, 119
Prólongo para Una Tragedia 85
Pueblo Nuevo 78

Queens, New York 20
Quitman, Cleo 31

racial trauma 229, 241, 243, 253
Racism Without Racists: Colorblind Racism and the Persistence of Racial Inequality in America 230
Raleigh, North Carolina 22, 192
Ramirez, Tina 29
Ramos, Diana 250
Raymonda 159
Reading Oral History: A Guide for the Humanities and Social Sciences 19
Red Angels 177
The Red Detachment of Women 31, 39, 225
Retta 119
Revelations 114, 119
Reyes, Xiomara 26
Riessman, Catherine 21
Roach, Max 119
Robbins, Jerome 59
Robertson, De Shona Pepper 103
Robinson, Renee 122
Rock School 172, 174
Rod Rodgers Dance Company 249
Rogers, Rod 249
Rome Opera Theater 32
Romeo and Juliet 14, 36
Royal Academy of Dancing Technique 39, 95, 241
The Royal Ballet 218
Royal Danish Ballet 198
Rubies 197
Ruiz, Pedro 166
Rushing, Shirley 249, 250
Russ Tallchief, Russ 26
Russians 18
Ruth Page School of Dance 134, 135

Sachane, Mahlatse 159
Sagan, Gene 31
San Francisco 14
San Francisco Ballet 14, 22–23, 19, 32, 38, 88, 111, 180, 201

Sansano, Gustavo Ramirez 145, 206, 212
Santiago, Chile 32
São Paulo, Brazil 156
São Paulo Companhia de Dança 157
Sapphire 17
Sasanka 116
Savage, Reginald 22, 133
School of American Ballet (SAB) 21, 31, 56–57, 192–197; Diversity Board 197
Schorer, Suki 195
Schwall, Elizabeth 23
Seo, Hee 180
Serenade 65, 115–116, 177
Serrano, Crystal 166
Serrano, Lupe 29, 32
Severin-Hansen, Margaret 22, 24, 192–202, 224, 235
Shellman, Eddie 125
Shook, Karel 29
Silva, Ingrid 167
Skhosana, Kristof 159
skin colored pointe shoes 128–129, 245
Sleeping Beauty 36, 56, 176, 196
sociology 18
Sounds in Motion Studio 250
South Africa 9, 29, 19, 39, 218, 222
South African training method 40
South Korea 28, 29, 222
South Korean National Ballet Company 31
Southern Methodist University (SMU) 97, 100, 104, 109
Spelman College 249–250
Spivak, Gayatri 2
Spriggs, Mozelle 249
Square Dance 195
Squirrel, Jenny 11
Stack Up 106
Steps on Broadway 115
The Steadfast Tin Soldier 195
stereotype(s) 7, 16–18, 37, 121, 179, 183, 199, 205, 213, 231, 233–236
Stevenson, Ben 2, 44, 46, 223–224, 239
Stevenson, Llanchie 249
Stravinsky, Igor 119
Stringer, Scott 132
SUNY Purchase 150
Sutton, Tommy 133
Swan Lake 10, 36, 56, 80, 83, 156, 174, 228
Swarthmore College 224
Les Sylphides 82, 83, 113, 229
Symphony in C 65
Szkutek, Carol 13

Tallchief, Maria 18, 25, 29, 172
Tallchief, Marjorie 18, 25, 29
Tan, Yuan Yuan 180
Tannen, Deborah 20
Tatum, Beverly Daniel 6, 35; *see also* Why Are All the Black

Index

Kids Sitting Together in the Cafeteria?
Taylor, Endalyn 6, 21, 13, 23, 112, 125, 128–140, 224, 228–231, 233, 237, 239
Taylor, Paul 6
Teacher's College, Columbia University 250
Temple University 11, 249
Tennessee 22
Tetley, Glen 137
Theatro Municipal do Rio de Janeiro 157
Thompson, Elizabeth 31
Thor, Melin 15
Tivoli Theatre 249
Tool, Rene 96, 102
Tornow, Hildegarde 249
tragic mulatto 233
La Traviata 158–159, 189
Trisler, Joyce 1
Trueblood, Cindy 239
Tumkovsky, Antonina 195
Tyrus, Judy 116, 118, 131, 140, 228
Tyson, Cecily 49

United Kingdom 27, 31
United States 9, 13, 16–17, 19, 25, 27–28, 31–35, 38, 223–226, 230, 232, 234, 235, 242, 244, 249
University of Illinois Urbana-Champaign 21
University of South Carolina 172
University of the Arts 22

Vadelka, Erica 159
Vaganova Technique 39, 206, 225, 241
Valdés, Cecilia 86
Valdés, Viengsay 71
Valls, Eila 211
Vamp 17
Van Heerden, Augustus 130
Varone, Doug 105
Verdecia, Lyvan 210
Verdecia, Melissa 22, 23, 144, 203–219, 227, 230, 239
Verdi, Giuseppe 36
Verdy, Violette 172
Vernon, Michael 115
Vessels 167
Vilaro, Eduardo 149
Villella, Edward 66
Villeneuve, Nicholas 142
Violin Concerto 65–66

Wang Theatre 134
Ward, Kevin 106
Washington Ballet 32
Wei, Shen 148
Weiss, Ricky Weiss 195
Weiss, Robert 195; *see also* Weiss, Ricky
Welsh, Kariamu 22
West, Cornel 17
Whelan, Wendy 66
white-presenting 173, 226
white privilege 35
whiteness 14, 28–29, 31–34, 36–38, 40, 174, 183, 225, 226, 229–234, 241–241, 246
Who Cares? 177
Why Are All the Black Kids Sitting Together in the Cafeteria? 35
Wilkerson, Isabel 6, 35, 230
Wilkinson, Raven 14, 18, 29, 31, 35, 49, 185, 228, 230, 237
Williams, Sheri "Sparkle" 103
Williams, Stanley 195
Wilson, Reggie 105
Winston-Salem, North Carolina 128
Women of the Global Majority 5
Wynn, Zelda 132

Youth America Grand Prix (YAGP) 155
Yow, Valerie 19
Yun, Shen 143

Zollar, Jawole Willa Jo 105

www.ingramcontent.com/pod-product-compliance
Lightning Source LLC
Chambersburg PA
CBHW060338010526
44117CB00017B/2880